Best Bike Rides
Las Vegas

The Greatest Recreational Rides in the Metro Area

PAUL W. PAPA

FALCONGUIDES

GUILFORD, CONNECTICUT
HELENA, MONTANA

FALCONGUIDES®

An imprint of Rowman & Littlefield
Falcon, FalconGuides, and Outfit Your Mind are registered trademarks of Rowman & Littlefield.

Distributed by NATIONAL BOOK NETWORK

Photos by Paul W. Papa

Maps: Melissa Baker © Rowman & Littlefield

British Library Cataloguing-in-Publication Information Available

Library of Congress Cataloging-in-Publication Data Available

ISBN 978-1-4930-0388-4 (paperback : alkaline paper)
ISBN 978-1-4930-1470-5 (e-book)

∞™ The paper used in this publication meets the minimum requirements of American National Standard for Information Sciences—Permanence of Paper for Printed Library Materials, ANSI/NISO Z39.48-1992.

Contents

Overview

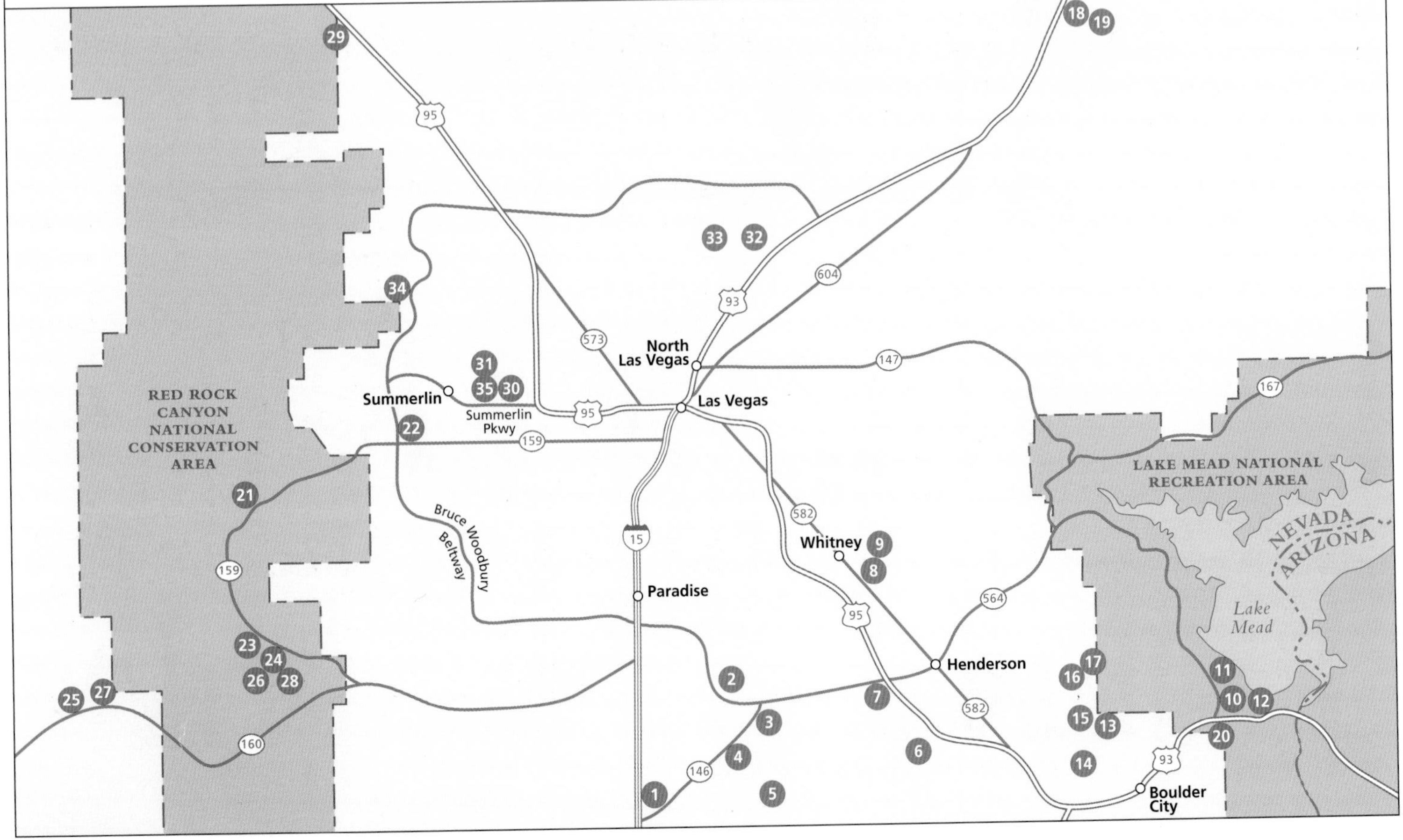

0 2 4 km.
0 2 4 mi.
N
RED ROCK CANYON NATIONAL CONSERVATION AREA
LAKE MEAD NATIONAL RECREATION AREA
NEVADA
ARIZONA
Lake Mead
North Las Vegas
Las Vegas
Summerlin
Summerlin Pkwy
Bruce Woodbury Beltway
Paradise
Whitney
Henderson
Boulder City
95
573
93
604
147
167
159
15
582
564
146
160

Acknowledgments

Thanks to Jeff and his crew at All Mountain Cyclery for all their help and especially to Dan Haskin for helping me select the best rides in Bootleg Canyon. Thanks also go out to Lisa Caterbone at bikinglasvegas.com and Terry and the crew at the Bike Shop for helping me select the best road bike rides around the valley and to Jon Blum and Erik Montville of the Southern Nevada Mountain Bike Association for linking me up with people who know the trails like the backs of their hands. Two of those people were Patrick Ellis and David Velez, who both took the time to ride with me and show me the trails I was unfamiliar with. Thanks guys, I couldn't have done it without you!

Thanks also go out to Chris at McGhie's Bike Outpost for helping me work out the names of the trails in Cottonwood and fixing my mountain bike when my brakes failed. A special thank-you to Debora Spano, who allowed me to tag along on a ride with some of the most outstanding people in the entire world—the men and women of Ride 2 Recovery, who work with wounded military members, helping in their therapy and letting them know that bike riding is not limited to people with four limbs. Riding with you all was a truly humbling experience—one I shall not soon forget.

I'd like to thank the wonderful people at FalconGuides, especially David Legere, who guided me through the process, and Lynn Zelem, for her obvious desire to make this the best guide it can be. Finally, I'd like to thank all the bicyclists I met on my rides, many of whom took the time to tell me about the trails, allowed me to take their picture—especially Lynetta and Joe—or just led me to some great places to eat. This book is for everyone who spends much of their lives on two wheels. Enjoy!

Introduction

I spend a good deal of my time trying to convince people that Las Vegas is more than an adult playground; more than contortionist shows, one-arm bandits, themed casinos, and free drinks. And even if I can get people to see past the Strip, I often have difficulty getting them to see past the desert—or more specifically, the desert heat. While everyone is familiar with the 100-plus temperatures that invade the valley every summer, few of those same people know the year-round average temperate in Las Vegas is only 66.3 degrees Fahrenheit.

The truth is, Las Vegas has much more to offer than the entertainment found on the famous "Strip." To find what else Las Vegas has to offer, you need simply to look out into the valley past the flashing neon lights. Most places pull you into the city with bike trails and rides; however, Las Vegas is a different beast entirely. Surrounding almost the entire valley is land owned by the Bureau of Land Management (BLM), and it is on this land where the best and most scenic rides can be found.

Las Vegas is home to both the largest man-made lake in the United States and the largest national forest in the Lower 48. Additionally the valley has no less than three national recreation areas, a state park, a conservation area, wetlands, and a dam that was considered a modern marvel when it was constructed in 1935. While tourists spend their days on the Strip—gambling, watching shows, eating in world-class restaurants, or lounging at the pool—locals are outside hiking, biking, horseback riding, boating, jet-skiing, or bird-watching. Besides, how many places offer you an opportunity to see both wild horses and wild burros while riding your bike?

When most people think of a desert, they think of cactus, sand, and, well, not much else. If you see the desert as a place Mother Nature abandoned, look again. The desert has a beauty all its own. A ride through Bootleg or Red Rock Canyon will expose you to some of the most intriguing colors you've ever seen. There are rich reds, yellows, browns, oranges, pinks, and blues . . . yes, blues. Travel to the Valley of Fire and see for yourself the bright red rocks that gave the area its name or the rich pastels that sweep down through the valley.

The Las Vegas valley has world-class mountain bike trails and is the site of both a Silverman triathlon and an XTERRA championship. Las Vegas and Henderson have spent millions of dollars building multipurpose trails around the valley, and they have been so successful that the League of American Cyclists awarded them the bronze level as a Bicycle Friendly Community. Las Vegas also has some hidden gems that are only known to locals and those who care to do a bit of exploring. One of these is the Historic Railroad Trail where you can ride through the very tunnels used to transport men, equipment, and supplies to the Hoover Dam construction site more than eighty years ago.

Yes, Vegas is "Sin City," and yes, you can come to Vegas for a once-in-a-lifetime experience; however, if you're looking for a different kind of "Vegas" experience, all you have to do is hop on a bike, strap on a helmet, and head out into the hills surrounding the valley. Just don't forget to bring sunscreen, water, and this guide. Oh, and take lots of pictures.

SAFETY

Best Bike Rides Las Vegas is meant as a guide to bike routes and not a how-to book on cycling. That being said, there are some safety factors about biking in general and biking in Las Vegas specifically that should be addressed to make your ride safer and more enjoyable.

On the Roads

While Las Vegas has been named a "bicycle-friendly community" by the League of American Bicyclists, riding on any road poses certain inherent dangers—mainly from distracted drivers or motorists who simply do not care about cyclists. Las Vegas has made great strides in creating bike lanes and paths that limit the cyclist's exposure to traffic; however, that is not always possible and when it's not possible, it is vitally important to always be aware of traffic. Remember, it's easier for a person on a bike to see a car than it is for a person in a car to see a bike, and it is never wise to assume the driver sees you. If you are passing in front of a vehicle for any reason, always make eye contact with the driver. If he or she looks you in the eye, you can be assured they see you.

While many of the rides in this guide are on paths not accessible by motor vehicles, many others are along established roads and state routes. When riding on these roads, it is wise to avoid the busiest times of the day—this is especially important on weekends and holidays. Wearing bright-colored or reflexive clothing will help motorists see you better, as will reflective devices on your bike. Additionally, if it'll become dark before you finish your ride, you should plan to have a headlamp or handlebar lamp and red flashers to help you be seen in the dark.

As a cyclist, it is important to remember that even though you may be riding in an approved bike lane, you are still considered a vehicle and subject to the same rules and regulations as every other vehicle on the road. This includes signaling your intention to turn—especially important when making left-hand turns. Here again it is important to make eye contact with any motorists who may be in the lane you are passing into or crossing. If you have to get out of the bike lane to make a left-hand turn, get in line behind the cars and then move back to the right, into the bike lane, once the turn is complete.

On Multipurpose Trails

Las Vegas and the surrounding communities have gone to great lengths to create multipurpose trails that are available to runners, cyclists, and people just out for a stroll. These trails are great places for cyclists; however, there are some precautions that should be taken. Many of these trails are well-used by families with strollers and small children, people walking their dogs, and runners trying to avoid running in traffic. Few of these people pay attention to bikes on the trail, and for this reason it is best to always look out for them and to give them a wide berth. Just as with vehicles, eye contact is important; however, you can also use your voice to let people know you are behind them. Additionally a bell on the handlebars or a whistle is useful in alerting people that you are approaching them, especially from behind.

When biking on multipurpose trails, follow the established traffic patterns used on regular roads. That is, always ride to the right side of the trail—especially with trails that have dividing lines—and pass on the left. Also, remember it is typically easier for you as the cyclist to get out of the way of oncoming traffic. Even if someone is in your lane, if it is easier for you to move, you should do so. Try to move as soon as possible and make it obvious where you are going. This will help the people on the trail not to panic and move in front of you. Be sure to ride at a reasonable speed and slow down when you are approaching people or pets, especially small children.

Watch out for bollards—posts installed in the ground to prevent vehicles from entering the trail. These are most often placed at intersections. You can typically ride between them, but it is always best to slow down when approaching any obstacle in the road. If you ride in a pair or a group, let those behind you know of any obstacles you encounter.

On Singletrack

Singletrack is a term used to indicate the trail is only wide enough to ride single file. Most of the mountain bike trails in this guide are singletrack. Because only one rider can fit on the trail at a time, there is a certain etiquette that must be followed. In most cases riders climbing have the right-of-way over riders going downhill—though this is not a steadfast rule. If you are the one staying on the trail, always announce if there are other riders in your party.

Almost all the mountain bike trails in this guide are open to runners, hikers, and equestrians, and cyclists should always yield way. You should always get off the trail when you see a runner or hiker and allow them to pass. In my experience runners will heed this rule, while most hikers will get off the path and yield way to cyclists. Just remember that this a courtesy allowed by some hikers, but the rule is for the cyclists to get off the path. If you encounter an equestrian, announce yourself from a distance so as not to spook the horse. Stand off the trail on the downhill side; this will make the horse feel more comfortable, as carnivores typically attack from an uphill position.

Stay on the trail. Don't create your own trails, and always respect the trail by skidding your tires as little as possible to avoid loosening the dirt. Stay off muddy trails, as riding through the mud can create deep grooves and ruts. If you cannot navigate an obstacle on the bike, do so on foot. Don't create another path around the obstacle. Other riders will follow the path, and it can have a detrimental effect on the ecosystem. Remember, the obstacles were planned into the ride and are meant to test the rider and be part of the riding experience. You should always respect the trail and never, ever forge your own trail.

Preparing for Las Vegas Weather

The Las Vegas Water Authority has a slogan they use to remind people not to waste water. The slogan, "It's a Desert Out There," is especially applicable when riding on the trails in and around the Las Vegas valley. This city is one of the few places where you can ride all year long—January 1 through December 31. The only thing that changes is the time of day you choose to ride. While the average temperature in Las Vegas is 66.3 degrees Fahrenheit, temperatures can reach well into the 100s, with 115 degrees or more being common in summer. Another thing to consider is that in most parts of the United States, the hottest part of the day is noon. That's not true for Las Vegas: Here the hottest part of the day is 5 p.m.

When riding in Las Vegas, water is essential—especially in the summer months. You should always make sure to carry an adequate supply of water for the time you will be riding. My advice is to take more water than you think you'll need, especially if you've never ridden in Las Vegas. Biking in the heat can easily get you dehydrated—a condition that can be life-threatening in the desert. When riding in May through September, you should plan your rides early in the morning or late at night. Another important item to have when riding in Las Vegas is sunblock. Regardless of the time of year, the sun is especially hot in the desert and it takes no time at all to develop a severe sunburn.

While Las Vegas only experiences 4.13 inches of rain a year, when that rain does come, it's hard and fast. Flash flooding is a definite possibility in many areas. If signs exist warning of riding in the rain or specifically telling you not to ride the trail in the rain, they should be heeded. If you are in Bootleg Canyon when it starts to rain, it's always safer to get off the trails and follow the wider dirt roads back to your car. For the most part, if it's raining in Las Vegas, you shouldn't ride.

Dealing with Las Vegas Critters

One of the best things about riding in the desert is that you encounter all manner of critters. In some areas this can mean desert tortoises, lizards, rabbits, tarantulas, and birds. In other areas it can mean bats, bighorn sheep, snakes, burros, and wild horses. While it is great to observe animals in the wild, they should always be left alone. Feel free to take a photo or two, but don't approach or feed the animal. In some cases, feeding animals can result in a significant fine. While you might think you're helping the animal by feeding it, you're actually teaching it to rely on people instead of nature as a food source. This can cause the animal to become dependent upon people as a food source, and people are unreliable.

Additionally, handling some animals may actually cause them to die. One of these is the desert tortoise, which is an endangered and protected species in Nevada. Desert tortoises resemble a small brown turtle, and if you encounter one on the trail, never touch it or pick it up. Doing so can cause the animal to urinate, and when that happens it loses precious water it may not be able to get back. Losing water can cause the animal to die. Desert tortoises, as you might expect, move slowly and when confronted with a loud noise—such as your bike tire on the trail—tend to freeze in place. It is best to dismount and walk around these critters or, better yet, block the trail from other riders with your bike until the tortoise passes safely.

A common desert dweller is the rattlesnake, and Las Vegas is home to three types: speckled, sidewinder, and Mojave. These snakes are most active in the mornings and at dusk when temperatures are between 70 and 90 degrees Fahrenheit. Their most active months are April and October. While I have only seen rattlesnakes a couple of times on the trail, I never ride the mountain bike trails without a snakebite kit. Snakes are more commonly seen on dirt trails or the trails that border dirt trails, such as the River Mountains Loop. If you hear that rattle, it is best to avoid the area where it came from. Snakes typically don't attack unless they have to, so you can usually avoid them pretty easily once they've given you their warning.

Another common desert dweller is the desert tarantula. Females are typically all brown or tan, while males have black legs. These critters are more commonly seen at night, especially in areas such as Bootleg Canyon or Cottonwood. Tarantulas are, for the most part, docile; however, they will aggressively defend themselves if picked up—and they're faster than you think. Like lizards, they will typically get out of your way when you are riding, and it is best to simply avoid them.

Wild burros are common in the Red Rock and Cottonwood areas, and they will usually avoid you. However, many people feed them—though it is illegal to do so—and that sometimes encourages them to approach

Desert tortoises are endangered and protected in Nevada.

people, looking for food. It is important to remember they will typically not move for you if on the trail so you will have to go around them, and it is best to do this while walking your bike, not riding, because riding your bike as you pass could spook them. If the burro is not on the trail, feel free to ride past it. They'll usually just stare at you. As a side note, these animals are not camera shy.

Bats are another common critter that can be seen on some of the trails. Bats typically fly above you, feeding on insects your bike tires kick up. There are more than twenty species of bats in Las Vegas. None of them will bother you when you ride, and it is actually kind of cool to be followed by a couple of bats.

Other animals you might see include white-tailed antelope squirrels, coyotes, foxes, and many, many different types of lizards—including Gila monsters, though they are not common. Most, if not all, of these animals will stay out of your way.

EQUIPMENT

While helmets aren't required in Las Vegas, it is simply foolish to ride without one—on any trail. When buying a helmet you should look for one that is approved by the Consumer Product Safety Commission (CPSC) or by private

A lizard suns itself on a rock.

organizations—such as the American Society for Testing and Materials (ASTM) or the Snell Memorial Foundation—that develop safety standards for such things as helmets. As long as the helmet meets the standards set by these organizations, price is not a factor—meaning more expensive helmets aren't necessarily better.

When riding in Las Vegas, water is essential. Water bottles don't typically carry enough water, so you should look at some type of hydration system that can be carried with you—usually on your back. Many of these are large enough for you to carry extra items such as energy bars, a hand pump, tools, and sunscreen.

Some trails, such as those in Bootleg Canyon, are extremely rocky and it is always a good idea to have at least one spare tube and the tools needed to change a flat. The desert is also known for its cactus, and many of our dirt trails are decorated with these thorny plants. I never ride without at least one spare tube. I also typically choose tubes with some type of anti-flat filler inside. Shin guards are also a useful item when riding in Bootleg Canyon, because of the large sharp rocks in many areas. They don't sell T-shirts that say "I gave blood at Bootleg" for nothing.

Several of the trails can be ridden at night, and night riding is common in many places in the valley. Riding at night requires lights; however, lights are a good safety feature day or night because they get the attention of motorists. Lights typically work better on road bikes, as the constant vibration singletrack causes can damage the light or break the bracket that connects the light to the handlebars. When you choose a light, make sure you factor in the type of riding you'll be doing. When riding on the road at night, a white lamp that can be seen at least 500 feet away is required by state law. In addition, a red tail reflector or light visible from at least 300 feet away must be used. Reflective material that can be seen at least 600 feet away must also be placed on the bike when riding at night in Las Vegas.

Mirrors placed on the handlebars or worn on the eyeglasses or helmet will help you monitor traffic behind you. These work best on road bikes and are useful when you have to veer into traffic to avoid debris or to stay out of the door zone of parked cars. They are also useful to help you see other cyclists who may come up behind you. Eyeglasses should always be worn to protect the eyes from the sun and the drying wind created by cycling.

If you want to follow the mileage given in this guide, you will need some type of GPS or a cyclometer. GPS units come in many styles—and prices—and

Riders prepare for a group ride in Cottonwood Canyon.

can be mounted on the bike or worn on the body. I wear mine on my wrist. If you plan on leaving your bike while you take in a view, go for a hike, or get something to eat, you'll probably want some type of lock to secure the bike. There are many different types of locks, and you should spend some time checking into which type and brand has the best rating for your needs.

How to Use This Guide

Like everything else in Las Vegas, the guide is divided geographically by Las Vegas Boulevard, commonly known as the "Strip." The other dividing line is Sahara Avenue, which is actually the official boundary of the city of Las Vegas. Everything above Sahara is north and everything below is south. Everything to the left of the Strip is west and everything to the right is east.

Most of the rides in this book are in the 5- to 35-mile range and can be finished within four hours or less, depending on the skill of the cyclists. While hour time frames are given, these are just estimates and it may take you longer or less time to actually complete the ride. Additionally, mountain bike trails are typically more difficult to ride, and it may take you just as long to ride a 5-mile mountain bike trail as it does to ride a 20-mile road bike trail.

One of the best things about riding a bike is the freedom it offers. This freedom allows you to travel into areas not accessible by motorized vehicles. When riding a trail, especially a new trail, it can be easy to concentrate on the trail itself and not on your surroundings. Take the time to pay attention to the area through which you are riding. One of my greatest joys in riding is seeing things I wouldn't normally see when riding in my Jeep. I chose the trails included in this guide with that thought in mind.

While most rides can be completed in one day, many of them travel through areas that allow camping and you may want to make a two-day event out of the ride. This can be done on either of the Valley of Fire rides or the Cold Creek ride. Other rides can be connected to create one long ride. For example, you can actually ride from the Strip to the outskirts of Boulder City by simply connecting trails together. On some of the longer rides, I have given you options to make the ride shorter, as is the case with both the Valley of Fire rides. Know your limits and only ride as far as you feel comfortable. Remember that many of the loops can be ridden clockwise or counterclockwise. Riding a trail essentially backwards provides a different view of that trail and can be a great experience.

Las Vegas is still a town progressing in its understanding of bicyclists. The city is doing its best to build more trails and to link those trails together, allowing cyclists to ride around the entire valley without having to deal with traffic. Don't be surprised if a trail described in this guide goes farther than what is outlined or takes a different route. For the most part I have chosen established trails, but anyone who knows Las Vegas knows we are a city of change and what was here today may be gone tomorrow—just ask the Stardust, the Sands, the Dunes, or the Aladdin.

GPS

The distances for Miles and Directions were calculated from a wrist-mounted GPS I wore while navigating the trails. While mileages should match your own GPS device, it is important to note that readings can be affected by things such as satellite positions, weather, and natural barriers—all of which can cause errors in readings. Taking side trips off the trails can also affect the mileage. Finally, cyclometers may give slightly different readings than do GPS devices, and this should be taken into account if you choose to use one.

This guide marks the trail in miles and tenths of a mile. As you might suspect, few of the landmarks pointed out on the trail land directly on either a mile or a tenth of a mile. In cases where the landmark didn't fall on these established guide points, I have rounded to the closest tenth of the mile.

A pair of cyclists pass a pair of wild burros in Blue Diamond.

Ride Finder

BEST ROAD RIDES

10. River Mountains Loop
11. Lakeshore/Northshore to Callville Bay
18. Valley of Fire: White Domes
19. Valley of Fire: Overton
21. Red Rock Scenic Loop
22. State Route 159
29. Cold Creek

BEST MOUNTAIN BIKES RIDES

5. Anthem East Trail
6. McCullough Hills Trail
13. Middle and Lower Lake View Loop
14. POW/Par None/IMBA Loop
15. Girl Scout/West Leg/Mother Loop
16. Caldera Loop
17. Inner Caldera Loop
23. Landmine Loop
24. Landmine/Middle Fork Loop
25. Beginner Loop
26. The Mini Hurl Loop
27. Badger Pass/3 Mile Smile Loop
28. Inner Loop

BEST RIDES FOR SIGHTSEEING

2. Pittman Wash Trail
8. Wetlands Park Trail
9. Outer Wetlands Trail
10. River Mountains Loop
11. Lakeshore/Northshore to Callville Bay
16. Caldera Loop
18. Valley of Fire: White Domes
19. Valley of Fire: Overton
20. Hoover Dam
21. Red Rock Scenic Loop
29. Cold Creek

BEST RIDES FOR FAMILIES

1. St. Rose Parkway Trail
2. Pittman Wash Trail
3. Paseo Verde Trail
4. Amargosa Trail
8. Wetlands Park Trail
10. River Mountains Loop
12. Historic Railroad Trail
35. Pueblo Park Trail

BEST RIDES FOR SEEING BIRDS AND WILDLIFE

2. Pittman Wash Trail
8. Wetlands Park Trail
9. Outer Wetlands Trail
11. Lakeshore/Northshore to Callville Bay
12. Historic Railroad Trail
18. Valley of Fire: White Domes
19. Valley of Fire: Overton
21. Red Rock Scenic Loop
29. Cold Creek

BEST PAVED TRAIL RIDES

1. St. Rose Parkway Trail
2. Pittman Wash Trail
3. Paseo Verde Trail
4. Amargosa Trail
7. Union Pacific Railroad Trail
8. Wetlands Park Trail
9. Outer Wetlands Trail
10. River Mountains Loop
30. Lone Mountain Trail
31. Angel Park Trail
32. Lower Las Vegas Wash Trail
33. Upper Las Vegas Wash Trail
34. Western Beltway Trail
35. Pueblo Park Trail

Map Legend

Transportation

Interstate/Divided Highway	
Featured US Highway	
US Highway	
Featured State, County, or Local Road	
Primary Highway	
County/Local Road	
Featured Bike Route	
Bike Route	
Featured Trail	
Trail/Dirt Road	
Railroad	

Hydrology

Reservoir/Lake	
River/Creek	
Spring	
Wetlands	

Land Use

National Recreation Area/Conservation Area	

Symbols

Interstate	15
US Highway	2
State Highway	202
Trailhead (Start)	10
Mileage Marker	17.1
Capital	✪
Large City	◉
Small City/Town	○
Visitor Center	❓
Point of Interest	■
Parking	P
Direction Arrow	→
Tunnel	⊢⊣
Airport	✈
Bridge	≍
Picnic Area	🛆
Mountain	▲
Dam	▬
Restrooms	🚻
State/Local Park	🌲

Green Valley

Many of the trails in Green Valley offer great views of the Las Vegas Strip.

Green Valley is an area of Henderson, which is a town connected to Las Vegas. Henderson in general and Green Valley in particular have made great efforts in developing a community where bikes are a welcome part—so much so that Henderson has been awarded the bronze level as a Bicycle Friendly Community by the League of American Cyclists.

Many of the trails in Green Valley take advantage of space that would otherwise not be used, such as the common areas between communities. These trails are beautifully landscaped and easily accessible. Other trails follow natural washes or roadways, allowing cyclists to transverse the valley easily and, for the most part, without having to worry about vehicular traffic. In fact, many of the trails are so close to each other that you could travel from Las Vegas Boulevard—the Strip—to the farthest part of Henderson without ever having to ride on a street.

Henderson is also home to Sloan Canyon, a national conservation area. While this area is still being developed for recreational use, there are currently two good dirt trails that are used by both cyclists and hikers. The canyon is also considered one of the premier petroglyph sites in southern Nevada.

1

St. Rose Parkway Trail

This ride takes advantage of an area that would normally be left undeveloped. To make the ride more enjoyable, art has been places in strategic places and a child's fairytale has been incorporated into the ride. As you start the ride, listen carefully and you may just hear the roar of big cats in the distance.

Start: Parking lot for the M Casino

Length: 10.4 miles

Approximate riding time: 30 to 45 minutes

Best bike: Road or hybrid bike

Terrain and trail surface: Asphalt

Traffic and hazards: This is a multipurpose road open only to walking, running, and biking. There are some intersections with traffic lights and some without.

Things to see: Desert scenery, wildlife, public art

Getting there: By car: Take I-15 to the St. Rose Parkway exit. Head east and cross Las Vegas Boulevard. Turn right into the driveway for the M Resort & Casino and follow the signs to the parking garage. **GPS:** N35 57.903' / W115 09.986'

THE RIDE

In the 1980s and 1990s, Las Vegas was a boom town—one with severe growing pains. At that time there was only one road that allowed residents to quickly travel from the east to the west part of the valley—Lake Mead. The road, so named because it eventually led to the lake, was the main thoroughfare for motorists and was a heavily traveled road. As the city grew, an east–west beltway was eventually constructed, taking up much of what was then the Lake Mead road. What was left became St. Rose Parkway, being named after the nearby St. Rose Hospital.

St. Rose Parkway turned into a busy 55 mph, eight-lane thoroughfare that begins roughly at Las Vegas Boulevard and goes until it eventually becomes Pecos Road at the newly created beltway. In an effort to make the city more bike friendly, a two-lane, 12-foot, multiuse trail was built along St. Rose Parkway. While the trail isn't in the most scenic spot in Las Vegas, the city has gone to great lengths to make it well worth the trip. Instead of relying on scenery, the city has installed art and incorporated on an old children's tale to make the trail more interesting.

Positioned at several places where the trail intersects a main road are decorative iron pieces showcasing the desert-tolerant plants that grow freely in the area. There are also benches, some of which have covers to provide shade and are adorned with iron-encased decorative stone. While the benches are nice, they only really give a view of St. Rose Parkway. You don't

Lion Habitat

Casinos are known for their constant remodeling, making themselves over with every new idea that comes along. For a while Las Vegas booked itself as a family attraction. The MGM Grand and Circus Circus both built theme parks, trying to attract families. The MGM Grand also built a very elaborate lion habitat inside its casino to show off its company namesake, "Leo the Lion," and his progeny. Leo was famous for roaring at the end of every MGM movie and television show. But where do old lions go when their movie careers are over?

The answer to that is an 8.5-acre ranch just outside Las Vegas called the Lion Habitat. The habitat is a facility accredited by the Zoological Association of America, and for almost eleven years, exotic animal trainer Keith Evans brought his big cats to the habitat at the MGM Grand so tourists could watch them roar, play, or, usually, just lay around. When the MGM Grand closed its habitat in 2012, Evans and his wife, Beverly, built glass enclosures and safety barriers to house their close to forty lions, including seven cubs born in separate litters in November 2012.

The habitat is now open on weekends for tours and educational experiences. Heck, you can even hand-feed the lions if you so choose; that is, if they're not getting groomed or shampooed to keep their coats clean. Not only can you learn about these 300- to 600-pound animals, but you can also take photos, book a private tour, or even become a trainer for a day.

View along St. Rose Parkway

get very far down the trail before you encounter a couple of competitors on your left. One has long ears and a bushy tail, while the other is carrying his own home. Across the trail you'll also see a starting line, and it is at this point that you realize the pair waiting at the starting line are the famed tortoise and hare. This version of the duo is made of colored rock encased in an iron frame. The two sit, motionless, waiting for some silent start signal.

As you make your way down the trail, you'll find other pieces of art before the racing pair are spotted again. One of these is a coyote climbing on some rocks above an unsuspecting roadrunner—a common bird in the area. Along the way you'll also find colorful educational signs that provide a great deal of information about the plants and animals—such as burrowing owls, coyotes, roadrunners, and rabbits—that still make the area their home.

About halfway through the trail you find more sculptures of the race competitors. The rabbit is taking a siesta while the tortoise is making its way—slow and steady—along the trail. At the end of the trail, the pair is seen a third and final time. A finish line crosses the asphalt, and over to the left the tortoise is crossing that line while the hare runs at top speed, doing everything he can in a vain attempt to pull ahead of the tortoise before the finish line is crossed. But alas, slow and steady truly wins the race.

The trail starts at the parking lot by the M Resort & Casino. It then makes its way down the south side of St. Rose Parkway on a trail that is set aside for runners, walkers, and bicyclists. While some main streets have to be crossed at lights, the trail is, for the most part, protected from vehicles. There are, however, a couple of places where the trail crosses entrances to shopping plazas, and it is important to make sure any vehicles in the area see you before you proceed across these intersections.

The trail makes its way down to Paseo Verde Parkway, where you can link up with either the Paseo Verde Trail or the I-215 East Beltway Trail. You can also cross Paseo Verde Parkway and ride the trail back up St. Rose Parkway on the north side of the road. This guide does not follow the trail back up St. Rose Parkway on the north side, mainly because the trail is not yet complete. While there are many places where the trail is finished, well-decorated, and worth the ride, in other places you will have to either ride through gravel or on the sidewalk to meet up with another complete section of the trail. This trail, however, is continually being constructed, so it may be worth checking to see if it has been completed yet when you ride it. The trail is also well-lit on the south side, meaning it can be ridden day or night.

Bike Shop

Bike Shop: 2630 Windmill Pkwy., Henderson; (702) 897-1618; bikeshop-lv.com

MILES AND DIRECTIONS

0.0 Start at the trailhead at the parking lot outside the M Resort & Casino. In 0.2 mile, cross Bruner Avenue.

1.2 Cross Bermuda Road. In 0.3 mile, cross Executive Airport Drive.

2.8 Cross Alper Center Drive.

3.1 Cross the entrance to the shopping plaza on the right, then cross Seven Hills Drive with the light.

3.7 Cross Jeffreys Street with the light. Follow the trail onto the sidewalk, then go to the right and head back to the asphalt trail.

3.9 Cross the entrance into St. Rose Hospital on the right. In 0.2 mile, cross S. Eastern Avenue with the light.

4.8 Cross the "finish line."

5.1 Cross Coronado Center Drive with the light, then follow the sidewalk back to the asphalt trail. The trail ends at Paseo Verde Parkway.

5.2 Turn around and take the trail back to the trailhead.

10.4 Arrive back at the trailhead in the parking lot of the M Resort & Casino.

1

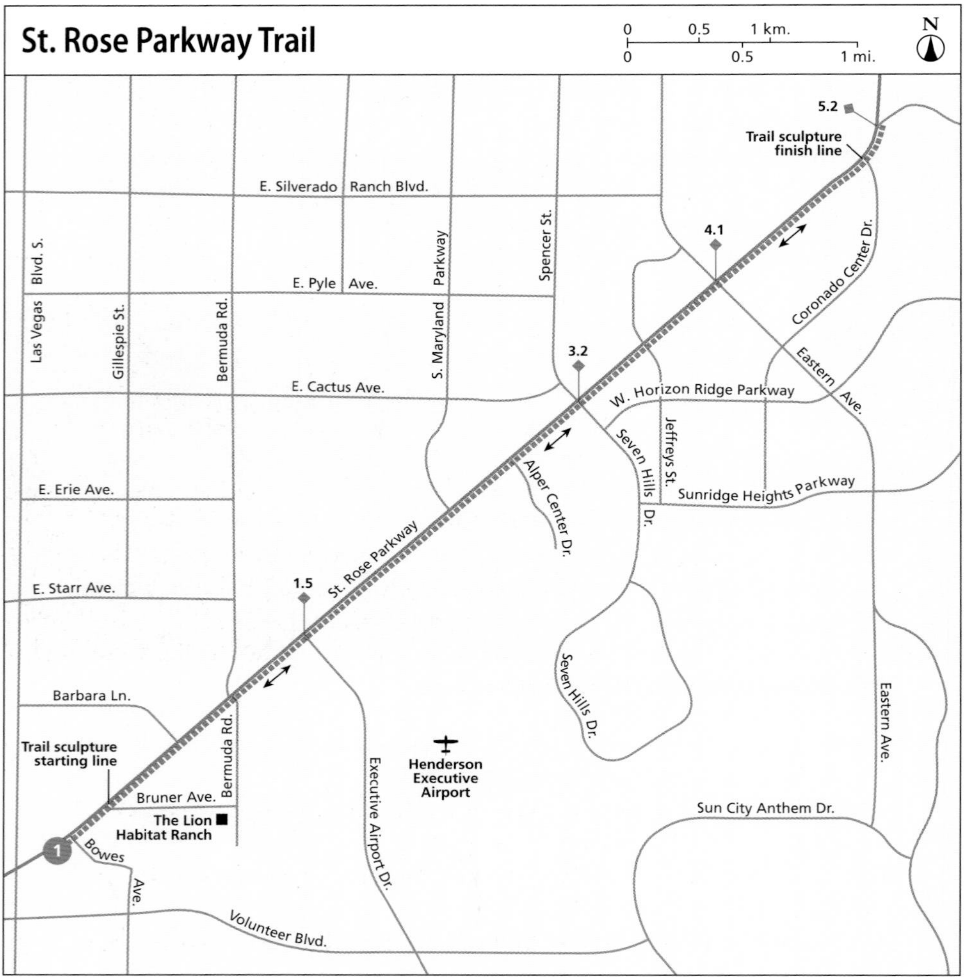

RIDE INFORMATION

Local Events and Attractions

Hostile Grape: Located inside the M Resort & Casino, this wine-tasting bar offers 160 different wines by the glass and over 400 wines by the bottle.

Lion Habitat: Probably the only place outside a zoo where you can hand-feed a lion or pet a lion cub; thecathouse.us.

The tortoise and hare at the start line readying for the race.

Restaurants

Burgers and Brews: Located in the M Resort & Casino; 12300 St. Rose Pkwy., Henderson; (702) 797-1000; themresort.com
Ten Saints Tavern: Located along the trail; 3265 St. Rose Pkwy., Henderson; (702) 982-3720
32 Degrees Draft Bar: Located in the M Resort & Casino; 12300 St. Rose Pkwy., Henderson; (702) 797-1000; themresort.com

Restrooms

Mile 0.0: Gas station at the trailhead
Mile 3.1: Inside shopping plaza
Mile 4.8: Sienna Heights Park

2

Pittman Wash Trail

This ride follows a natural wash that makes its way through the valley on its way to Lake Mead. The beautifully landscaped trail offers more than just a bike ride down an asphalt road. And as you make your way down the trail, it's hard to believe you're in the heart of the desert.

Start: Pebble Park

Length: 8.8 miles

Approximate riding time: 1 to 1.5 hours

Best bike: Road or hybrid bike

Terrain and trail surface: Asphalt

Traffic and hazards: This is a multipurpose road open only to walking, running, and biking. There are some intersections with traffic lights.

Things to see: Desert scenery, wildlife

Getting there: By car: Take the Bruce Woodbury Beltway (I-215) to the Eastern Avenue exit. Head north on Eastern and continue on to Pebble Road. Turn right on Pebble Road and then right again onto Topaz Street. Park in the small parking lot for Pebble Park or on Topaz Street. **GPS:** N36 01.533' / W115 06.850'

THE RIDE

When you're writing a guide about trails, you really should try to be impartial as you describe the trails, making sure not to favor one over the other. That said, if I could choose a favorite paved trail in Las Vegas, it would be the Pittman Wash Trail. In my opinion, this is one of the best laid-out trails in the entire valley.

The trail follows a cement wash called Pittman Wash. A wash is a water channel that is filled with water at certain times of the year. The purpose of the Pittman Wash is to provide a safe passage for water runoff generated after a storm. The trail makes great use of an area that would otherwise be left vacant. It is also constructed in such a way as to avoid a steep climb no matter which direction you travel. This is even more impressive when you realize the trail changes 264 feet in elevation from start to finish.

As the cement portion of the Pittman Wash progresses, it eventually finds its way to a natural wash populated with all manner of birds and other wildlife, as well as plants, trees, and shrubs. This area is one of the most beautiful in the valley, and the trail is one of those that makes you forget you're even in a desert. As the trail progresses, the wash gets wider and wider, appearing almost as a wooded valley running through the heart of Henderson—the town neighboring Las Vegas. While on the trail, take the time to notice the many birds in the area, including roadrunners, which, true to their name, often run across the trail.

The Pittman Wash Trail is one of those trails that doesn't require you to leave the asphalt once you get on it. In a couple of places there are offshoot trails leading to the surrounding communities. These trails should not be taken. On three occasions, the trail also goes down into the wash under bridges. If it is, or has been, raining, these trails should be avoided. Washes—both natural and man-made—allow water to flow through channels down to Lake Mead. When it rains in Las Vegas, it rains hard and fast, making flash floods not at all uncommon. When water flows in washes, it can build speed, acting much like a raging river. Getting caught in that river can not only be dangerous, but also life-threatening.

Whenever the trail goes into the wash, there is an alternate route that passes over the street. Some of these crossover opportunities are easy to spot, while others are a little more difficult. Luckily, the trail on either side of every road is marked with large, round, rusty metal trail markers that say Pittman Wash Trail. It is a simple matter of looking for these markers to find the trail. Additionally, all street crossings are aided by crosswalks, many of which have warning lights that can be activated to notify cars you are crossing the street.

Bike Shops

Aspen Creek Cycling: 1590 W. Horizon Ridge Pkwy., #140, Henderson; (702) 893-2453; aspencreekcycling.com

Bike Shop: 2630 Windmill Pkwy., Henderson; (702) 897-1618; bikeshop-lv.com

McGhie's Ski, Bike, and Board: 19 S. Stephanie St., Ste. 100, Henderson; (702) 800-3636; mcghies.com

REI: 2220 Village Walk Dr., #150, Henderson; (702) 896-7111; rei.com

VegasVelo Bicycles: 691 N. Valle Verde Dr., Ste. 130, Henderson; (702) 503-9005; vegasvelo.com

Project GREEN

Riding along the Pittman Wash Trail takes you past one of the few remaining large areas of natural habitat left in Green Valley. Instead of trying to develop the land in this area that forms a natural wash, the City of Henderson decided to create a program that would protect this 2.5-mile ecosystem and keep it natural. The result is Project GREEN (Green Valley Ecology, Environment, and Nature). The stated goal of the project is "to restore one of the few remaining large areas of natural habitat in the Green Valley area."

The project was supported by the people of Henderson, who voted to spend $7,250,000 for the construction of recreational trails, with Pittman Wash being one of those trails. The Eastman Kodak Company granted Project GREEN $1,000 for the purchase of plants and trees to be planted along the trail. Additionally, educational trails, which travel right into the wash, were created as a way of helping visitors become more knowledgeable about the wash and its ecosystem.

Start the trail at Pebble Park. The parking lot is small, but there is space on Topaz Street to park. Ride down Topaz Street toward Pebble Road. Cross Pebble Road at the crosswalk and go to the trailhead to the left of the wash. You'll know you're on the trail because of the marker and the yellow dashes that run along the asphalt trail. The trail makes its way between communities of houses on one side and the wash on the other. Follow the trail to Wigwam Parkway and cross Wigwam at the lighted crosswalk.

Pecos Road is the first place where you can either go under the road by heading down into the wash or cross the road at the crosswalk. Going under the road is a great way to avoid traffic; however, you should only take the trail into the wash if it is not, or has not been, raining. About 1.5 miles into the ride, you'll see a set of stairs that lead down into the wash. This is one of the hiking trails that actually go into the wash. This trail has educational markers that give hikers information on the wash and all it has to offer. It is a great activity for families.

About 2 miles into the ride, the trail turns to the right, making a large U-shaped bend. Follow the trail to the left after the bend and head to Green Valley Parkway. As you travel on this portion of the trail, you'll ride under a canopy of trees. Be sure to notice the many birds that make these trees their home. At Green Valley Parkway you can again choose to either go under the road or over the road. If you choose to cross Green Valley Parkway at the

Both cyclists and runners use the Pittman Wash Trail.

crosswalk, you'll pick up the trail again to the left of the wash. If you go under, follow the cement trail as it crosses the wash and comes out on the other side.

Here the trail makes its way past one of the widest parts of the wash. The trail also winds its way through a grassy area filled with trees. There is a small amphitheater on one side of the trail and a sports complex on the other. Follow the trail to Valle Verde Drive, where you will again have the choice of going under the road or crossing the road at the crosswalk. From here you'll follow the trail to Arroyo Grande Boulevard, where the trail ends. If you prefer, you can also cross Arroyo Grande Boulevard and head into Arroyo Grande Park, or you can simply head back up the trail to the trailhead.

MILES AND DIRECTIONS

0.0 Start at Pebble Park. Turn left onto Topaz Street and follow it down to Pebble Road.

0.1 Cross Pebble Road at the lighted crosswalk. Turn right and pick up the trail at the trailhead on the left. The asphalt trail is marked with yellow dashed lines.

0.5 Cross Wigwam at the lighted crosswalk.

Pittman Wash Trail

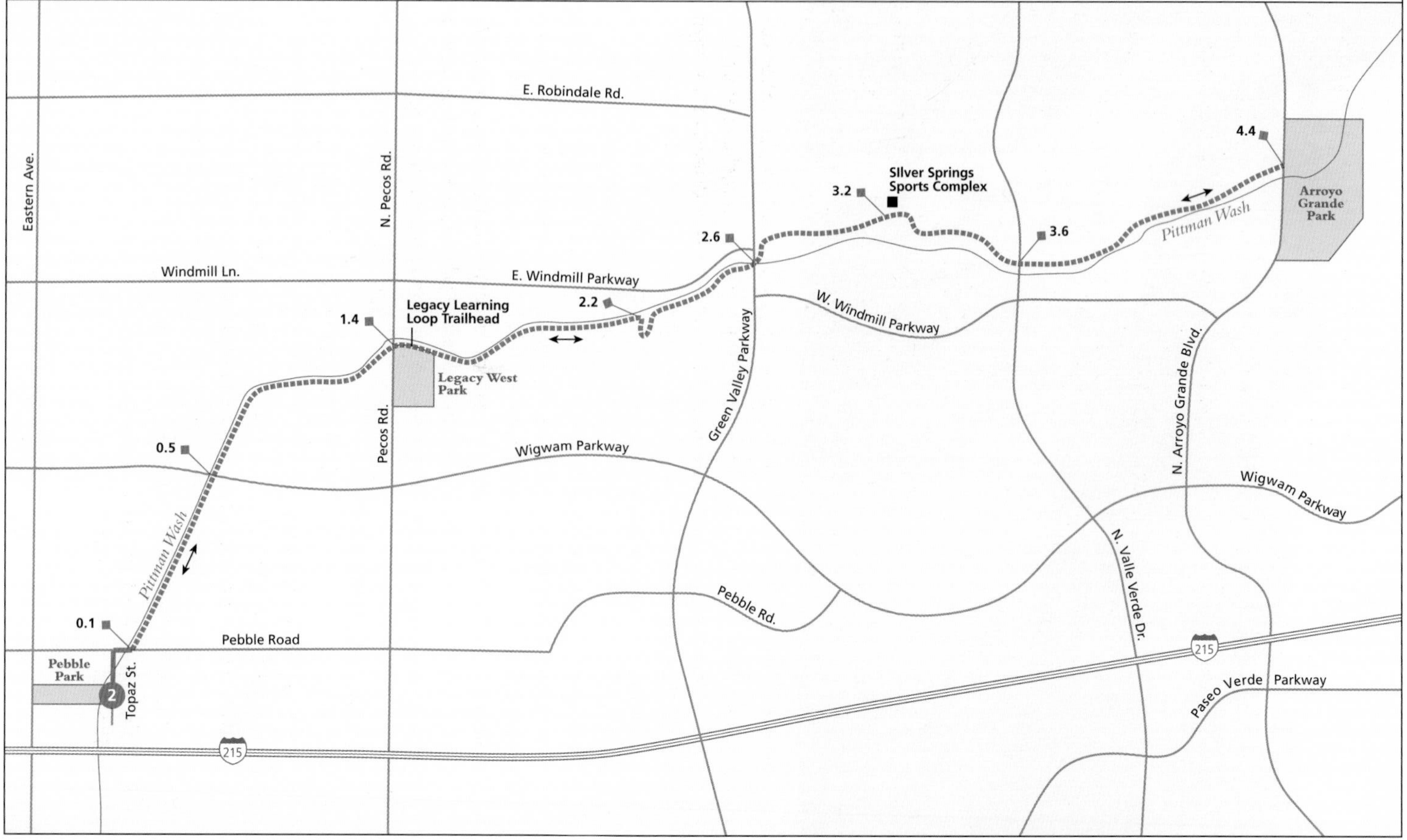

1.4 Take the trail under Pecos Road or cross Pecos Road at the lighted crosswalk. Turn right after crossing Pecos and pick up the trail on the left.

1.5 Pass the entrance to the Legacy Learning Loop on the left.

2.2 Follow the trail as it curves to the right, making a large U-shaped bend. In 0.3 mile, follow the trail to the left.

2.6 Take the trail under Green Valley Parkway or cross that street at the lighted crosswalk. If you take the trail under the street, turn left and cross the wash, picking the trail back up at the end of the bridge on the opposite side of the wash. If you cross the street, turn left at Green Valley Parkway to find the crosswalk.

3.2 Pass the Silver Springs Sports Complex. In 0.2 mile, pass the Eagle Scout Trail on the right.

3.6 Cross Valle Verde Drive at the lighted crosswalk or take the trail under the street to the right. On the other side of Valle Verde, take the asphalt trail and continue straight. Do not take the wide cement trail to the right of the asphalt trail.

4.0 Follow the trail into a quick drop and a short climb on the other side.

4.4 The trail ends at Arroyo Grande Boulevard. This is the turnaround point for the ride. You can also cross the street and head into Arroyo Grande Park.

8.8 Arrive back at Pebble Park.

RIDE INFORMATION

Local Events and Attractions

Two trails lead into the wash from the Pittman Wash Trail: the Legacy Learning Loop and the Eagle Scout Trail. Both of these trails provide great opportunities to learn a little more about the ecosystem thriving in the wash.

Restaurants

Havana Grill: 8878 S. Eastern Ave., #100, Las Vegas; (702) 932-9310; havanagrillcuban.com

Island Sushi and Grill: 9400 S. Eastern Ave., Las Vegas; (702) 221-1600; islandsushiandgrill.com. Hawaiian and Japanese cuisine.

Restrooms

Mile 1.4: Legacy West Park

Mile 4.4: Arroyo Grande Park

3

Paseo Verde Trail

This family-friendly trail is one of the most commonly used trails in all of Green Valley, probably because when riding the trail, it's easy to forget you're in a desert. The trail also passes several parks, making it a perfect thoroughfare for families going to and from the park.

Start: Cumorah Plaza parking lot

Length: 5.0 miles

Approximate riding time: 45 minutes to 1 hour

Best bike: Road or hybrid bike

Terrain and trail surface: Asphalt

Traffic and hazards: This is a multipurpose road open only to walking, running, and biking. There are some intersections with traffic lights and some without.

Things to see: Desert landscaping, parks

Getting there: **By car:** Take the Bruce Woodbury Beltway (I-215) to the Pecos Road exit. Head south onto St. Rose Parkway and then left onto Paseo Verde Parkway. Park in the Cumorah Plaza. **GPS:** N36 01.085' / W115 05.992'

THE RIDE

This is probably one of the most often used trails in all of Green Valley, due in part to two factors: The trail passes no less than three parks, and Paseo Verde is a main thoroughfare. The other thing that makes the trail popular is that it is just beautiful. It is decorated with established plants, grass, and trees and there is even a rose garden on part of the trail. The trail is so well landscaped that when riding under the canopy of trees, it's easy to forget you're in a desert.

Another thing that makes the trail popular is that the wide asphalt section is separate from the cement sidewalk. This means people walking can take the sidewalk, allowing runners and cyclists almost exclusive use of the asphalt trail. This is, however, a popular runner's trail, so it is best to watch for pedestrians while riding. For this reason, a bell is a useful piece of equipment when riding the trail. While the trailhead is officially at the corner of St. Rose Parkway and Paseo Verde, the trail can be accessed at any point; for example, Discovery Park or Paseo Verde Park. Each of these two parks have restroom facilities and parking lots which allow easy access to the trail.

The trail itself consists of a downward slope from the trailhead to the end. The slope is gradual, though you can gain quite a bit of speed if you allow the bike to run freely. This isn't always the best idea because you do have to cross some streets and there are pedestrians that don't always react well to fast-moving bikes. The climb back to the trailhead is more gradual than the descent might lead you to believe, meaning almost anyone can ride the trail, regardless of their level of fitness.

The trail starts at Paseo Vista Park. There are yellow bollards in the road indicating the trailhead. It begins on a cement sidewalk, but quickly turns to asphalt. The trail winds its way down Paseo Verde Parkway, and while you do have to cross some streets, you don't ever have to get off the trail. As you make your way down the trail, you'll cross a couple entrances to gated communities. It is a good idea to watch for vehicles pulling into these communities from behind you. Although they are required to do so, drivers don't always yield to bicyclists, so it is always best to make sure they stop before you enter any intersection.

The first major intersection you cross is Green Valley Parkway. This street is busy and must be crossed with a light. After you cross Green Valley Parkway, you'll eventually make your way down to Discovery Park, the largest park on the trail. Not much farther down the trail is Paseo Verde Park, a smaller but

Bike Shops

Aspen Creek Cycling: 1590 W. Horizon Ridge Pkwy., #140, Henderson; (702) 893-2453; aspencreekcycling.com

Bike Shop: 2630 Windmill Pkwy., Henderson; (702) 897-1618; bikeshop-lv.com

McGhie's Ski, Bike, and Board: 19 S. Stephanie St., Ste. 100, Henderson; (702) 800-3636; mcghies.com

REI: 2220 Village Walk Dr., #150, Henderson; (702) 896-7111; rei.com

Riding the Paseo Verde Trail makes you forget you're in the desert.

well-used park. The trail ends shortly after that on South Valle Verde Drive. From here you turn around and make the steady but gradual climb back to the trailhead.

The trailhead for this trail is a short distance from the St. Rose Trail and if you wanted, you could combine the two trails into one long, 20-mile loop. In fact, many of the trails in the Green Valley area link to other trails, allowing offshoot and alternate routes that provide a great deal of variety when riding around the valley.

Bicycle Friendly Community

The city of Henderson has worked hard over the years to establish itself as bike friendly. Recently they have been recognized for their efforts by being awarded the bronze level as a Bicycle Friendly Community by the League of American Cyclists. To qualify for this award, Henderson needed to demonstrate they had created safer roadways for cyclists, convenient bicycling amenities, recreational activities, and bicycle-related events. The city of Henderson now offers 184 miles of hiking and biking trails. They also have a program called Bike It or Hike It in which taking a selfie at any trailhead and uploading it to the city's website will qualify you for a chance to win prizes.

Paseo Verde Trail

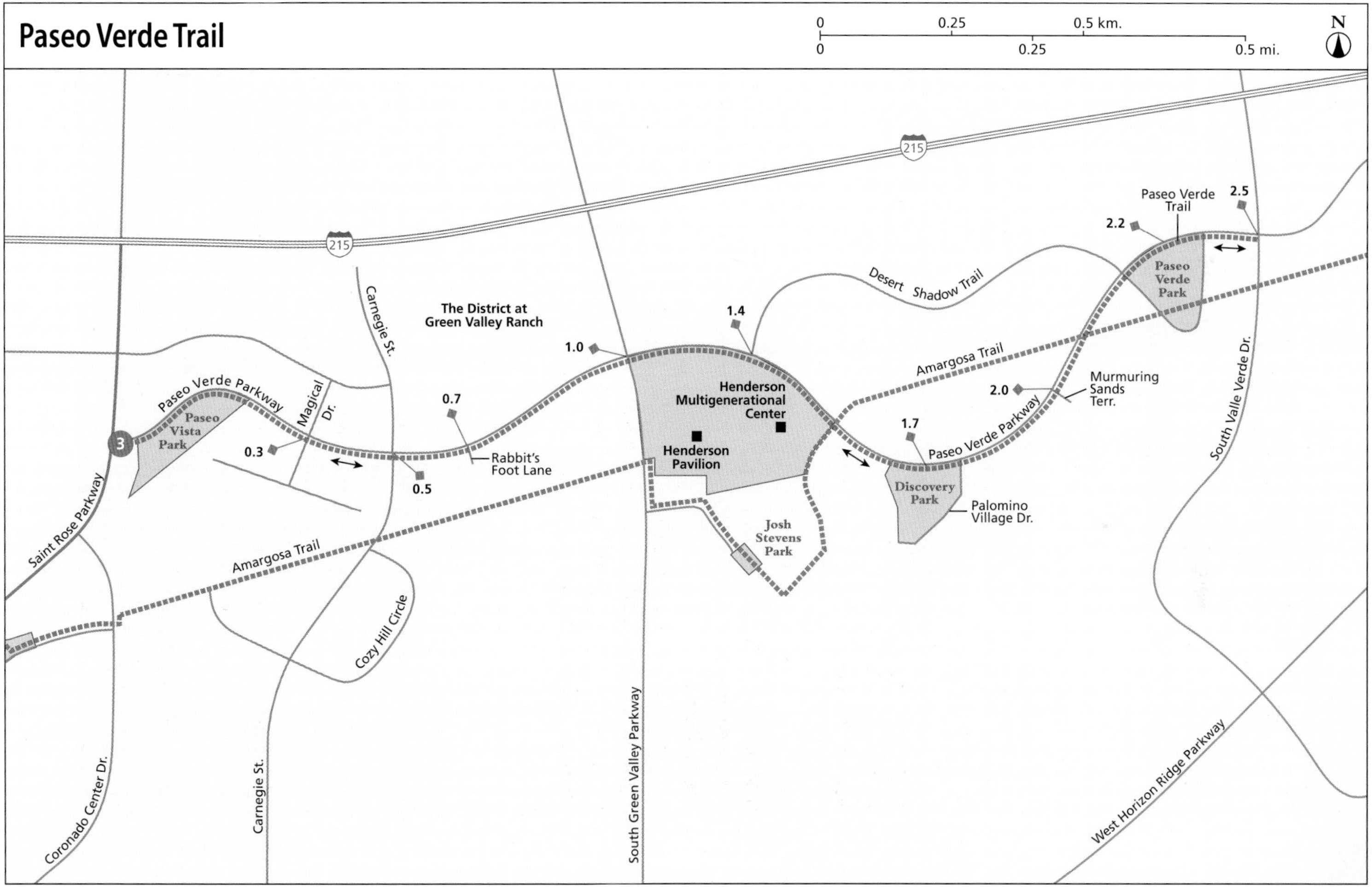

MILES AND DIRECTIONS

0.0 Start at the trailhead at the corner of St. Rose Parkway and Paseo Verde Parkway.

0.3 Cross Magical Drive. In 0.2 mile, cross Carnegie Street.

0.7 Cross Rabbit's Foot Lane. In 0.3 mile, cross Green Valley Parkway with the light.

1.4 Cross the entrance to the Henderson Multigenerational Center and follow the trail to the right.

1.7 Pass Discovery Park and cross Palomino Village Drive.

2.0 Cross Murmuring Sands Terrace. In 0.2 mile, cross Desert Shadow Trail and pass Paseo Verde Park.

2.4 Cross Desert Shadow Trail a second time and follow the trail to South Valle Verde Drive.

2.5 Turn around and head back up the trail to the trailhead.

5.0 Arrive back at the trailhead.

RIDE INFORMATION

Local Events and Attractions

The Gallery: The Gallery is a free-to-the-public art gallery located inside the Henderson Multigenerational Center; cityofhenderson.com.

Henderson Pavilion: The largest outdoor amphitheater in Nevada is a state-of-the-art venue for both visual and performing arts; cityofhenderson.com.

Henderson Multigenerational Center/Aquatic Complex: The 84,120-square-foot facility has a demonstration kitchen, jogging track, adult lounge, and dance room, as well as an outdoor aquatic complex; cityofhenderson.com.

Restaurants

Balboa Pizza: Located in the District; 2265 Village Walk Dr., #141, Henderson; (702) 407-5273; districttaverngroup.com

Lucille's Smokehouse Bar-B-Que: Located in the District; 2245 Village Walk Dr., Henderson; (702) 257-7427; lucillesbbq.com

Restrooms

Mile 0.0: Trailhead in Paseo Vista Park

Mile 1.4: Inside the Henderson Multigenerational Center

Mile 1.7: Discovery Park

Mile 2.4: Paseo Verde Park

4

Amargosa Trail

The Amargosa Trail snakes its way behind and between many different communities, using land that would otherwise be left vacant. Unlike many of the Green Valley trails, this trail is actually divided into several sections, requiring you to travel on some streets to make the connections. Still, the trail is well-landscaped and is just a fun trail to ride.

Start: Siena Heights Park

Length: 9.5 miles

Approximate riding time: 1 to 1.5 hours

Best bike: Road or hybrid bike

Terrain and trail surface: Asphalt

Traffic and hazards: This is a multipurpose road open only to walking, running, and biking. There are some intersections with traffic lights and some without.

Things to see: Desert landscaping, parks

Getting there: By car: Take the Bruce Woodbury Beltway (I-215) to the Pecos Road exit. Head south onto St. Rose Parkway, left onto Coronado Center Drive, and right onto Siena Heights Drive. Park at Siena Heights Park. **GPS:** N36 00.763' / W115 06.344'

THE RIDE

This $2.2 million trail system winds its way through the back neighborhoods of Green Valley. Except for a couple of short parts, the trail is a wide, two-lane asphalt trail that is well protected from motor vehicles—because they are not allowed on the trail. The trailhead is in Siena Heights Park, which is a little, out-of-the-way park just off St. Rose Parkway. The park includes restroom facilities, tennis courts, a playground, a disc golf course, and several bocce courts. There is also a small parking lot where you can leave your car.

This trail makes its way from St. Rose Parkway all the way to Stephanie Street through meticulously landscaped areas designed to take advantage of what would otherwise be wasted space. There are many benches along the way, and the entire trail is well lit so it can be ridden day or night. This is a very popular trail, and it is not uncommon to see families strolling along with their children in tow.

The trail officially starts at Siena Heights Park. From there you turn left and travel a short distance down Siena Heights Drive. You can ride on either the sidewalk or the street. This is not a very busy area, so street travel is not necessarily treacherous. However, the road curves, so it is best to make sure traffic sees you before you pull out. From here you follow Siena Heights Drive until it dead-ends at Coronado Center Drive. If you look over to your left, you will easily see the asphalt trail across the street.

At this point you will be traveling along the trail and once you get on it, you won't really get off except for a couple of places where the trail isn't continuous. This first part of the asphalt trail is one of the longest. It stretches from Coronado Center Drive to Green Valley Parkway, following wooden power-line poles. The first road you cross is Cozy Hill Circle, which is an offshoot of a roundabout leading to a housing community. The next street is Carnegie, which is not a busy street, but does have more traffic than Cozy Hill Circle. Following Carnegie Street is a longer portion of the trail leading to Green Valley Parkway. This is a busy street, and to assist in crossing, a lighted crosswalk has been installed. It is best to use the crosswalk because it is not always easy to be seen on the side of the road.

After you cross Green Valley Parkway, turn right and go up the sidewalk to Benji Drive. Turn left on Benji Drive and follow it to Josh Stevens Park, located at the point where Benji Drive intersects with Sunset Crossing Lane. Take the sidewalk through Josh Stevens Park, heading back through the park. The sidewalk narrows a bit as it goes between a couple of communities, but the asphalt trail is clearly visible just ahead. Once you reach the asphalt trail, take it to the left and follow it down as it makes its way between communities on each side. Cross Radiant Lane, which is a

Bike Shops

Aspen Creek Cycling: 1590 W. Horizon Ridge Pkwy., #140, Henderson; (702) 893-2453; aspencreekcycling.com
Bike Shop: 2630 Windmill Pkwy., Henderson; (702) 897-1618; bikeshop-lv.com
McGhie's Ski, Bike, and Board: 19 S. Stephanie St., Ste. 100, Henderson; (702) 800-3636; mcghies.com
REI: 2220 Village Walk Dr., #150, Henderson; (702) 896-7111; rei.com

Lush landscaping along the Amargosa Trail

gated-off road, and follow the trail to the left. Just as the trail turns, an offshoot leads to Pavilion Park, a small community park. Continue following the trail, past the park, down to where it meets up with the Paseo Verde Trail.

Once the trails meet, turn left and cross Paseo Verde Parkway using the established crosswalk. Paseo Verde Parkway is a four-lane road separated by a barrier. The walkway allows you to pass through the barrier while crossing the street. Note that you'll actually have to cross Paseo Verde Parkway twice: at the start of the crosswalk and then at the end of the crosswalk. Paseo Verde Parkway is a busy street, so watch carefully for traffic before crossing.

Once you cross Paseo Verde Parkway, you'll meet back up with the Amargosa Trail. Shortly into the trail, it forks. Going straight is a fun offshoot that only adds about 0.2 mile to the trip. This guide follows that offshoot on the way down the trail, but not on the way back to the trailhead. Follow the offshoot by going straight instead of taking the trail to the right. From here you cross Deer Crossing Way and then make your way down a hill toward Bobtail Circle. There is a small park on the corner.

After you cross Bobtail Circle, continue straight on the sidewalk, crossing Desert Shadow Trail. From here you turn right to meet back up with the asphalt trail a short distance ahead. Take that trail, following it downward to its end at Windfall Avenue. You will also pass another small park towards the bottom of the hill. Once you reach Windfall Avenue, turn around and climb back out to the point where the trail splits after you crossed Paseo Verde Parkway.

When you reach the split, turn left and follow the trail downward as it makes its way toward Paseo Verde Parkway. When you reach Paseo Verde Parkway, turn left and cross that street using the crosswalk. On the other side of the crosswalk you'll again meet up with the Paseo Verde Trail. Turn left and follow that trail down to Valle Verde Drive, where it ends. Cross Valle Verde Drive and turn right, following the sidewalk up until you find the asphalt trail on your left. This is the next section of the Amargosa Trail and it leads all the way to Stephanie Street, where the trail ends. From here you can turn around and go back to the trailhead.

MILES AND DIRECTIONS

0.0 Start at the trailhead at Siena Heights Park. In 0.1 mile, turn left on Siena Heights Drive.

0.3 Turn left onto Coronado Center Drive and then take the asphalt trail to the right.

0.5 Cross Cozy Hill Circle. In 0.3 mile, cross Carnegie Street.

1.4 Cross Green Valley Parkway using the crosswalk, then turn right and follow the sidewalk up to Benji Drive.

1.5 Turn left on Benji Drive and follow the road to the right.

1.7 Cross Sunset Crossing and enter Josh Stevens Park. Follow the sidewalk to the back of the park.

1.8 Meet up with the asphalt trail and take it to the left. Cross Radiant Lane.

1.9 Stay straight on the trail as it curves to the left. Do not take the offshoot trail to the park on the right.

2.2 The Amargosa Trail meets the Paseo Verde Trail. Take the Paseo Verde Trail to the left and cross Paseo Verde Parkway with the crosswalk.

2.3 When the trail splits, stay straight. Cross Deer Crossing Way and meet up with the asphalt trail on the other side of the road.

2.5 Go down the hill, pass the small park on the right, and cross Bobtail Circle. Follow the sidewalk and cross Desert Shadow Trail. Turn right and follow the sidewalk to the asphalt trail on the left.

2.6 Cross Golden View Street and meet back up with the asphalt trail. Follow the trail down to Windfall Avenue.

2.9 Turn back around at Windfall Avenue and climb back up the trail. In 0.1 mile, cross Golden View Street.

Amargosa Trail

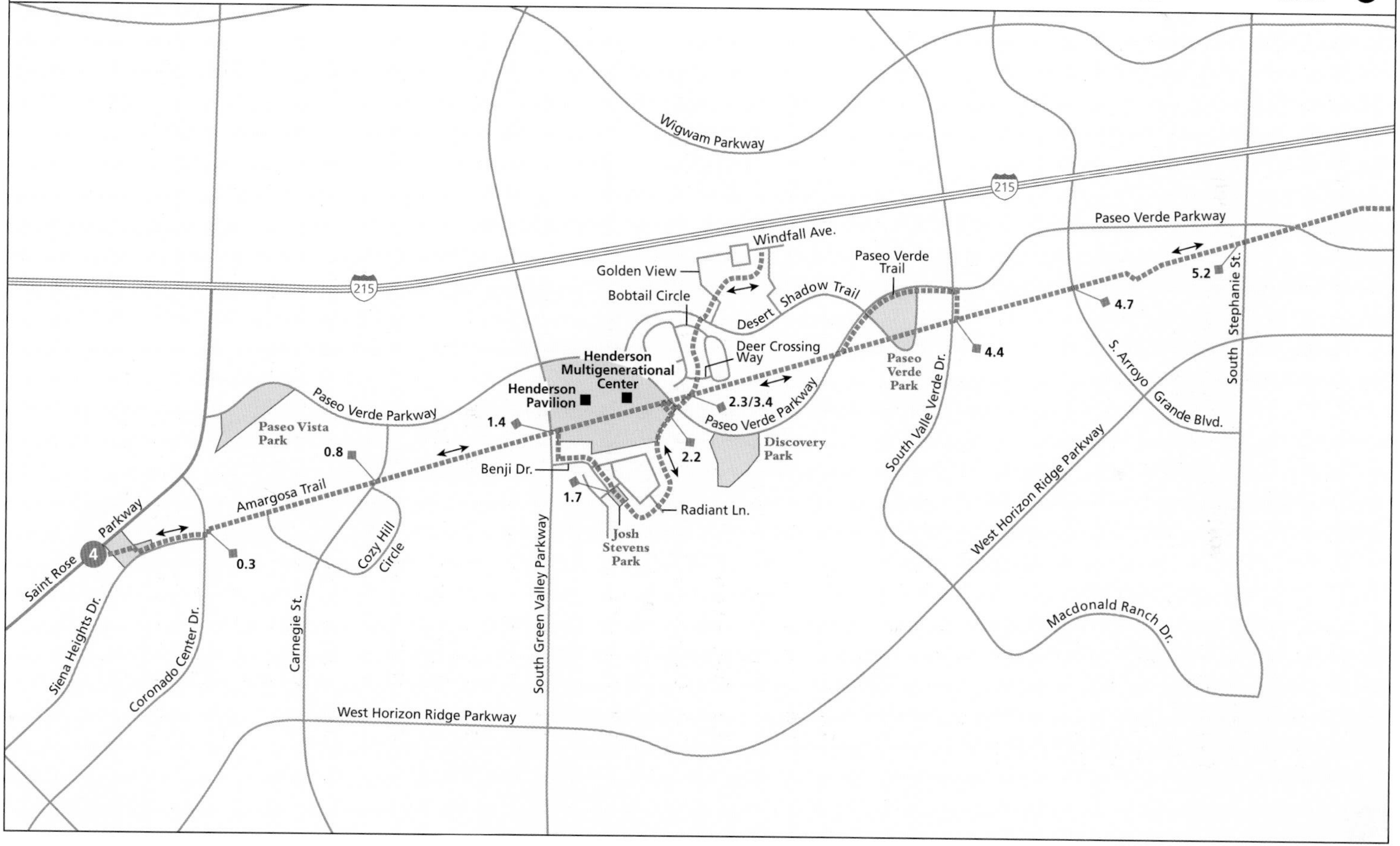

3.1 Turn right on Desert Shadow Trail and use the crosswalk to cross Desert Shadow and then Bobtail Circle. At mile 3.3, cross Deer Crossing Way.

3.4 Meet back up with the Amargosa Trail (where it split previously) and take the trail to the left.

3.8 Turn left on the sidewalk to Paseo Verde Parkway and use the crosswalk to cross the parkway. In 0.1 mile, turn left onto Paseo Verde Trail and follow it down.

4.0 Cross Desert Shadow Trail. In 0.2 mile, cross Desert Shadow Trail again.

4.3 Cross Valle Verde Drive and turn right, following the sidewalk to the asphalt trail on the left.

4.4 Turn left onto the asphalt trail, which is the last section of the Amargosa Trail. In 0.3 mile, cross Arroyo Grande Boulevard.

5.2 End at Stephanie Street. This is the turnaround point for the ride.

5.7 Cross Arroyo Grande Boulevard.

6.0 Turn right onto Valle Verde Drive and follow the sidewalk to the crosswalk, where you cross Valle Verde Drive in 0.1 mile.

6.2 Cross Desert Shadow Trail. In 0.2 mile, cross Desert Shadow Trail again.

6.5 Cross Paseo Verde Parkway with the crosswalk. Turn left after crossing Paseo Verde Parkway on the other side of the crosswalk and meet back up with the asphalt trail on your right.

7.0 Take the trail to the left at the split and then cross Paseo Verde Parkway using the crosswalk.

7.2 Turn left after crossing Paseo Verde Parkway, meeting up with the Paseo Verde Trail. Take the trail to the right after passing the seating area.

7.5 Follow the trail, crossing Radiant Lane.

7.6 Follow the asphalt trail to the end and then take the sidewalk to the right, going through Josh Stevens Park.

7.7 Cross Sunset Crossing and follow Benji Drive.

7.9 Turn left on Green Valley Parkway and follow the sidewalk to the crosswalk. In 0.1 mile, cross Green Valley Parkway at the crosswalk.

8.6 Cross Carnegie Street. In 0.1 mile, cross Cozy Hill Circle.

9.2 Turn left on Coronado Center Drive. In 0.1 mile, turn right on Siena Heights Drive.

9.5 Follow the sidewalk to Siena Heights Drive, back to the trailhead.

RIDE INFORMATION

Local Events and Attractions

The Gallery: The Gallery is a free-to-the-public art gallery located inside the Henderson Multigenerational Center; cityofhenderson.com.

Henderson Pavilion: The largest outdoor amphitheater in Nevada is a state-of-the-art venue for both visual and performing arts; cityofhenderson.com.

Henderson Multigenerational Center/Aquatic Complex: The 84,120-square-foot facility has a demonstration kitchen, jogging track, adult lounge, and dance room, as well as an outdoor aquatic complex; cityofhenderson.com.

Restaurants

Lucille's Smokehouse Bar-B-Que: Located in the District; 2245 Village Walk Dr., Henderson; (702) 257-7427; lucillesbbq.com

Settebello Pizzeria Napoletana: Located in the District, serving official pizza from Italy; 140 S. Green Valley Pkwy., Henderson; (702) 222-3556; settebello.net

Restrooms

Mile 0.0: Trailhead in Siena Heights Park

Mile 4.0: Paseo Verde Park

Mile 5.2: Gas station on Stephanie Street

5

Anthem East Trail

The Anthem East Trail makes its way into the hills and valleys of the Sloan Canyon right behind houses, a school, and a park. Even though it's close to many homes, when riding the trail, it is easy to forget you are anywhere near an established community.

Start: Anthem Hills Park

Length: 4.4 miles

Approximate riding time: 45 minutes to 1 hour

Best bike: Mountain bike

Terrain and trail surface: Asphalt and dirt trail

Traffic and hazards: This is a multipurpose trail open to hiking, running, horseback riding, and biking. You should always give the right of way to hikers, runners, and those riding horseback.

Things to see: Desert plants and animals

Getting there: By car: Take the Bruce Woodbury Beltway (I-215) to the Eastern Avenue exit. Head south onto Eastern, left onto Reunion Drive, and left onto McCullough Hills Parkway. Take the first left and then the right to Anthem Hills Park. Park at the trailhead. **GPS:** N35 58.974' / W115 05.027'

THE RIDE

The Anthem East Trail is so named because it makes its way into the hills of Sloan Canyon behind the Anthem community. Even though you are riding in the hills just behind a well-established community, you get the feeling you are riding your trusty steed, just like the cowboys of old, out in the open desert. In fact, when on this trail, it's easy to forget you are anywhere near Las Vegas. That is, of course, once you get back into the hills. Before that you are presented with wonderful views of the Las Vegas valley as it opens up in front of you.

The first part of the trail is asphalt and is heavily used by people just walking, so be courteous and move out of the way for pedestrians. A little over a half mile into the trail, the road turns to a dirt trail that winds its way up into the hills. As it travels through the canyon, the trail makes its way into and out of a wash that runs through the canyon. There are signs along the trail warning of riding in the wash while it is raining. Be sure to heed these signs. Flash floods are common in the Mojave Desert, and these washes are where the water flows. Faster than you can imagine, water can come rushing down a wash, sweeping away everything in its path—including bike riders and their bikes.

When riding in the wash, be sure to keep a firm grip on the bike's handlebars and continue pedaling. This particular wash, in many places, is filled with deep gravel that can bog down the bike and make it hard to move. It is not uncommon for the front tire to jump from one groove in the gravel to another, causing the handlebars to turn sharply, which can cause you to fall. Other than the warning signs, there are few obstacles along the trail. There is one tricky downhill section where the trail narrows into singletrack and travels into the black rocks alongside the hill. There are also some significant climbs, but other than that, the trail is relatively easy.

When riding the Anthem East Trail, it is important to follow the trail markers. Many unofficial trails have been blazed in this area. Not only are these trails illegal, but following them can be confusing and it is easy to get lost. Luckily, the Anthem East Trail is simple to follow because it is well-marked with square, rusty metal markers that have the name of the trail as well as directional arrows. As long as you follow these markers, you'll be fine.

The trail starts in the parking lot at Anthem Hills Park. The trailhead is clearly marked, and there is a covered bench right next to the trail. The first part of the trail is asphalt. Follow this trail as it winds up into the hills through a series of switchbacks. Not far up the trail, you'll find a hiking trail to the right called Bear Paw Trail. This is a fun trail that can be hiked before starting your ride; however, do not take your bike on this trail.

Bike Shops

Aspen Creek Cycling: 1590 W. Horizon Ridge Pkwy., #140, Henderson; (702) 893-2453; aspencreekcycling.com

Bike Shop: 2630 Windmill Pkwy., Henderson; (702) 897-1618; bikeshop-lv.com

McGhie's Ski, Bike, and Board: 19 S. Stephanie St., Ste. 100, Henderson; (702) 800-3636; mcghies.com

REI: 2220 Village Walk Dr., #150, Henderson; (702) 896-7111; rei.com

A rider makes his way down the first downhill section of the Anthem East Trail.

Located at a couple of spots on the asphalt trail are scenic overlooks that give terrific views of the Las Vegas valley. These are great places to stop and take in those views. About halfway up the trail, the asphalt path splits. It's best not to take the split to the right. Although it will lead you to the dirt part of the trail, you'll have to climb a steep hill to get there. Instead, continue on the left split to the top of the hill. When the asphalt dead-ends at a dirt road, cross the dirt road and pick up the little-bit-wider-than-singletrack trail. Take this trail to the left and follow it as it climbs up the hill. The large dirt road is commonly used by horseback riders who use the trail as well.

Once you reach the top of the hill, about a mile into the ride, the trail turns to the right and starts a tricky downhill section. Follow this trail as it narrows and snakes its way through the black rocks that decorate the canyon. This trail is narrow and tight, and inexperienced riders may want to walk this section. Close to the end of this downhill section, the trail widens as it drops into the wash.

Follow the trail into the wash, making sure to continue pedaling and keeping a firm grip on the handlebars. On the other side of the wash, take the sharp right turn and head up onto the hill, following the trail to the left as it climbs up the hill. At the top of the hill, take the singletrack to the right. About 2 miles into the ride, the trail makes its way back down into the wash. Follow the trail through the wash up to the other side. The trail ends where the singletrack comes out of the wash and meets the dirt road. You'll know you are at the end of the trail because there is a marker with the name of the trail but no directional arrow. Here you turn and ride back.

Be careful not to be fooled by the dirt road. This road travels through Sloan Canyon and at times is actually part of the trail. The dirt road continues to travel up the hill, back into the canyon. If you want to make the ride longer, you can take the road. Just be aware, the dirt road is not as well-groomed as the trail and is not intended to be ridden as part of the trail.

MILES AND DIRECTIONS

0.0 Start at the Anthem Hills Trailhead. Take the asphalt road next to the covered bench.

0.2 Stay straight. Do not take the trail to the right.

0.4 Follow the trail as it curves to the right and continue to follow the switchbacks.

0.5 Follow the trail to the left. At 0.6 mile, cross the dirt road and take the narrower trail on the other side. Turn left and follow that trail up the hill.

0.7 Take the drop into the steep climb. In 0.1 mile, take the small drop and follow the trail as it climbs the hill.

0.9 Follow the narrower singletrack trail to the right at the trail marker. Begin a tricky downhill section along the side of the hill.

1.0 Follow the trail to the right when it widens and continue the downhill section.

1.2 Cross the wash, following the trail markers. Pick up the trail to the right and climb the hill. Do not follow the dirt road to the right or the left.

1.3 Follow the trail as it turns to the left at the trail marker. Continue straight at the trail marker at 1.4 miles and climb to the top of the hill.

1.6 Follow the singletrack trail to the right and start another downhill section of the trail. Stay straight at the trail marker at 1.8 miles.

1.9 Follow the trail as it goes down into the wash. Continue straight into the wash at the trail marker at 2.0 miles.

2.1 Stay straight. Do not take the offshoot trail to the right.

2.2 Cross the wash and meet up with the dirt road. Turn around and head back the way you came, following the trail markers to the trailhead.

4.4 Arrive back at the trailhead.

5

Anthem East Trail

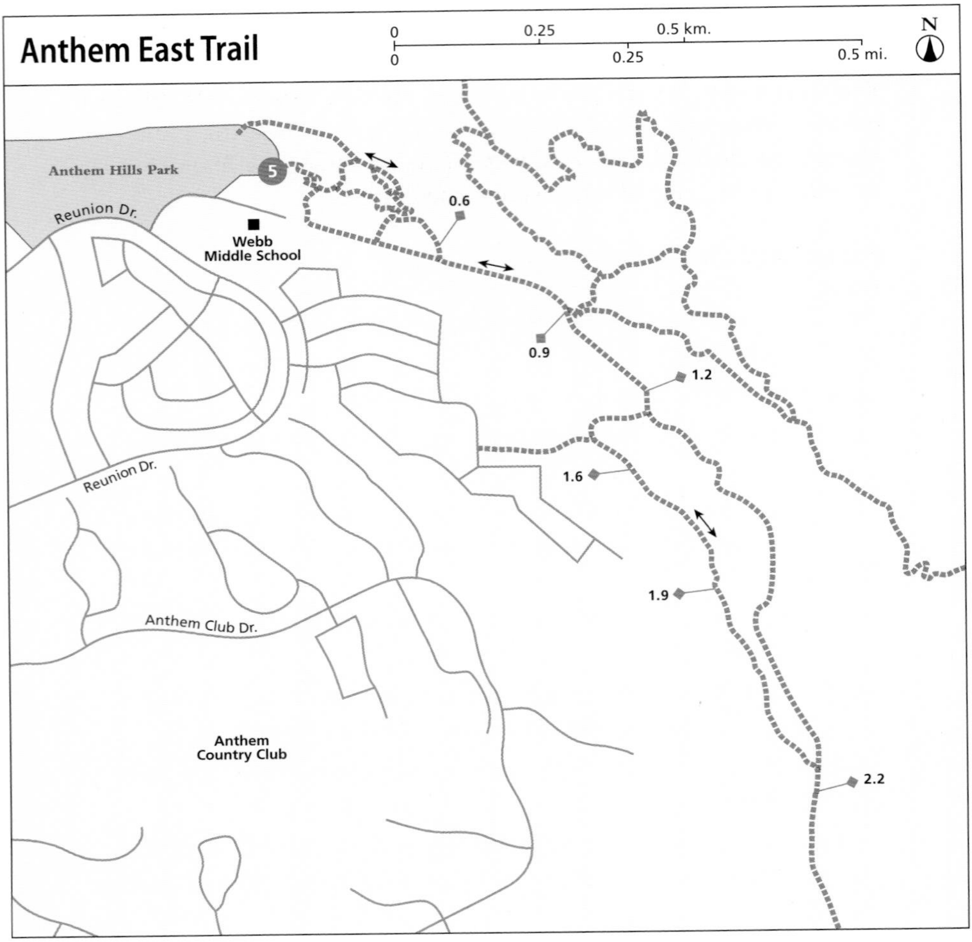

RIDE INFORMATION

Local Events and Attractions

The Gallery: The Gallery is a free-to-the-public art gallery located inside the Henderson Multigenerational Center; cityofhenderson.com.

Henderson Pavilion: The largest outdoor amphitheater in Nevada is a state-of-the-art venue for both visual and performing arts; cityofhenderson.com.

Henderson Multigenerational Center/Aquatic Complex: The 84,120-square-foot facility has a demonstration kitchen, jogging track, adult lounge, and dance room, as well as an outdoor aquatic complex; cityofhenderson.com.

Restaurants

Crepe Expectations: 9500 S. Eastern Ave., Ste. 150, Las Vegas; (702) 583-4939; crepeexpectations.com

The Cupcakery: 9680 S. Eastern Ave., Ste. 100, Las Vegas; (702) 207-2253; thecupcakery.com

Island Sushi and Grill: Hawaiian and Japanese cuisine; 9400 S. Eastern Ave., Las Vegas; (702) 221-1600; islandsushiandgrill.com

Restrooms

Mile 0.0: Anthem Hills Park

6

McCullough Hills Trail

This well-groomed dirt trail winds its way into the hills of Sloan Canyon National Conservation Area, offering a completely different view of the Nevada desert, one where volcanic action played a large part. The trail is one of the few multipurpose trails in the southern part of the valley that accommodates hikers, mountain bike riders, and equestrian enthusiasts.

Start: McCullough Hills Trailhead

Length: 13.8 miles (14.8 optional)

Approximate riding time: 1.5 to 3.5 hours

Best bike: Mountain bike

Terrain and trail surface: Well-groomed dirt

Traffic and hazards: This is a multipurpose trail open to hiking, running, biking, and in many areas, horseback riding. You should always give the right-of-way to hikers, runners, and those riding horseback. Rocks placed intentionally in the washes have the potential of causing pinch flats, so it is a good idea to bring extra tubes.

Things to see: Desert plants and animals

Getting there: By car: Take the Great Basin Highway south to the Horizon Drive exit. Head south on Horizon Drive and then left on Horizon Ridge Parkway. Turn right on Mission Drive and follow the road to the McCullough Hills Trailhead on the left. **GPS:** N35 59.870' / W114 59.872'

THE RIDE

In 2002 Congress set aside 48,438 acres of land with the intent of protecting a portion of southern Nevada's Mojave Desert for the benefit and enjoyment of present and future generations. This area became known as the Sloan Canyon

National Conservation Area. The North McCullough Wilderness is part of the conservation area, and it is through this wilderness that the McCullough Hills Trail runs.

The McCullough Hills Trail is a good place to start for anyone looking to get into mountain biking. Unlike most mountain bike trails, this one is fairly wide. In fact, it's wide enough for bikers to ride side-by-side. This means it is not considered singletrack. Additionally, the trail is well-groomed and is, for the most part, free of many of the obstacles, such as rocks, commonly found on most mountain bike trails. In fact, about the only time you encounter rocks is in the washes, where they have been placed intentionally to prevent the trail from becoming washed out. Riding over these rocks creates the potential of causing pinch flats, so it is a good idea to bring extra tubes or to use tubes with some type of flat repellant.

While the trail is relatively easy, it does have some tricky parts. There are some steep climbs and sharp turns—some of which are fairly difficult to navigate. However, most climbs are gradual and have been designed with flat spots, making the climb easier. Located at two points on the trail are shaded benches designed to provide a break in the long trail. These benches are strategically positioned to provide great views of the Las Vegas and Henderson valleys. Each rest stop is also complete with a hitching post for horses. The structure providing shade is artistically designed to fit in nicely with the desert landscape.

The McCullough Hills Trail is well-marked for the first 7 miles. The markers are made of metal posts that have been allowed to rust, and they are strategically placed to help riders stay on the correct trail. The trail itself starts at the McCullough Hills Trailhead—an area specifically designed for people using the trail. There is a small parking lot, a restroom, a map kiosk, and a drinking fountain. The trail starts on the north side of the parking lot, right behind the map kiosk, and turns right into the hills.

The trail is easy to follow, mainly because of its width. All offshoot trails are much narrower and shouldn't be followed. In most cases where there is a question about where the trail heads, there is a trail marker with directional arrows showing the way. Follow the trail as it makes its way up into the hills. The first 3 miles are a gradual climb and the next mile is an alternating climb and downhill section. A little over

Bike Shops

Aspen Creek Cycling: 1590 W. Horizon Ridge Pkwy., #140, Henderson; (702) 893-2453; aspencreekcycling.com

Bike Shop: 2630 Windmill Pkwy., Henderson; (702) 897-1618; bikeshop-lv.com

McGhie's Ski, Bike, and Board: 19 S. Stephanie St., Ste. 100, Henderson; (702) 800-3636; mcghies.com

REI: 2220 Village Walk Dr., #150, Henderson; (702) 896-7111; rei.com

6

4 miles into the ride, you'll find a sign warning riders of the impending switchbacks. Follow the switchbacks as the trail climbs up the hill and then turns to the right as it makes its way over the top of the hill. Once you're at the top of the hill, follow the trail as it winds down into the valley. The Las Vegas valley, including the Strip, will start to open up in front of you at this point. Follow the trail as it starts to climb after mile marker 6.

Shortly after this marker—in about 0.8 mile—the wide trail meets up with a convergence of singletrack trails. There is a trail marker here, but it is a little confusing and doesn't really tell you which trail to take. There is only about a half mile of the trail remaining, and the terrain gets difficult and confusing from here. I would recommend stopping at this point and heading back. However, if you wish to continue, take the singletrack trail to the left and follow it as it curves to the right. Be careful to stay on the correct trail as the trail splits not far after the turn. If you keep to the right, you'll be on the proper trail. You should be able to see the trail marker for mile 7 a short distance ahead.

Follow the trail as it climbs the hill and then goes down the other side. The trail ends at the marker a little less than 7.5 miles into the ride. However,

The McCullough Hills Trail winds through Sloan Canyon.

the marker is also a bit confusing at this point—which is why I recommend turning back when the wide trail ends. At this marker you can also continue straight, turning right when you get to a portion of the trail that resembles a dirt road. This can be ridden down to another trailhead, but it is a little confusing as to whether this is the McCullough Hills Trail or the Anthem East Trail. In my opinion, the extra portion of the trail is not worth the ride, so I would turn back at either the marker at the bottom of the hill or the point where the wide trail ends.

MILES AND DIRECTIONS

0.0 Start at the McCullough Hills Trailhead. You'll find the trail behind the map kiosk.

0.2 Stay straight and climb the hill. Do not take the trail to the right.

0.4 Follow the trail as it snakes around the hills and starts a short downhill section.

0.6 Climb the hill and continue with the short downhill section. At 0.7 mile, cross the wash—which is also used by horseback riders—at the trail marker.

0.9 Cross the dirt road at the trail marker and then follow the trail to the left, crossing the dirt road a second time at the next trail marker.

1.2 Follow the trail to the left. Do not take the offshoot trail to the right.

1.5 Follow the trail to the right, crossing the wash at 1.9 miles.

2.1 Follow the trail up the small hill. Continue on the trail, staying straight at the next trail marker at 2.2 miles.

2.3 Take the drop, follow the trail to the left, and then climb the hill.

2.5 Pass the shaded rest area. In 0.1 mile, take the drop and the climb on the other side.

3.4 Stay straight as the trail levels out a bit. Do not take the offshoot trail to the right.

4.2 Follow the trail into a switchback section up the hill.

4.7 Pass the elevation marker, marking the highest point on the trail—3,120 feet—then start a downhill section. Do not take the offshoot trail to the right.

5.3 Follow the trail to the left. Pass the second shaded rest area at 5.4 miles and head into the downhill switchbacks.

5.6 Cross the wash and the dirt road at the trail marker, then follow the trail up the hill.

McCullough Hills Trail

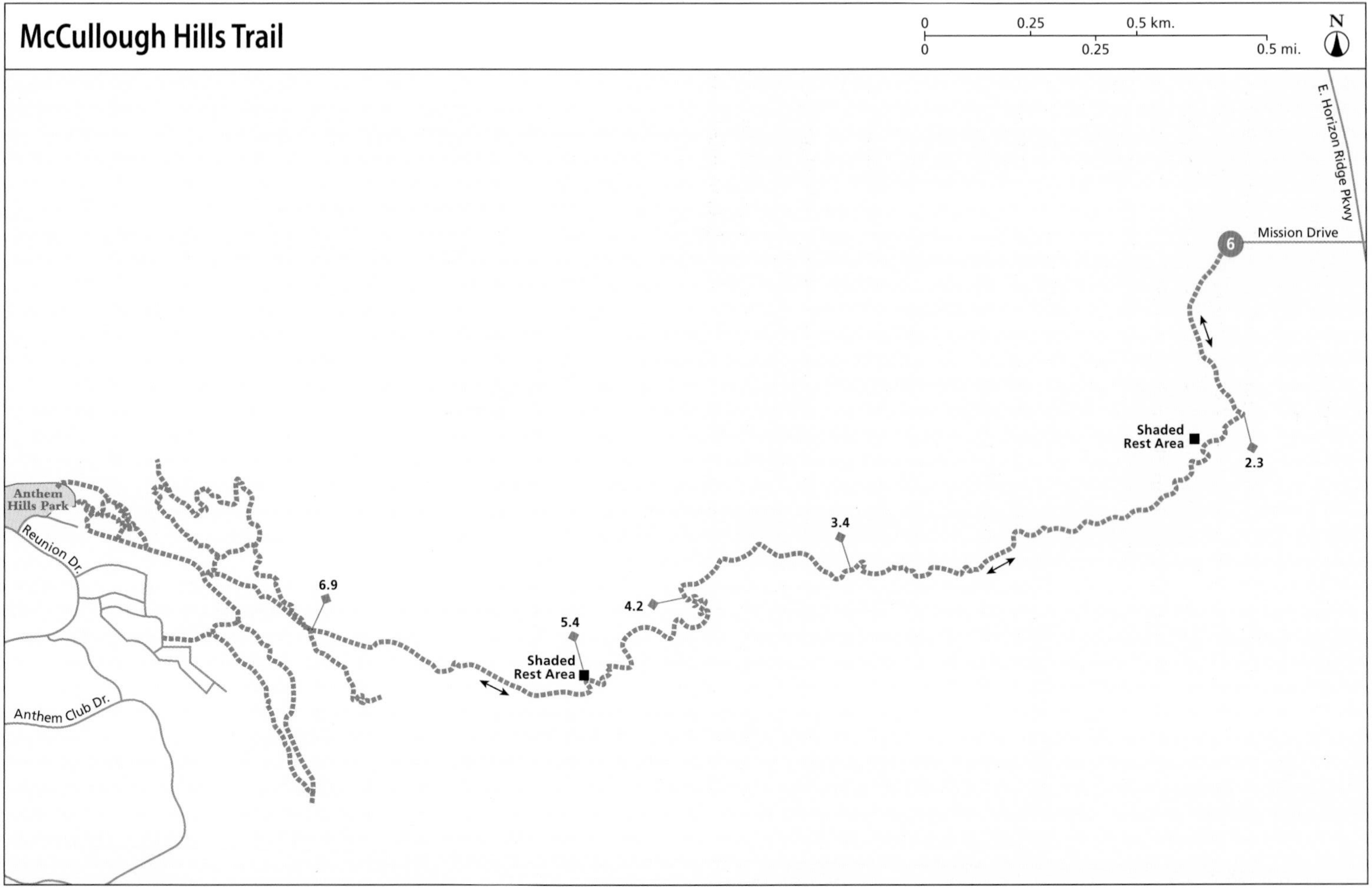

6.1 Stay straight and cross the dirt road at the marker.

6.6 Begin a steep climb.

6.9 The wide trail ends at the convergence of singletrack trails. I recommend turning back at this point. **Option:** If you continue, take the trail to the left and stay on it as it curves to the right. Do not follow the trail that offshoots from that trail on the left.

7.2 Climb the steep and rocky section up the hill for 0.1 mile, then follow the trail down the hill on the other side. The trail is extremely rocky.

7.4 Stay straight at the trail marker and follow the trail down to the next marker. Here the trail ends. Turn around and ride back to the trailhead, following the trail markers.

14.8 Arrive back at the trailhead.

RIDE INFORMATION

Restaurants

Lucille's Smokehouse Bar-B-Que: Located in the District; 2245 Village Walk Dr., Henderson; (702) 257-7427; lucillesbbq.com
Settebello Pizzeria Napoletana: Located in the District, serving official pizza from Italy; 140 S. Green Valley Pkwy., Henderson; (702) 222-3556; settebello.net

Restrooms

Mile 0.0: McCullough Hills Trailhead

7

Union Pacific Railroad Trail

This ride pays homage to Las Vegas's past and the integral role played by the Union Pacific Railroad. One end of the trail is meant to resemble a train station, and all the rest areas are cleverly designed with a railroad theme.

Start: Acacia Park

Length: 13.1 miles

Approximate riding time: 1 to 1.5 hours

Best bike: Road or hybrid bike

Terrain and trail surface: Asphalt

Traffic and hazards: This is a multipurpose road open only to walking, running, and biking. There are some intersections with traffic lights.

Things to see: Desert landscaping, parks

Getting there: By car: Take the Bruce Woodbury Beltway (I-215) to the Gibson Road exit. Turn south onto Gibson and then east onto Las Palmas Entrada Avenue. Follow that street to Acacia Park and park in any of the lots. **GPS:** N36 01.816' / W115 00.989'

THE RIDE

The history of Las Vegas is intertwined with the railroad. In fact, when the gavel crashed down in the May heat, selling the first plot in a two-day land auction orchestrated by brothers William Andrews and J. Ross Clark, it was to establish the township of Las Vegas as a refueling station for their San Pedro, Los Angeles & Salt Lake Railroad. At the time, the brothers could hardly foresee the city that would grow from the humble seeds they planted on the 15th and 16th of May, 1905. Since then, the railroad has played an integral part in the development of Las Vegas. The Clark brothers eventually

Rest areas on the Union Pacific Railroad Trail are meant to look like train tracks.

sold their railroad to the Union Pacific, and the railroad has had a presence in the valley ever since.

This trail follows the tracks of the Union Pacific Railroad as it makes its way into the east part of the valley. The trail is accessed by taking the small, white metal bridge at the end of Acacia Park. Once you start on the asphalt trail, you'll stay on it, not taking any of the trails or paths that shoot off the main trail. Along the way, a well-groomed dirt trail parallels the main asphalt trail. This trail crosses the main trail at several locations and isn't always continuous. For this reason, it's best to simply stay on the asphalt trail, unless you're riding with young children, then it may be fun for the kids to ride on the dirt trail.

As you follow the trail, you'll cross a wash and then go under the Great Basin Highway. The trail makes its way behind the Fiesta Henderson Hotel and Casino, steadily heading up into the hills. Even though the climb is continuous from the trailhead to the end, it is very gradual and not difficult at all. Cross Fiesta Henderson Boulevard at the crosswalk. You'll have to go across the train tracks to get to the crosswalk, which will now place you on the opposite side of the tracks. From here you'll pass Burkholder Park and Lyal Burkholder Middle School. As you make your way down the trail, you'll find benches located on either side. At each bench the trail will turn to cement. Take the time to notice the impressions in the cement. They are meant to resemble train tracks

Bike Shops

Aspen Creek Cycling: 1590 W. Horizon Ridge Pkwy., #140, Henderson; (702) 893-2453; aspencreekcycling.com
Bike Shop: 2630 Windmill Pkwy., Henderson; (702) 897-1618; bikeshop-lv.com
McGhie's Ski, Bike, and Board: 19 S. Stephanie St., Ste. 100, Henderson; (702) 800-3636; mcghies.com
REI: 2220 Village Walk Dr., #150, Henderson; (702) 896-7111; rei.com
VegasVelo Bicycles: 691 N. Valle Verde Dr., Ste. 130, Henderson; (702) 503-9005; vegasvelo.com

and railroad ties—the wood the train tracks are attached to. The benches themselves are also molded to look like stacked railroad ties.

Cross Pacific Avenue at the crosswalk and stay straight, then cross Greenway Road and College Drive at the crosswalks before also crossing Horizon Drive at the lighted crosswalk. Take the bridge over the wash, cross the railroad tracks a second time, and then go across Arrowhead Trail at the crosswalk. Along the trail you'll find several educational markers that tell the tale of the railroad and the town of Henderson—the neighboring town through which the trail passes. Take the time to read these markers, as they make the trail more memorable.

Cross the wash, but only if it isn't raining. Rain in Las Vegas can be very dangerous. While it doesn't rain much in the valley, when it does rain, it comes down hard and fast—creating flash floods. Riding through running water in Las Vegas is not only dangerous, but can also be life-threatening. Once you cross the wash, follow the trail under the Great Basin Highway, also called Veterans Memorial Highway. Follow the trail to Nevada State Drive and cross the road with the lighted crosswalk. Here the trail splits. You can either continue straight or take the alternate trail to the left. It doesn't matter which trail you take because both trails meet back up a short distance ahead.

After the trails meet, cross Paradise Hills Drive at the lighted crosswalk. Once across the street, pick up the trail to the left. The trail ends at the top of the hill. This trailhead is designed to resemble the outside of a train station. It consists of a covered section with seating under the cover. The trail in front of the area is cement and has the train track and railroad tie imprint, making it look as if anyone seated under the canopy is waiting for a train. Once you've reached this mock train station, turn and head back down the trail to the trailhead.

The Union Pacific

The roots of the Union Pacific Railroad in Las Vegas go back to 1921, when the Clark brothers sold their San Pedro, Los Angeles & Salt Lake Railroad to the Union Pacific Railroad (UPRR). Unfortunately, the relationship between the UPRR and Las Vegas hasn't always been cordial. Five years after they took over the railways in Las Vegas, the UPRR's employees grew dissatisfied with how they were being treated. The Clark brothers had founded Las Vegas solely as a stop for their railroad between Salt Lake and Los Angeles. Because of this, they treated Las Vegas more as a company town than an emerging city—something that suited their employees very well. When the UPRR took over, they didn't see Las Vegas the same way, and the employees who had been riding high under the Clarks were now largely ignored.

Less than a year after the UPRR bought out the Clarks' railroad, their employees joined 400,000 other railroad workers and went on a nationwide strike. When the strike was finally over and the dust cleared, the UPRR was less than happy with the actions of their employees. In what could only be viewed as retaliation, the UPRR pulled their repair shops from the valley, replacing them with smelly stockyards. The move not only cost hundreds of jobs, it almost caused Las Vegas to shrivel up and die. In fact, if it wasn't for the building of the Hoover Dam in the early 1930s, Las Vegas may not have made it. Luckily the construction of the dam brought money and opportunity to the valley, repairing the relationship between Las Vegas and the Union Pacific.

MILES AND DIRECTIONS

0.0 Start at the trailhead at Acacia Park. Begin the trail at the white bridge on the east side of the park. Go over the bridge and continue straight.

0.1 Stay straight; do not take the offshoot trail to the right. Cross the wash at 0.3 mile.

0.4 Follow the trail to the left and then under the Great Basin Highway. Continue to follow the trail as it climbs slightly and curves to the right.

0.6 Cross the train tracks and then cross Fiesta Henderson Boulevard at the crosswalk.

0.9 Stay straight on the asphalt trail. Do not take the dirt trail to the right.

Union Pacific Railroad Trail

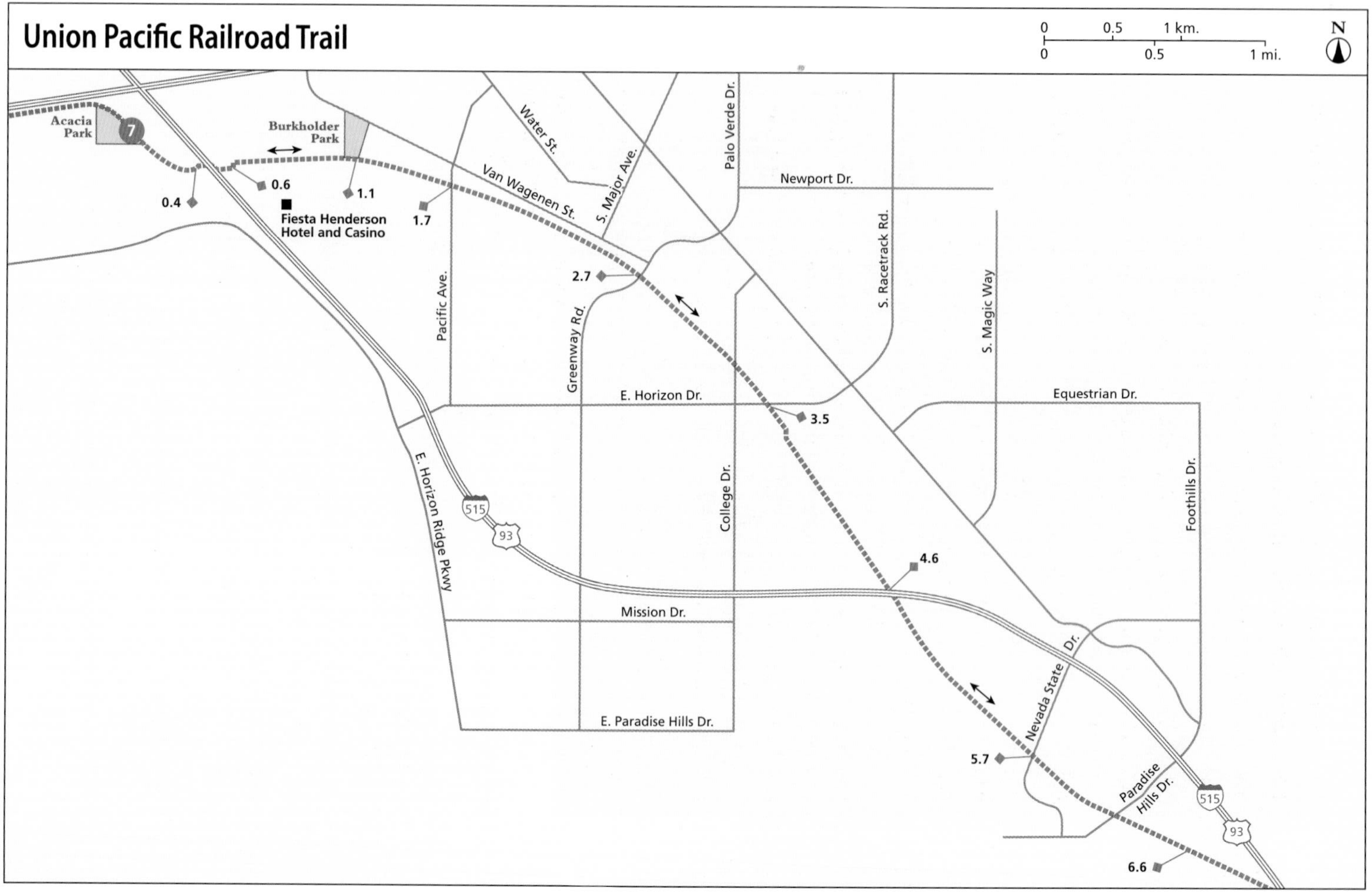

1.1 Pass Burkholder Park and Lyal Burkholder Middle School on the left.

1.7 Cross Pacific Avenue at the crosswalk.

2.2 Stay straight. Do not take the offshoot trail to the right.

2.7 Cross Greenway Road at the crosswalk and stay straight.

3.3 Cross College Drive at the lighted crosswalk.

3.5 Cross Horizon Drive at the lighted crosswalk. In 0.1 mile, cross the bridge going over the wash.

3.7 Cross the railroad tracks, then cross Arrowhead Trail at the crosswalk.

4.1 Cross the wash—but only if it is not raining.

4.6 Go under the Great Basin Highway.

5.1 Stay straight. Do not take the offshoot trail to the right.

5.7 Cross Nevada State Drive at the lighted crosswalk. Stay straight or take the trail to the left.

6.2 When the trails meet back up, cross Paradise Hills Drive at the lighted crosswalk. Turn left and pick up the trail on the right.

6.6 The trail ends at a rest stop designed to resemble a train depot. Turn around and ride back to the trailhead.

13.1 Arrive back at the trailhead.

RIDE INFORMATION

Local Events and Attractions

Demonstration Gardens: Located at Acacia Park, the demonstration gardens provide examples to help create water-efficient and desert-tolerant landscaping. The gardens also host a variety of workshops every spring and fall.

Restrooms

Mile 0.0: Trailhead in Acacia Park
Mile 1.1: Burkholder Park

Southeast and Northeast

The Hoover Dam is a Nevada icon.

The southeast and northeast parts of the valley have some of Las Vegas's greatest icons. Here you'll find Lake Mead, the largest man-made lake in the United States; the Hoover Dam; the wetlands—yes, there are wetlands in the desert; and the Valley of Fire, the oldest and largest park in the state of Nevada. The area is also home to a canyon that played an integral role in keeping Las Vegas wet during a dry spell in American history.

The trails in this area offer great opportunities to experience these icons. There are many road bike trails in and around the southeast. Some are along established trails, while others follow state routes and roadways. One of these trails leads to Hoover Dam and allows you to actually ride across the dam. Other trails circle Lake Mead. One trail even allows you to ride through large tunnels created specifically for the iron horses that carried supplies and equipment to the dam site. While still others take you past rock formations with colors so breathtaking, they have been described as being on fire.

Many of the trails in this area are mountain bike trails. Most of these are located in an area known as Bootleg Canyon. The small, narrow canyon—made mostly of molten rock uplifted over thousands of years—is home to a series of interconnected trails that are a favorite of mountain bikers from all over the world. Due to the efforts of cycling enthusiast Brent Thomson and brothers Dan and Jeff Haskin, a series of world-class trails—which the International Mountain Biking Association (IMBA) deemed an "epic" ride—now run through the canyon. These trails host multiple racing events throughout the year, and while they are challenging, they are accessible to all levels of riders.

Wetlands Park Trail

8

This ride makes its way through the wetlands in southeast Las Vegas. It is one of the best rides for seeing the many different species of birds, mammals, and reptiles that call this unique area home, making it one of the top family bike rides in Las Vegas.

Start: Wetlands Park parking lot

Length: 6.2 miles

Approximate riding time: 20 to 30 minutes

Best bike: Road or hybrid bike

Terrain and trail surface: Cement and asphalt

Traffic and hazards: This is a multipurpose trail open only to walking, running, and biking.

Things to see: Desert scenery, wildlife, wetlands

Getting there: By car: Take US 95, also called the Veterans Memorial Highway, to Tropicana Avenue. Go east on Tropicana Avenue to Wetlands Park Lane. Follow Wetlands Park Lane to the Clark County Wetlands Park. **By bike:** Ride east down Tropicana Avenue to Wetlands Park Lane. Follow Wetlands Park Lane to the Clark County Wetlands Park. **GPS:** N36 05.097' / W115 01.392'

THE RIDE

One of the things deserts are famous for is mirages. Picture a weary traveler, head wrapped in a white linen scarf in a vain attempt to block the flesh-burning rays of the sun, stumbling through sand that seems to deepen with every step. Suddenly, off on the horizon, an oasis appears; one with trees,

The river that runs through the wetlands on its way to Lake Mead

shade, and, of course, life-giving water. Well, if you travel to the east of the valley, you'll find a park that might just make you think you've found that same mirage. Here are acres of plants, trees, ponds, and streams, populated with all manner of birds, waterfowl, and reptiles. But this is no mirage—it's the Clark County Wetlands Park Nature Preserve, and it is truly an oasis in the Las Vegas desert.

The wetlands park comprises 2,900 acres of water, trails, and trees along the Las Vegas Wash. The purpose of the park is to reduce the environmental impact of reclaimed water—wastewater and storm water runoff—before it enters Lake Mead. The wetlands plants slow the movement of reclaimed water, in the process filtering much of the impurities and pollutants from that water before it enters the lake. The plants, in turn, benefit from the slow-moving water by receiving vital nutrients.

The park is home to many soaring birds, such as turkey vultures, red-tailed hawks, and northern harriers. Waterfowl are also plentiful at the wetlands. Here you can find mallard ducks, American coots, snowy egrets, and great blue herons. At times you can even find beavers,

Bike Shops

Bike Shop: 2630 Windmill Pkwy., Henderson; (702) 897-1618; bikeshop-lv.com
Bike World: 2320 E. Flamingo Rd., Las Vegas; (702) 735-7551; bikeworldlv.com

raccoons, coyotes, crayfish, spiny soft-shell turtles, and, of course, desert cottontail rabbits—lots of desert cottontail rabbits.

Most of the trails at the wetlands park are meant to be enjoyed on foot. However, some trails are meant for horses and at least two are designed to be used by cyclists. The Wetlands Park Trail is one of those. This trail starts at the parking lot outside the park's visitor center, near the outside restrooms. It is easily found by the trail markers and because it is the only trail with a yellow line running down the center. This trail does not go through the park itself, but it does hug the outskirts of the park, allowing great views of plants, ponds, streams, and animals. However, as the trail progresses, it eventually makes its way north, heading out of the park and into the desert.

The Wetlands Park Trail is not typically crowded, making it one of the best trails for families. Additionally, when the trail starts to leave the park—at the large bridge—you can simply turn and head back to the park. If you choose to continue the ride, you will find a nice, easy trail that offers great desert views as well as views of the wetlands park at a distance. Once you get on the cement trail, you stay on the trail. The only tricky transition is turning left

A rider makes his way along the Wetlands Park Trail with views of the Strip in the distance.

on the long bridge, mainly because the trail looks like it goes to the right—it does, but that part isn't open to bikes.

The first part of the trail makes its way through trees and plants, offering a great view of one of the wetland's ponds. There is a seating area near the pond that is an ideal place to see the animals that make the pond home. If you're riding with a family, be sure to take advantage of the seating area. The trail eventually makes its way to a long bridge. Turn left and follow the trail across the bridge—the yellow stripe will disappear. Make sure to take the time to stop on the bridge and look at the wide creek running below. It is not uncommon to see great blue herons sitting on the bank, blending into the plants, waiting for just the right fish.

On the other side of the bridge, the cement road turns to asphalt. Take the trail to the right. Like the cement trail, once you get on the asphalt, you'll stay on the trail until it ends. There are many offshoot trails on both sides of the main trail, and most of them have trail markers indicating what is allowed on that trail. The markers are made of rusted metal—rusted on purpose—with cutouts showing walking, cycling, or equestrian denotations, indicating the type of activity allowed on the trail. It is important to pay heed to the markers and only ride the trails that allow bikes. Some of these trails are still under construction, so they may not go very far before they end.

Bird-Watching

Clark County Wetlands Park was created in 1991 with the charge to protect and enhance the Las Vegas Wash ecosystem and offer a place for people to enjoy nature. One of the favorite activities at the park is bird-watching. Living among the shrubs, thickets, southern cattails, and marshes are 212 species of waterfowl, desert birds, and soaring birds. Here in the ponds and streams you'll find mallard ducks, American coots, common moorhens, pied-billed grebes, great blue herons, snowy egrets, belted kingfishers, and black phoebes, to name but a few. You can also find birds common to the desert like Anna's hummingbirds, thrashers, house finches, Gambel's quail, mourning doves, black-throated sparrows, blue-gray gnatcatchers, and Albert's towhees. Soaring birds such as turkey vultures, northern rough-winged swallows, red-tailed hawks, and northern harriers all fly high above the marsh.

The park is open from dawn till dusk and offers guided walking tours. Cameras and binoculars are encouraged, and there is even a bird-watching blind. You can go as an individual or with many of the bird-watching groups—such as Birding Vegas—that meet at the park on a regular basis. Just be sure to bring water and sunscreen—even in the winter.

Once you reach the end of the trail at the Sunrise Trailhead, you simply turn and head back. The ride to the Sunrise Trailhead is uphill, but gradual. However, on the ride back you can generate quite a bit of speed. Make sure when traveling back that you watch for animals on the trail, as well as other people enjoying the ride. Be sure to be courteous and slow down when approaching and passing others, especially families with children.

MILES AND DIRECTIONS

0.0 Start at the trailhead at the north end of the Wetlands Park parking lot. The cement trail is marked by a yellow stripe. Do not take the cement trail without the stripe.

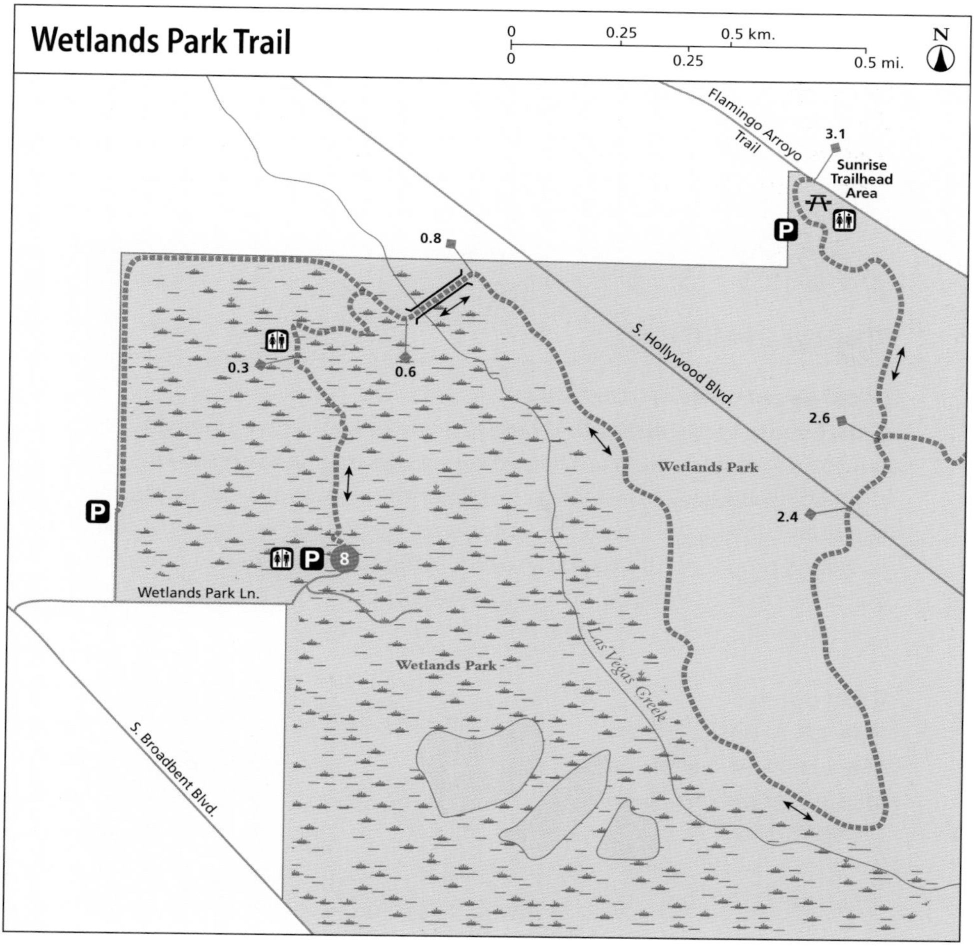

0.1 Stay on the yellow-striped trail. Do not take the dirt trail to the right or the dirt trail to the left farther up.

0.2 Stay on the yellow-striped trail. Do not take the dirt trail to the left.

0.3 Stay on the yellow-striped trail. Do not take the cement trail to the left before the restrooms.

0.4 Stay on the yellow-striped trail. Do not take the dirt trail to the left here or the dirt road to the left that follows in 0.1 mile.

0.6 Where the trail splits, take the trail to the left and cross the long bridge. The yellow stripe will be gone. Do not follow the cement trail to the shorter bridge on the right.

0.8 Take the asphalt trail to the right on the other side of the bridge.

1.2 Continue straight. The scenery changes to desert.

2.4 Cross the road and stay straight.

2.6 Stay straight. Do not take the asphalt trail to the right or the dirt trail to the left.

3.0 Pass a small park.

3.1 The trail ends at the Sunrise Trailhead. Turn around and head back to Wetlands Park.

6.2 Arrive back at the trailhead.

RIDE INFORMATION

Local Events and Attractions

Clark County Wetlands Park: There are many things to do at the park. You can go on a photo safari, take a guided nature walk, take your dog on an early-morning "wolf walk," bird-watch, or just enjoy the plants and wildlife. You can also spend time in the interactive visitor center, which has won awards for its education programs. There you can also watch an immersive orientation film that showcases the wildlife, trails, and river-like Las Vegas Wash. One of the best things about the park is that nothing has an entry fee.

Restrooms

Mile 0.0: At the trailhead
Mile 0.3: Alongside the trail
Mile 3.0: At the small park

9

Outer Wetlands Trail

This ride makes its way through the wetlands in southeast Las Vegas. It is one of the best rides for seeing the many different species of birds, mammals, and reptiles that call this unique area home, making it one of the top family bike rides in Las Vegas.

Start: Wetlands Park parking lot

Length: 20.2 miles

Approximate riding time: 2 to 3 hours

Best bike: Road or hybrid bike

Terrain and trail surface: Cement and asphalt

Traffic and hazards: This is a multipurpose trail open only to walking, running, and biking.

Things to see: Desert scenery, wildlife, wetlands

Getting there: **By car:** Take NV 95, also called the Veterans Memorial Highway, to Tropicana Avenue. Go east on Tropicana Avenue to Wetlands Park Lane. Follow Wetlands Park Lane to the Clark County Wetlands Park. **By bike:** Ride east down Tropicana Avenue to Wetlands Park Lane. Follow Wetlands Park Lane to the Clark County Wetlands Park.
GPS: N36 05.097' / W115 01.392'

THE RIDE

Clark County Wetlands Park is truly an oasis in the desert. Spend any time in this area, and you just might forget you're right smack in the middle of one of the hottest deserts in America. If the shoulder-high cattails and marshes don't clue you in, the ponds and streams should do the trick. These aren't small ponds and narrow streams. The ponds are a decent size, and the creek is wide enough that two large metal bridges were built so it could be crossed.

A large portion of this trail is the same as the Wetlands Park Trail. However, at a certain point, the Outer Wetlands Trail turns off from the Wetlands Park Trail and winds its way around the perimeter of the wetlands, eventually making its way into the Las Vegas desert. This is an enjoyable trail that is a gradual climb until it reaches the River Mountains Loop. On the way back, the trail offers a pleasing downhill section that allows you the time to take in and thoroughly enjoy the scenery.

The Outer Wetlands Trail starts with the Wetlands Park Trail, which is at the north end of the parking lot, just to the right of the outside restrooms. The trail is easy to find due to the trail marker and the yellow stripe running up the center of the trail. The first part of the trail makes its way through trees and plants, offering a great view of one of the wetland's ponds. There is a seating area near the pond that is an ideal place to see the animals that make the pond home. If you're riding with a family, be sure to take advantage of the seating area. The trail eventually makes its way to a long bridge. Turn left and follow the trail across the bridge—the yellow stripe will disappear. Make sure to take the time to stop on the bridge and look at the wide creek running below. It is not uncommon to see great blue herons sitting on the bank, blending into the plants, waiting for just the right fish.

On the other side of the bridge, the trail turns from cement to asphalt as it veers off to the right. About 2.5 miles into the trail, there is a turnoff to the right. It's fairly easy to find because it is the only part of the Wetlands Park Trail that has an offshoot trail on both sides. The trail on the right is asphalt and the one on the left is dirt. The trail on the right is the trailhead for the Outer Wetlands Trail. Turn right and follow that trail as it makes a short but fairly steep climb up a hill.

Like the Wetlands Park Trail, once you're on the Outer Wetlands Trail, you don't get off or take any of the offshoot trails. Most of the offshoot trails on both sides of the main trail have markers indicating what is allowed on that trail. The markers are made of rusted metal—rusted on purpose—with cutouts showing walking, cycling, or equestrian denotations, indicating the type of activity allowed on the trail. It is important to pay heed to the markers and only ride the trails that allow bikes. Some of these trails are still under construction, so they may not go very far before they end.

Bike Shops

Bike Shop: 2630 Windmill Pkwy., Henderson; (702) 897-1618; bikeshop-lv.com
Bike World: 2320 E. Flamingo Rd., Las Vegas; (702) 735-7551; bikeworldlv.com

As the trail progresses, it runs along Las Vegas Creek, getting very close at some points. A couple of times the trail runs alongside or crosses a dirt road used by the workers who care for the wetlands and the park. Be sure to stop in these areas and take notice of the wildlife that live near the creek. However, if you do, make sure you stay on the trail and not venture off into unmarked areas.

The trail is designed to closely follow the natural terrain of the area. This means, like the land it crosses, the trail has lots of little hills and valleys. There are also a couple of steep climbs, one of which, located towards the end of the trail, is especially steep. A little over 8 miles into the ride you'll come across the second bridge. On the other side of the bridge the trail seems to dead-end at another trail. Taking that trail to the left will take you to Lake Las Vegas, an area complete with hotels, restaurants, and shopping. The trail to the right is the Wetlands Connector Trail. Take this trail and follow it through the tunnel. On the other side of the tunnel, the trail climbs steadily upward until it reaches the River Mountains Loop, about 1.5 miles up the trail. Once you reach the River Mountains Loop, turn around and ride back.

The Outer Wetlands Trail snakes through the lush wetlands.

Riprap

Where do imploded casinos go to die? Apparently they go to the wetlands. Imploding a hotel creates a great deal of rubble and debris—much of which is in the form of large pieces of cement. These cement pieces are carried away to make room for new, modern hotels and casinos. But instead of ending up in landfills, many of the Las Vegas casinos imploded over the years have found a new home as riprap along the wetland's washes and weirs. A wash is a channel that is filled with water at certain times of the year. A weir is a barrier placed across a river that is designed to alter the flow characteristics of the river.

Large cement pieces, called riprap, that were once the Aladdin, the Desert Inn, the Dunes, the Castaways, and the Stardust are placed along washes to control erosion or used to create weirs. These cement pieces can be seen when riding along the Outer Wetlands Trail and especially when crossing the bridge near the Wetlands Connector Trail. The riprap not only controls erosion, it also creates habitats for the birds and reptiles who live in the wetlands. While the "Strip" may still be firmly planted on Las Vegas Boulevard, its counterpart is alive and well in the wetlands.

MILES AND DIRECTIONS

0.0 Start at the trailhead at the north end of the Wetlands Park parking lot. The cement trail is marked by a yellow stripe. Do not take the cement trail without the stripe.

0.1 Stay on the yellow-striped trail. Do not take the dirt trail to the right or the dirt trail to the left farther up.

0.2 Stay on the yellow-striped trail. Do not take the dirt trail to the left.

0.3 Stay on the yellow-striped trail. Do not take the cement trail to the left before the restrooms.

0.4 Stay on the yellow-striped trail. Do not take the dirt trail to the left here or the dirt road to the left that follows in 0.1 mile.

0.6 When the trail splits, take the trail to the left and cross the long bridge. The yellow stripe will be gone. Do not follow the cement trail to the shorter bridge on the right.

0.8 Take the asphalt trail to the right on the other side of the bridge.

1.2 Continue straight. The scenery changes to desert.

2.4 Cross the road and stay straight.

Outer Wetlands Trail

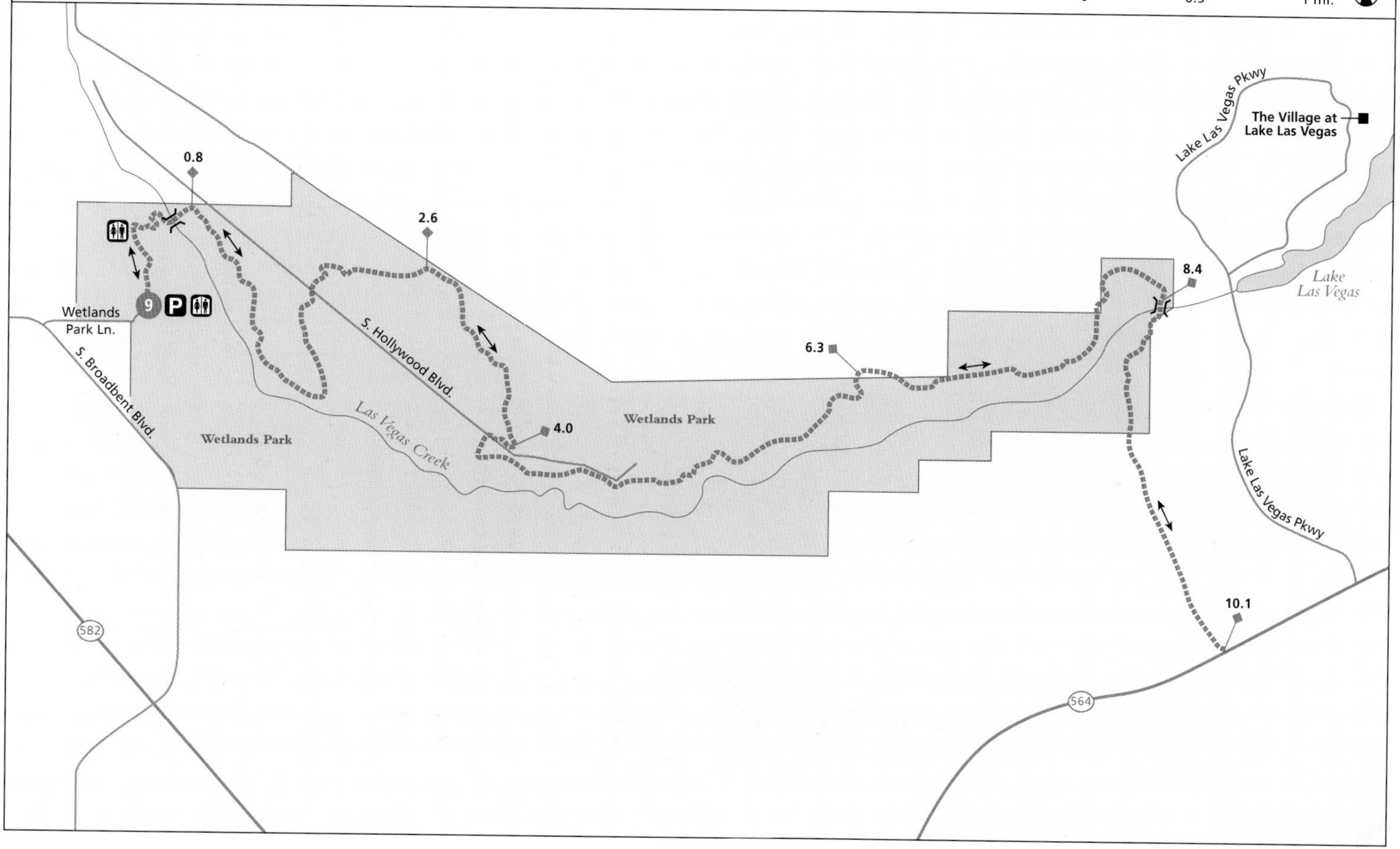

2.6 Take the asphalt trail to the right and make the short but steep climb.

2.8 Stay straight on the asphalt trail. Do not take the dirt road to the right.

3.2 Follow the trail over a series of small hills and across a wash.

4.0 Follow the trail as it makes a hairpin turn to the right.

4.4 Follow the trail as it curves to the left. Notice the pond on the right.

4.5 Stay straight on the asphalt trail across the dirt road. Follow the asphalt trail, staying to the left of the gravel road at mile 4.6.

4.8 Stay straight on the asphalt trail. Do not take the dirt roads on the left.

5.0 Follow the asphalt trail to the left. Do not take the dirt roads on either side of the trail.

5.4 Cross the dirt road and stay straight on the trail. In 0.2 mile, cross the dirt road again and stay straight on the trail.

6.3 Climb the steep hill, following the asphalt trail to the left. Do not take the dirt road to the right.

6.5 Climb the second steep hill. Momentum will get you up the other side.

7.3 Follow the trail to the right, through the opening in the fence. Do not take the dirt road to the left.

7.7 Climb another steep hill. Do not take the gravel road to the right.

8.4 Cross the bridge.

8.5 Take the asphalt Wetlands Connector Trail to the right. In 0.1 mile, go through the tunnel and begin the gradual climb.

8.8 Cross the cement wash.

10.1 The Wetlands Connector Trail ends at the River Mountains Loop. Turn the bike around and head back to the trailhead.

20.2 Arrive back at the trailhead.

RIDE INFORMATION

Local Events and Attractions

Clark County Wetlands Park: There are many things to do at the park. You can go on a photo safari, take a guided nature walk, take your dog on an early-morning "wolf walk," bird-watch, or just enjoy the plants and wildlife. You can also spend time at the interactive visitor center, which has won awards for its education programs. There you can also watch an immersive orientation film that showcases the wildlife, trails, and river-like Las Vegas Wash. One of the best things about the park is that nothing has an entry fee.

The Village at Lake Las Vegas: The village offers numerous entertainment opportunities, including the Lakeside Music series. Here you can enjoy live music every Saturday night on the shores of the man-made lake that gives the resort community its name.

Restaurants

Bernard's Bistro by the Lake: 15 Via Bel Canto, Henderson; (702) 565-0843; bernardsbistro.com. French-California cuisine.

The Pub Auld Dubliner: 40 Via Bel Canto, Ste. 100, Henderson; (720) 567-8002; http://vegas.thedubpubs.com. Classic Irish-American food.

Sonrisa Grill: 30 Via Brianza, #100, Henderson; (702) 568-6870; sonrisagrill.com. Mexican cuisine.

Restrooms

Mile 0.0: At the trailhead

Mile 0.3: Alongside the trail

Mile 3.0: At the small park

10

River Mountains Loop

The River Mountains Loop makes its way around the hills outside of Las Vegas, offering great views of the Las Vegas valley and Lake Mead. The loop is a favorite of road bikers because it has several challenging climbs.

Start: Parking lot just below the Alan Bible Visitor Center

Length: 34.4 miles

Approximate riding time: 2.5 to 5 hours

Best bike: Road or hybrid bike

Terrain and trail surface: Asphalt and cement

Traffic and hazards: This is a multipurpose trail open only to walking, running, biking, and, in some areas, horseback riding. Pay attention to runners and people walking and make sure to give them the right-of-way.

Things to see: Lake Mead, desert scenery, wildlife, Las Vegas valley

Getting there: By car: Take US 93 toward the Hoover Dam (Boulder City). Turn onto Lakeshore Road and follow it to the parking lot just below the Alan Bible Visitor Center. Do not go so far that you reach the entrance fee station. **GPS:** N36 00.707' / W114 47.609'

THE RIDE

The River Mountains Loop is a trail that was created to connect Lake Mead National Recreation Area, Hoover Dam, Henderson, Boulder City, and the Las Vegas valley into one enjoyable ride. The trail might not have happened if it weren't for the combined efforts of private landowners, citizens, and many of Nevada's resource management agencies to link several separate unofficial trails into one. The 12-foot-wide trail is asphalt in most areas and cement in some, with a dashed yellow line running down the center almost the entire length of the trail. The official trailhead is located at the Railroad Pass Hotel & Casino, which is mile marker 1. However, most riders will tell you to start at the parking lot below the Alan Bible Visitor Center because it puts one of the longest climbs at the beginning of the trail instead of at the end, where you're more apt to be tired and not want to make a long climb.

The trail actually has several trailheads. You can access the trail at the parking lot below the Alan Bible Visitor Center, at Bootleg Canyon, at Pacifica Way (a parking lot created just for the trail), at the Railroad Pass Hotel & Casino, at Equestrian Park, and at Mountain Lake Park. Each of these trailheads is located at points around the trail, allowing you to make the loop at several different starting points. This lets you access the trail and make the loop no matter what part of the Las Vegas valley you live in—meaning you don't have to start the trail where this guide starts it. Each of these trailheads, along with directions to get there, can be found on the River Mountains Loop website at rivermountainstrail.com.

A rider makes his way up the cement wash along the River Mountains Loop.

Bike Shops

All Mountain Cyclery: 1404 Nevada Hwy., Ste. C, Boulder City; (702) 453-2453; allmountaincyclery.com
Aspen Creek Cycling: 1590 W. Horizon Ridge Pkwy., #140, Henderson; (702) 893-2453; aspencreekcycling.com
JT's Bicycle: 76 W. Horizon Ridge Pkwy., Henderson; (702) 564-5345; jtsbicycle.com
McGhie's Ski, Bike, and Board: 19 S. Stephanie St., Ste. 100, Henderson; (702) 800-3636; mcghies.com
REI: 2220 Village Walk Dr., #150, Henderson; (702) 896-7111
River Mountains Bike Shop: 2310 E. Lake Mead Pkwy., Henderson; (702) 564-3058; rivermountainsbikeshop.com

Park your car at the Alan Bible Visitor Center and access the trail at the top of the parking lot—toward the visitor center. Take the cement trail as it winds its way upward, turning right and going under Lakeshore Road before heading up into the hills. The trail turns to asphalt on the other side of the tunnel under Lakeshore Road. Once you get on this trail, you don't get off, so if you see any offshoot trails, don't take them. The only time you won't be on asphalt is when you cross a wash or when the trail goes into the wash as it travels next to the Great Basin Highway on its way to Bootleg Canyon.

This trail has several climbs, and the one that follows the wash is the first. Right before the trail turns into the wash, there is a painted marker that is the River Mountains Loop symbol. The marker consists of a bighorn sheep on the face of a mountain and a ring—representing the trail—going over the top of the mountain. Follow the trail to the left and head into the wash. Just before you make that left-hand turn, you'll pass the Pacifica Way Trailhead on your right.

Once in the wash, turn right and follow the wash up toward Boulder City and Bootleg Canyon. Do not take this wash if it is raining. In fact, the trail really shouldn't be ridden in the rain, but if you wish to do so, you can jump onto the Great Basin Highway and ride it up to the top of the hill. While this road is an official highway, the speed limit in this section is only 45 mph and there is a bike lane on the road. Many cyclists choose this route instead of riding in the wash even when it is not raining. At the top of the hill you'll see the trail to the right, and you can easily hook back up with the River Mountains Loop.

Once you climb out of the wash, continue the climb up into Bootleg Canyon. Mountain bike trails cross the loop at many points, so be sure to watch out for mountain bikers, as they will be moving faster than you and it is often more difficult for them to see you than for you to see them. Follow the trail to the roundabout, connecting back with the trail on the opposite side. Be sure not to take the trail to the right, which leads to the Bootleg Canyon mountain bike trails. As the trail heads downward, you'll pass the Bootleg Canyon trailhead, which is a parking lot on the right.

From here the trail heads downward and then climbs again right before it passes the Railroad Pass Hotel & Casino. This is the official beginning of the trail, and you'll see an asphalt trail that leads into the hotel's parking lot. While this is where you'll find mile marker 1, few people access the trail at this trailhead. As you travel along the trail, you'll find markers that have directional arrows, tell you who is allowed on the trail, and give you the mileage at that point. These markers are placed every mile and half mile along the trail. There are also several educational markers on the side of the trail. These markers provide a great deal of information about the history of the trail and the area through which the trail passes.

Once you pass the Railroad Pass Hotel & Casino, you actually enter a bit of a downhill section that lasts for close to 6 miles until you reach a portion of the trail known as "Three Sisters." These three mountain ridges where given their name by bike riders competing in the annual Silverman Triathlon, in which this portion of the trail is used. The average grade of the Sisters is 15 percent up and down. You can bypass a couple of the Three Sisters by taking the trail to the left when it splits and connecting onto the Lake Mead Parkway Trail through the tunnel going under Lake Mead Parkway. If you take the Three Sisters, you'll still pass under Lake Mead Parkway after you complete the third one.

Follow the trail as it eventually crosses back under Lake Mead Parkway and winds its way into and out of the River Mountains. There are a lot of

Railroad Pass Hotel & Casino

The Railroad Pass Hotel & Casino has the distinction of being issued the fourth gaming license in the state of Nevada. The first two licenses were never issued, and the casino that got the third license is no longer in existence. This means Railroad Pass is the oldest running casino in the state. Celebrating its eightieth birthday in 2011, the hotel and casino—named after the railroad that ran behind it—was built in 1931 to serve the workers building the Hoover Dam in the nearby straight-laced town of Boulder City. The hotel and casino had a nightclub that was a popular spot for workers to unwind after a hard day's work. Located inside the hotel is a museum dedicated to the days of yore, where you can find vintage photos, old slot machines, and Railroad Pass memorabilia.

switchbacks and tight turns in this area. Be careful on this part of the trail, especially when traveling on the downhill sections, as it is easy to build up quite a bit of speed, which can be dangerous in the tight turns. After you complete the downhill section, you'll have a bit of a climb as the trail eventually turns toward Lake Mead. Follow the trail as it goes under Lakeshore Road and winds around the lake. Here you'll cross several entrances to Lake Mead and three cement washes. If it is raining, don't ride across the washes. Additionally, if it has rained recently, be careful, as the washes may be full of debris.

Follow the trail as it eventually makes its way back up into the hills and climbs toward the Alan Bible Visitor Center. While you'll cross several streets and pass a water treatment plant, the trail is easy to follow, and as long as you look for the trail markers, you won't get lost. Follow the trail as it climbs the gradual hill into the parking lot below the visitor center, where you started.

MILES AND DIRECTIONS

0.0 Start at the trailhead at the parking lot below the Alan Bible Visitor Center, and take the cement trail above the parking lot. In 0.1 mile, follow the trail to the right and into the tunnel, passing under Lakeshore Road.

0.9 Cross the dirt road and in 1.0 mile, follow the trail as it curves to the left and enters what looks like a little canyon.

2.6 Follow the trail to the left and begin a short downhill section. Do not take the dirt road.

4.0 Turn left at the painted trail marker when the asphalt trail turns to cement and head down into the wash. Turn right and head up the wash.

4.2 Stay straight; do not take the tunnel to the left. In 0.2 mile, stay straight again and pass through the tunnel.

4.6 Stay straight; do not take the trail to the left. At mile 5.0, take the trail to the right and cross St. Jude's Street at the crosswalk, then follow the trail back down into the wash.

5.1 Take the trail to the left and cross the entrance to St. Jude's at the crosswalk, then follow the trail back down into the wash.

5.3 Follow the trail as it climbs out of the wash on the right and head straight to the stop sign. Cross the road and pick up the trail on the left. In 0.2 mile, cross Lakeview Drive at the crosswalk.

5.6 Follow the trail to the right just before Katzenbach Drive.

River Mountains Loop

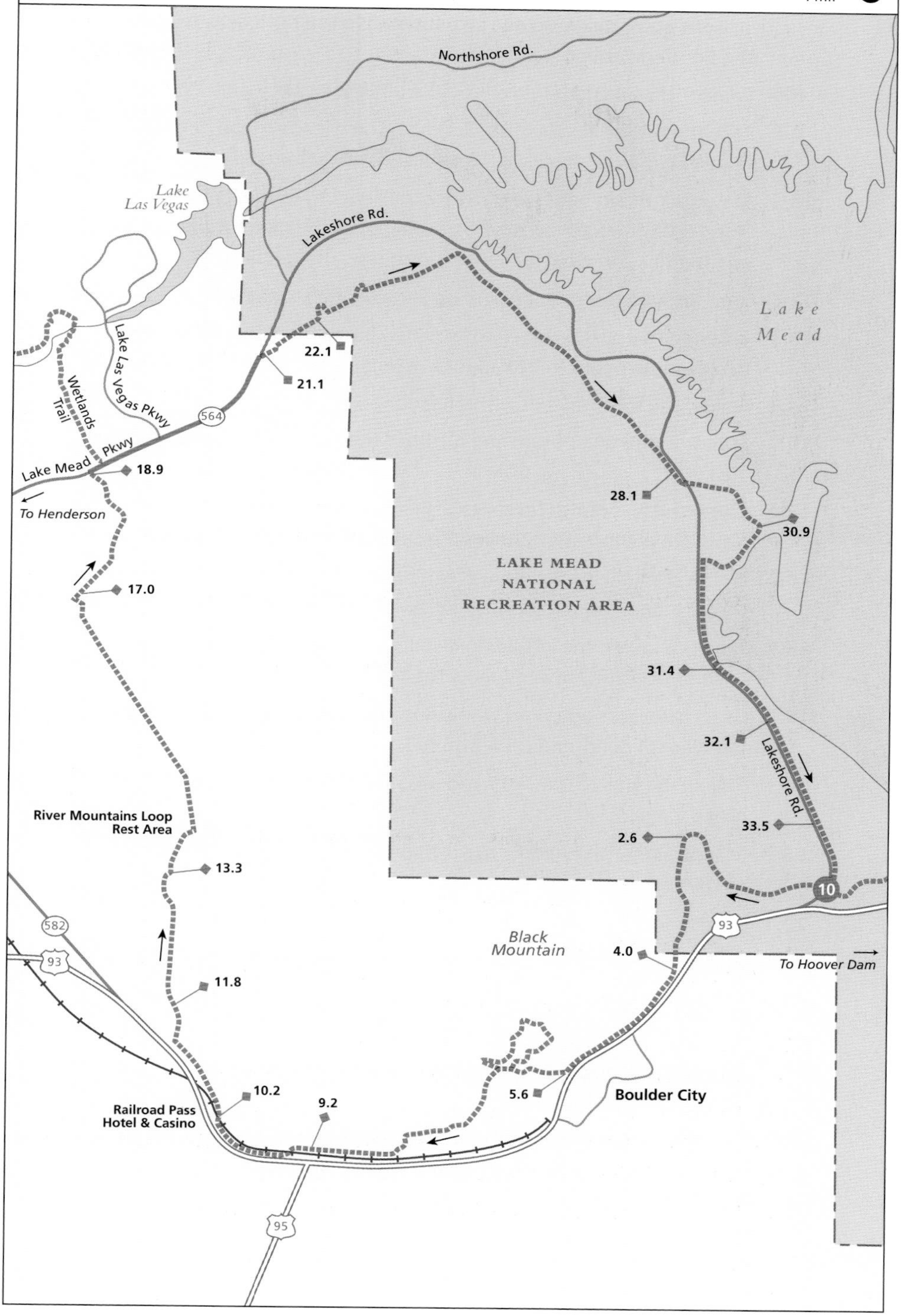

6.5 Enter the roundabout and pick up the trail on the opposite side. Stay straight at 6.7 miles; do not take the trail to the right, which leads to the Bootleg Canyon trailhead.

6.8 Cross the road and begin a little downhill section.

9.2 Take the bridge across Cascata Drive, which leads to the golf course. Cross the railroad tracks in 0.2 mile and follow the trail to the right.

10.2 Stay straight; do not take offshoot trail leading to the Railroad Pass Hotel & Casino parking lot. In 0.2 mile, cross the railroad tracks again and begin a short climb before a long downhill section.

11.8 Stay straight; do not take Lindsay's Corner trail to the left.

13.3 Take the trail to the right and cross the Equestrian Channel on the bridge, then begin a short climbing section.

14.4 Follow the trail into a downhill section.

16.0 Stay straight; do not take the offshoot trail leading to the Burkholder Trail.

17.0 Climb the first of the Three Sisters. Follow the trail into a very steep downhill section at 17.3 miles. Be careful and watch your speed.

18.3 Follow the trail into another steep downhill section. In 0.1 mile, cross the dirt road, then in 0.2 mile, follow the trail to the right.

18.9 Take the trail to the left when it splits. Go through the tunnel under Lake Mead Parkway and follow the trail to the right.

19.7 Cross Lake Las Vegas Parkway at the crosswalk. Take the trail to the left when it dead-ends in 0.2 mile.

21.1 Follow the trail to the right and pass through the tunnel under Lake Mead Parkway.

21.7 Stay straight. Do not take the cement trail to the left or the dirt trail to the right.

22.1 Start a downhill section into switchbacks with hairpin turns.

24.4 Follow the trail to the right and begin a climbing section.

28.0 Follow the trail as it goes down into the wash and pass through the tunnel, going under Lakeshore Road.

28.1 Pass through the tunnel going under Saddle Cove Road. In 0.6 mile, cross the cement wash.

29.3 Cross the asphalt road and continue straight.

30.9 Cross the road to the Lake Mead Marina. In 0.4 mile, cross the cement wash.

31.4 Cross the road to the Boulder Harbor.

32.1 Cross the first road to Boulder Beach, then in 0.3 mile, cross the second road to Boulder Beach.

32.6 Cross the road to Lake Mead RV Village, then cross the cement wash in 0.1 mile.

33.5 Cross Hemenway Road.

34.4 Arrive back at the trailhead.

RIDE INFORMATION

Local Events and Attractions

Alan Bible Visitor Center: Here you will find exhibits on Lake Mead, including the animals that make the lake their home, along with a full-size relief map of Lake Mead National Recreation Area; nps.gov/lake/planyourvisit/visitorcenters.htm.

Lake Mead Cruises: A popular attraction on Lake Mead is a cruise on a Mississippi River–style paddleboat; lakemeadcruises.com.

Restaurants

Boulder Dam Brewing Company: 453 Nevada Way, Boulder City; (702) 243-2739; boulderdambrewing.com. Local brewery and restaurant started by Seattle native Todd Cook.

Boulder Pit Stop: 802 Buchanan Blvd., Boulder City; (720) 293-7080; boulderpitstop.com. Best hamburgers in town, located a short distance from the trail.

The Harbor House Cafe: 490 Horsepower Cove, Boulder City; (702) 293-3081; boatinglakemead.com. Unique floating restaurant and bar on Lake Mead.

Restrooms

Mile 0.0: Alan Bible Visitor Center

Mile 13.3: River Mountains Loop rest area

Lakeshore/Northshore to Callville Bay

Callville Bay was originally established by Mormon pioneers looking to create a steamboat dock on the Colorado River. The area was eventually abandoned by the Mormons, but not before a couple of steamboat trips were successfully made. This is a long ride that provides great views of Lake Mead and the surrounding area.

Start: Parking lot just below the Alan Bible Visitor Center

Length: 53.2 miles

Approximate riding time: 3.5 to 5.5 hours

Best bike: Road bike

Terrain and trail surface: Asphalt

Traffic and hazards: This road is heavily traveled by cars and motorcycles.

Things to see: Lake Mead, desert scenery, wildlife.

Getting there: By car: Take US 93 toward the Hoover Dam (Boulder City). Turn onto Lakeshore Road and follow it to the parking lot just below the Alan Bible Visitor Center. Do not go so far that you reach the entrance fee station. **GPS:** N36 00.707' / W114 47.609'

Fees: A pass to enter Lake Mead National Recreation Area by bike costs $5 and is good for seven days. Yearly passes are $30 per person. National Park passes are also accepted. Payments are made at the guard booth at the entrance to Lake Mead.

THE RIDE

Lake Mead was created in 1935 when the Hoover Dam was built to tame the mighty Colorado River. Building the dam generated the largest man-made lake in the United States, comprising 1.5 million acres—200,000 of which are

Bike Shops

All Mountain Cyclery: 1404 Nevada Hwy., Ste. C, Boulder City; (702) 453-2453; allmountaincyclery.com
Aspen Creek Cycling: 1590 W. Horizon Ridge Pkwy., #140, Henderson; (702) 893-2453; aspencreekcycling.com
JT's Bicycle: 76 W. Horizon Ridge Pkwy., Henderson; (702) 564-5345; jtsbicycle.com
McGhie's Ski, Bike, and Board: 19 S. Stephanie St., Ste. 100, Henderson; (702) 800-3636; mcghies.com
REI: 2220 Village Walk Dr., #150, Henderson; (702) 896-7111

water. The Lake Mead National Recreation Area is now home to 900 species of plants and 500 species of animals, including 24 that are rare and threatened. This ride will take you around a significant part of Lake Mead providing great views of both the lake and the surrounding desert landscape. This is a long ride on curving roads that have gradual but significant climbs and long sections of downhill. The trail is easy to follow because once on it, you will not get off unless you want to do some sightseeing.

While the ride is long—almost 54 miles—you can turn around at any time if you don't want to complete the entire route. If you do choose to take the entire ride, it is best to time it so you arrive back towards the trailhead around sunset. If you've never experienced it before, this ride will help you understand the words in the song "America the Beautiful": "For purple mountain majesties." When the sun sets on the mountains surrounding Lake Mead, they turn the most magnificent shade of purple you have ever seen. It is something, I believe, unique to the Las Vegas valley.

As with many of the rides in the far southeast portion of the valley, the trailhead is the parking lot just below the Alan Bible Visitor Center, a place, by the way, well worth visiting. From the parking lot, turn right onto Lakeshore Road and head to the ranger collection booths, where you will need to pay a fee. The fee is nominal, and you should resist the temptation to get on the free River Mountains Loop at the parking lot and ride it until you can junction with Lakeshore Road.

It is important to note that while a bike lane does exist on Lakeshore Road, the lane is narrow and the speed limit of the road is 50 mph in some areas. Most people on the road are driving it for the scenic beauty, so it is important to pay attention to the traffic. At the start of the trail are many different docks, marinas, and overlooks, and while each of these adds to the total miles you'll need to ride, many are worth a visit. This is especially true for

Hemenway Harbor, which not only has a floating cafe and bar, but is a great place to see some of the largest carp you'll ever find in a lake. These carp swim right up next to the marina, eagerly awaiting chips, cheese puffs, and whatever food tourists throw into the water.

The trail continues around the west side of the lake, winding its way up toward several scenic overlooks. Take the time to visit at least one of these places designed to provide unique and interesting views of Lake Mead. As you ride along, you'll see the River Mountains Loop accompanying you on your right. That trail will eventually make its way to the other side of the road as it heads off to the west. As you go you'll pass the Alfred Merritt Smith Water Treatment Facility and the Lake Mead Fish Hatchery, both off to the right.

About 11.5 miles into the trip, you'll switch from Lakeshore Road, turning right onto Northshore Road, just before Lakeshore Road becomes East Lake Mead Parkway. About a mile into the trail, Northshore Road crosses Las Vegas Wash, which is known as an "urban river" because it's composed of urban runoff, shallow groundwater, reclaimed water, and storm water. The Las Vegas Wash is

The view of Lake Mead from the Sunset View Scenic Overlook

part of the wetlands that offer great bird-watching opportunities and is a habitat for many desert animals. From here you'll do a bit of climbing, steep in some places and more gradual in others. When riding in this area watch for animals, especially at night. It is not uncommon for bighorn sheep to cross the road or for reptiles, such as snakes and even scorpions, to do the same.

Callville Bay is about 22.6 miles into the ride and is accessed by turning right onto Callville Bay Road. Here you can take time to eat at the lounge, have a picnic, or just take in the views. Callville Bay was named after Anson Call, a member of the Church of Jesus Christ of Latter-Day Saints who was

Tortoise Fences

Lake Mead is home to an animal that has been on the earth for millions of years—the desert tortoise. If you're wondering, a tortoise differs from a turtle in that it lives entirely on land. While riding the Lakeshore/Northshore to Callville Bay route, you will see a series of long, low fences that run the length of almost the entire Lakeshore Road. These fences, called tortoise exclusion fences, are meant to contain the desert tortoises and prevent them from going out onto the busy street and getting hit by cars.

The 36-inch-high fences are buried at least 12 inches below the natural level of the ground, leaving 22 to 24 inches visible. This is done to prevent the tortoises from burrowing underneath the fence. Rocks are also placed against the fence, on the tortoise side—again to keep the tortoises from digging their way under the fence.

While these small creatures are fun to see, too many people try to handle them, or worse yet, make them pets. This is why the species is endangered and experienced a population decrease, which some estimate to be as high as 90 percent in the western Mojave Desert. At one time desert tortoises averaged 200 adults per square mile. That number has dropped to as low as five in some areas and only twenty in even the most populated areas. If you see a desert tortoise, leave it alone. Lifting or moving one of these animals can cause it to urinate, loosing precious water that, depending on its size, it may not be able to get back. If you find one injured, call a ranger and let them take care of the animal. In Nevada we like to say "Let the wild be wild."

If you'd like to do something to help the desert tortoise, you can adopt one through any of the following agencies:

- Defenders of Wildlife Adoption & Gift Center; secure.defenders.org
- Tortoise Group; tortoisegroup.org
- Reno Tur-toise Club; sierrawave.org/rttc

sent to Nevada in 1864 to establish a steamboat port on the Colorado. Two years later the steamboat *Esmeralda* completed a trip, delivering 100 tons of freight. In 1867 the US Army took over the area and established Fort Callville. The place was eventually abandoned with the construction of the Transcontinental Railroad. The National Park Service took over the site, calling it Callville Bay in 1967.

After you've taken the time to enjoy the bay, you can climb back out, following Callville Bay Road and then turning left onto Northshore Road. You'll eventually make your way back to Lakeshore Road, heading south back to the trailhead. Be sure to turn left when Northshore Road meets Lakeshore Road, as going right will take you the wrong way.

MILES AND DIRECTIONS

0.0 Start at the trailhead at the parking lot below the Alan Bible Visitor Center. Turn right onto Lakeshore Road and pay the fee at the ranger pay station in 0.6 mile.

0.7 Pass the road to Hemenway Harbor on the right.

1.6 Pass the road to Boulder Campground on the right. In 0.2 mile, pass a road to Boulder Beach on the right.

2.3 Pass another road to Boulder Beach on the right.

2.8 Pass the road to Boulder Harbor on the right.

4.2 Pass the road to the Alfred Merritt Smith Water Treatment Facility on the right.

5.0 Pass the road to the fire station entrance on the right. In 0.1 mile, pass the road to the Lake Mead Fish Hatchery on the right.

6.4 Pass the road to the Sunset View Scenic Overlook on the right.

7.4 Pass the road to the Long View Scenic Overlook on the right. In 0.5 mile, pass the road to the 33 Hole Scenic Overlook on the right.

9.4 Pass the road to Las Vegas Bay on the right.

11.5 Turn right onto Northshore Road.

12.4 Cross the bridge and begin a climb.

14.6 Pass the road to North Las Vegas via Lake Mead Boulevard on the left.

15.9 Pass the Upper Gypsum Wash Road on the right.

17.7 Pass the Government Wash Road on the right.

18.1 Pass the lookout on the right.

19.6 Pass the 8 Mile Road on the right.

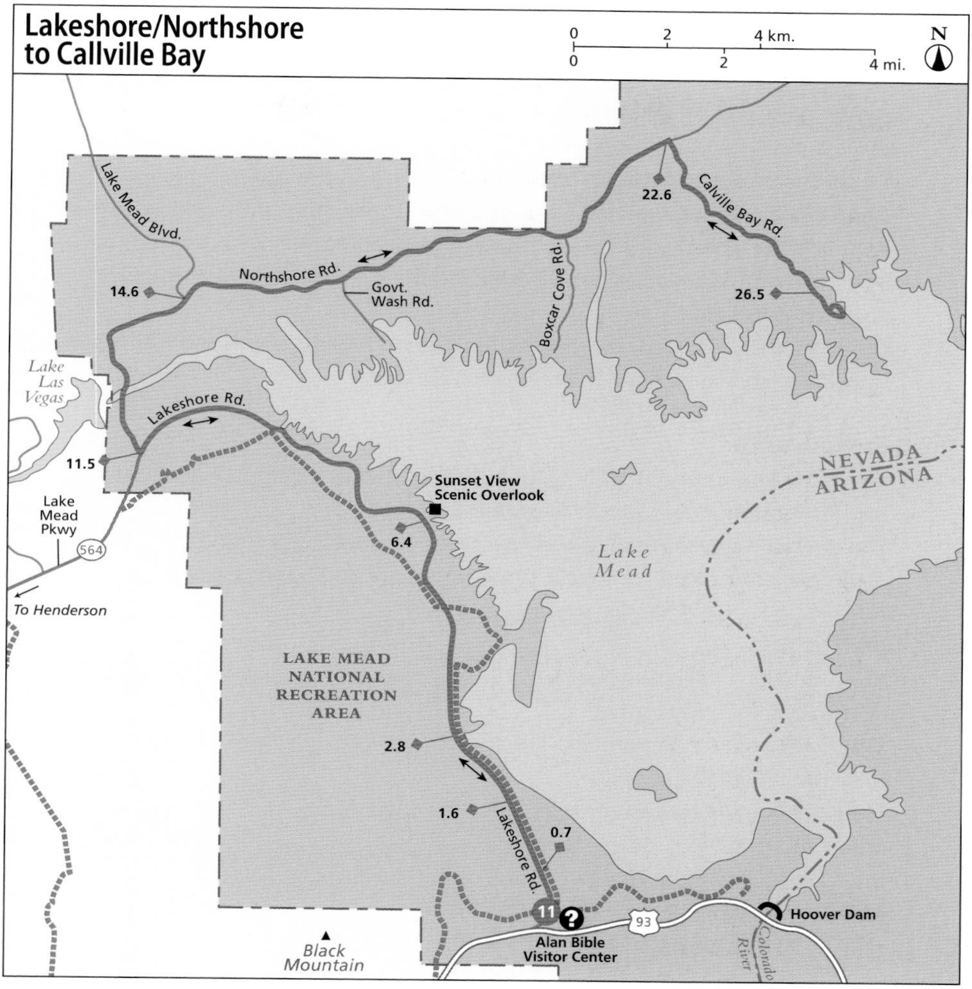

20.4 Pass the Boxcar Cove Road on the right.

22.0 Cross the bridge.

22.6 Turn right onto Callville Bay Road and head down the winding road to Callville Bay.

26.5 Turn left into the parking lot for Callville Bay or to return to the trailhead.

26.7 Turn left at the dead end.

26.8 Turn right at the stop sign and ride out of Callville Bay to the main road. The route is a retrace from here.

53.2 Turn left into the parking lot and the trailhead.

RIDE INFORMATION

Local Events and Attractions

Alan Bible Visitor Center: Here you will find exhibits on Lake Mead, including the animals that make the lake their home, along with a full-size relief map of Lake Mead National Recreation Area; nps.gov/lake/planyourvisit/visitorcenters.htm.

Lake Mead Cruises: A popular attraction on Lake Mead is a cruise on a Mississippi River–style paddleboat; lakemeadcruises.com.

Restaurants

Fountain Site Lounge: HCR-30, Box 100; (720) 565-8958; callvillebay.com. Lounge located at the Callville Bay Marina.

The Harbor House Cafe: 490 Horsepower Cove, Boulder City; (702) 293-3081; boatinglakemead.com. Unique floating restaurant and bar on Lake Mead.

Restrooms

Mile 0.0: Alan Bible Visitor Center
Mile 0.7: Hemenway Harbor
Mile 1.6: Boulder Campground
Mile 1.8: Boulder Beach
Mile 2.8: Boulder Harbor
Mile 6.4: Sunset View Scenic Overlook
Mile 7.9: Long View Scenic Overlook
Mile 9.7: Las Vegas Bay
Mile 26.5: Callville Bay

12

Historic Railroad Trail

In 1931 the federal government undertook the building of what was then the largest dam in the United States. While the dam remains, much of the roads and trails used to access the construction site have long since disappeared—that is, except for the Historic Railroad Trail. This trail not only offers unique views of the lake, but also allows you to pass through the very tunnels used by the railroad when traveling to the dam.

Start: Parking lot just below the Alan Bible Visitor Center

Length: 7.5 miles

Approximate riding time: 1.5 to 2.5 hours

Best bike: Mountain bike

Terrain and trail surface: Mostly dirt and loose gravel

Traffic and hazards: These trails are only open to human power and are used by mountain bikers, hikers, and runners. The road is wide enough to easily offer room for everyone on the trail.

Things to see: Lake Mead, large tunnels used for railroad passage, timbers used to support the tunnels, various wildlife

Getting there: **By car:** Take US 93 toward the Hoover Dam (Boulder City). Turn onto Lakeshore Road and follow it to the parking lot just below the Alan Bible Visitor Center. **GPS:** N36 00.707' / W114 47.609'

THE RIDE

The Historic Railroad Trail was once used to get many of the materials needed to build the Hoover Dam to the dam site. While the railroad tracks have long been removed, the overly large tunnels hewn into the iron-rich rocks still exist. In a town that quickly destroys its past, this trail is a bastion of history that has been around since 1931, when a conglomeration of six major western firms—called the Six Companies Inc.—got together to build almost 30 miles of railroad in five months. Once the tracks were laid, trains ran to and from the dam site twenty-four hours a day, carrying machinery, gravel, and supplies to the dam site.

There are five tunnels on the trail. Each tunnel is 18 feet wide and 27 feet high. The width and height were needed to allow massive pieces of pipe, turbine, and construction equipment to pass through unobstructed. Many of the tunnels were reinforced with timbers that were meant to prevent rock from falling onto the train. Unfortunately the original timbers in tunnel two burned down in 1990; however, they were replaced by the National Park Service. The timbers in tunnel five were also burned in 1978, after which the tunnel was sealed. In 2001 the walls were reinforced with shotcrete and the tunnel reopened.

Because the trail was used by trains to transport supplies, the dirt road that makes up the trail is very wide and relatively flat. While the trail does climb as it makes its way through the tunnels, that climb is gradual and relatively easy. This is also a great trail to see many animals native to Nevada. Here you may spot owls, bighorn sheep, coyotes, and bats. In fact, Mexican free-tailed bats roost in many of the tunnels. If you ride in the evening, you can often see the bats fluttering around. Bats, and all other wildlife, should be left alone.

The trailhead is just above the parking lot below the Alan Bible Visitor Center. It starts out as a cement trail, but quickly turns into dirt when you follow the trail sign as it breaks off the cement trail. This dirt trail takes you to the entrance of the main trail, which is a large metal gate. If the gate is not open, the trail cannot be ridden. Once on the trail, simply follow it as it winds its way into the mountains above Lake Mead, offing spectacular views of the lake to the left. You will pass through five tunnels. Just before you reach the first tunnel, look down the ravine to the right. Here you can see several concrete plugs taken out of the Hoover Dam to install the turbines. Between tunnels two and three is another large ravine. The large, loose rocks used to create the ravine were removed from the tunnels when they were being dug out.

At the end of the last tunnel, about 2 miles into the ride, there is another, smaller metal gate. This is where the trail goes from land owned by the National Park Service

Bike Shops

All Mountain Cyclery: 1404 Nevada Hwy., Ste. C, Boulder City; (702) 453-2453; allmountaincyclery.com

JT's Bicycle: 76 W. Horizon Ridge Pkwy., Henderson; (702) 564-5345; jtsbicycle.com

McGhie's Ski, Bike, and Board: 19 S. Stephanie St., Ste. 100, Henderson; (702) 800-3636; mcghies.com

A mother and daughter ride through a tunnel used by the railroad when building the Hoover Dam.

onto land owned by the Bureau of Reclamation. This gate is closed at sunset, and you should not go onto the trail if you cannot be back at the gate before sunset, because the Bureau of Reclamation will not open the gate again once it is closed for the night, and it is illegal to be on their land at night. If caught on the trail, you will have to ride to the asphalt parking lot and then climb the Great Basin Highway, back to the trailhead.

The trail is largely downhill after the second gate. Remember to plan for the time it will take to climb back out when you decide whether you have enough time to ride the entire trail. The trail loops at the end, allowing you to follow it back to the trailhead. There is a small portion of the trail that must be walked—mainly because it is very steep, but also because the signs tell you to walk. There is also a shortcut that you can take toward the end of the trail. This trail, which leads to the walking portion, is much steeper than the main trail.

Posted along the trail are plaques that provide information about the animals you might see. Be sure to look upward into the rocks, as well as downward toward the lake, for a chance to see animals such as bighorn sheep, antelope, ravens, owls, lizards, and ground squirrels. Other plaques tell the story of the railroad construction, complete with vintage photographs taken when the railroad was being built. In some areas along the trail, people have created offshoot hiking trails. These trails are illegal and should not be taken. Towards the end of the trail, there is a parts boneyard. Here you can see the large pieces of equipment used to build the turbines powered by the dam. Looking at these pieces of equipment, it's easy to see why the tunnels were built so wide and tall.

The Hoover Dam Tunnels

On December 30, 1929, President Herbert Hoover signed a bill authorizing the construction of a dam to tame the mighty Colorado River. The first problem was how to get the materials to the construction site. This task fell on a consortium of six major western firms, which together formed Six Companies Inc. A total of five tunnels were burrowed and blasted into the mountains leading to the construction site. Each tunnel was approximately 300 feet long and 25 feet in diameter. The size was needed to make sure the turbines used at the dam would fit through the tunnels. Once the system was complete in 1931, nine steam and four gas locomotives operated on a twenty-four-hour basis. It took seventy-one people to keep the railroad in operation.

The tracks were abandoned after the completion of the dam in 1935, although trains still ran up until 1961. A year later, in 1962, the tracks were taken up and sold for scrap, along with the Oregon fir trees used as ties. In 1984 the trail was placed on the National Register of Historic Places and is the only remaining section of the Hoover Dam Railroad system that is not highly disturbed or underwater.

In 1977 Clint Eastwood and Sondra Locke filmed parts of *The Gauntlet* in a section of the tunnel. In the movie, Eastwood played a cop assigned to escort prostitute Locke from Las Vegas to Phoenix so she could testify against the mob. In the scenes filmed at the tunnels, the couple are on a motorcycle being chased by an assassin in a helicopter.

Historic Railroad Trail

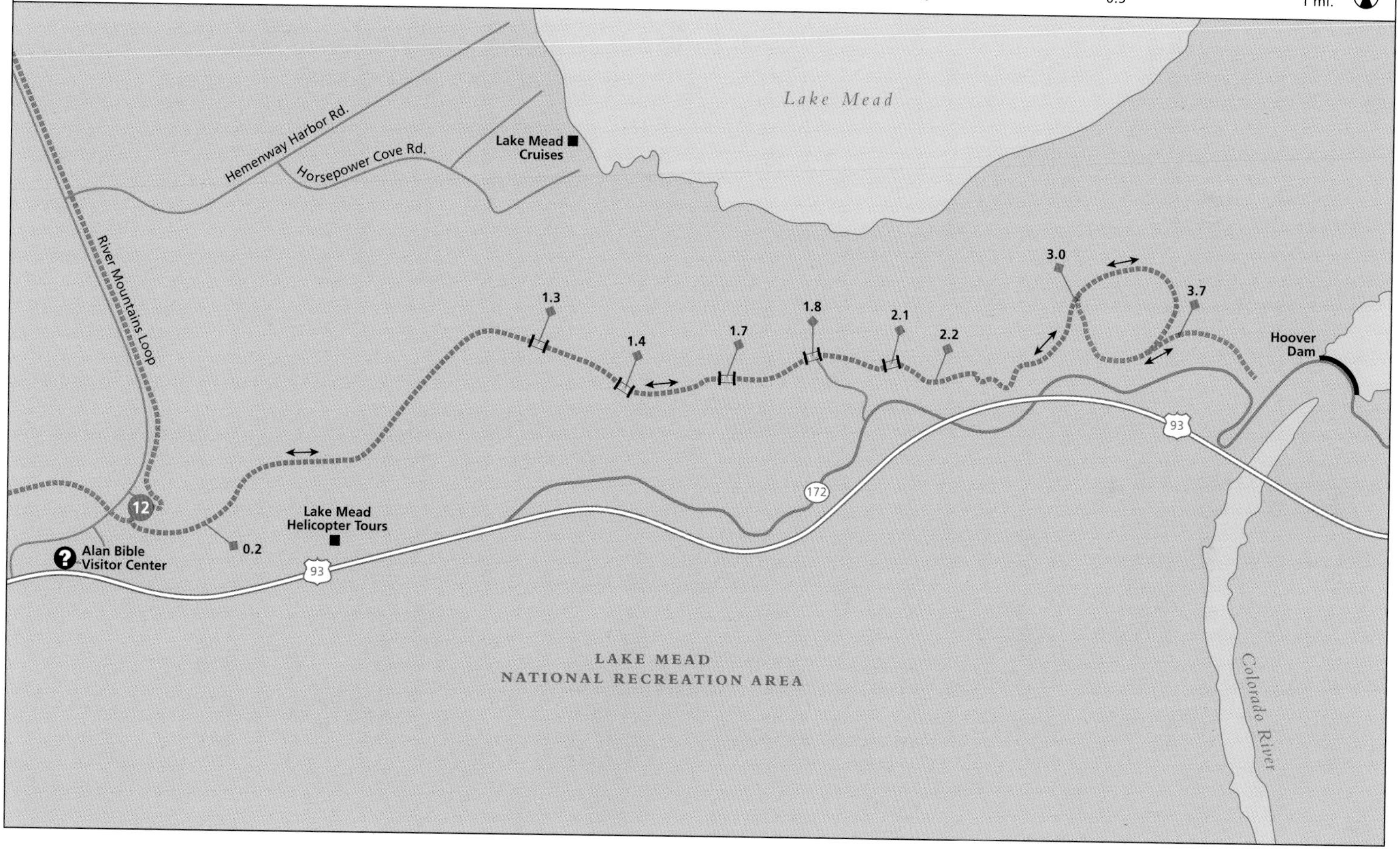

MILES AND DIRECTIONS

0.0 Start at the trailhead just above the parking lot. Follow the trail as it heads to the left.

0.2 Enter large metal gates.

1.3 Go through the first tunnel. This tunnel is not very long, and you can see the second tunnel as you enter.

1.4 Go through the second tunnel.

1.7 Go through the third tunnel.

1.8 Go through the fourth tunnel.

2.1 Go through the fifth tunnel. This is the longest of all the tunnels.

2.2 Go through the second gate, entering Bureau of Reclamation land.

2.8 Pass through another metal gate. Watch out for trucks on this portion of the trail.

3.0 Stay straight. Do not take the shortcut off to the right.

3.4 The trail splits; stay straight. In 0.2 mile, take the trail to the left.

3.7 Take the walking trail back up to the main trail, then follow the trail to the right back to the trailhead.

7.5 Arrive back at the trailhead.

RIDE INFORMATION

Local Events and Attractions

Alan Bible Visitor Center: Here you will find exhibits on Lake Mead, including the animals that make the lake their home, along with a full-size relief map of Lake Mead National Recreation Area; nps.gov/lake/planyourvisit/visitorcenters.htm.

Helicopter Tour of Lake Mead: Take a fifteen-minute tour of Lake Mead by air; grayline.com or papillon.com.

Lake Mead Cruises: A popular attraction on Lake Mead is a cruise on a Mississippi River–style paddleboat; lakemeadcruises.com.

Six Tunnels to Hoover Dam: This annual run through the tunnels of Hoover Dam takes place every year on St. Patrick's Day. There is a half marathon and two-person relay, a 5K run/walk, and a 1-mile stroll. There are even prizes for best costume; mountainmanevents.com.

Restaurants

Boulder Dam Brewing Company: 453 Nevada Way, Boulder City; (702) 243-2739; boulderdambrewing.com. Local brewery and restaurant started by Seattle native Todd Cook.

Boulder Pit Stop: 802 Buchanan Blvd., Boulder City; (720) 293-7080; boulderpitstop.com. Best hamburgers in town, located a short distance from the trail.

Milo's Cellar: 538 Nevada Way, Boulder City; (702) 293-9540; miloswinebar.com. Sidewalk cafe and wine bar.

Restrooms

Mile 0.0: Alan Bible Visitor Center

Mile 2.3: Just on the other side of the gate

13

Middle and Lower Lake View Loop

This loop provides some great views of Bootleg Canyon as well as Lake Mead. Here you can see the beauty of the desert in colorful rocks and flowering plants. Although the trail is relatively short, the lower portion consists of an easy but steady climb that takes a while to complete.

Start: Just behind and to the right of the restrooms at the entrance to Bootleg Canyon

Length: 2.7 miles

Approximate riding time: 45 minutes to 1.5 hours

Best bike: Mountain bike with suspension (either front or full)

Terrain and trail surface: Mostly dirt, some large rocks, and loose gravel—asphalt trail briefly crossed twice

Traffic and hazards: These trails are only open to human power and are mostly used by mountain bikers. However, hikers and runners also use the trail, and it is best to be courteous and give way to them when encountered. These trails are also some of the few that cross the many downhill trails in Bootleg Canyon. When riding this loop, it is a good idea to keep an eye up toward the top of the canyon to make sure no one is riding down one of the trails. Downhill riders go a lot faster than you, and it is more difficult for them to stop. Rocks can be hazards on this trail, and shin guards are a valuable accessory.

Things to see: Lake Mead, Bootleg Canyon, some old remnants of bygone bootlegging, desert plants and animals

Getting there: **By car:** Take US 93 toward the Hoover Dam (Boulder City). Bootleg Canyon is easily visible on left-hand side of the road. It is marked by a large white BC, which actually stands for Boulder City, not Bootleg Canyon. Turn left on Veterans Memorial Drive and follow the road around to Canyon Road. Turn left on Canyon Road and follow it all the way to the restrooms. There is a parking lot just below the restrooms. You'll know you are in the correct place because you'll see the parking lot, restrooms, and covered picnic tables. If you go far enough to hit a dirt road, you will have gone too far. ***Note:*** If the parking lot is full, you can park in the dirt lot just below the asphalt lot. **GPS:** N35 58.020' / W114 51.712'

THE RIDE

The Middle and Lower Lake View Loop is actually a combination of two trails which together form a loop through the middle and lower part of the canyon. While the Middle Lake View Trail has some technical challenges, the Lower Lake View Trail is a nice, easy, gradual ride back to the trailhead. Both trails offer scenic views of Lake Mead, which is how they got their name.

The trail starts just behind and to the right of the restrooms. It is well-worn and easy to see. The trailhead is between two large rocks that have been placed there specifically to mark the trail. Once you start down the first hill, stay to the right until you go over the next little hill. After you reach the top of the small hill, keep to the left because the right trail leads to a fairly difficult jump—one that can cause injury if missed.

As you come around the bend, there is a large ditch in the trail. The ditch is a remnant of the zipline that used to run from the top of the hill. The creators of the zipline were worried the dangling feet of their passengers would strike bike riders on the trail below, so they dug a ditch for bikers to ride into—thus avoiding those pesky feet. The zipline is gone, but the ditch was left behind because the bikers liked it. If you don't want to ride down the ditch, you can bypass it by taking the trail just to the right.

Coming out of the ditch, you arrive at a point where the trail splits into the Middle Lake View and the Lower Lake View—marked by small wooden signs. While this guide covers the loop clockwise following the Middle Lake View first, you can also take the loop counterclockwise following the Lower Lake View first. Either way the ride is very enjoyable, but the route outlined here is better for more experienced riders.

Bike Shop

All Mountain Cyclery: 1404 Nevada Hwy., Ste. C, Boulder City; (702) 453-2453; allmountaincyclery.com. Rents mountain bikes and gives guided mountain bike tours of all Bootleg Canyon trails.

Immediately after the sign, the trail takes the first of its deep dips. This one is pretty gradual, but momentum is needed to make it up the other side. As the trail progresses, there are many places where downhill trails cross the main trail. It's pretty easy to tell which trail is which, so there isn't much reason to worry about getting on the wrong trail. Shortly after the first big drop, there is another, much steeper drop. This one can be a little intimidating, so you may want to take the trail to the right, which is more gradual and, therefore, a little easier and less intimidating.

Once you've made it up the other side, you come to what is likely the best part of the ride. This portion is a series of small hills and dips that are fun to ride, and following the loop this way allows you to pick up a certain amount of speed. The section ends with a fairly steep but gradual climb that is not technical. From here the trail winds its way around the outside of the canyon, offering great views of the canyon walls on the left. Bootleg Canyon is quite scenic: It has some of the most unique colors of rocks in all of Nevada, and biking here allows one to experience the beauty of the desert.

Not too far along, the trail comes to another dip. While this drop is not steep, the climb on the other side is and it is also fairly technical—which is a fancy way of saying it requires a certain amount of skill. If you don't feel comfortable climbing the hill, you can simply get off your bike and walk. After the dip, follow the trail upward and around a hill to the next dip. This is probably the largest and most difficult of all the dips on the trail. Going downward, the trail splits in two and you can take either route. The key here is to build up momentum for the climb on the other side and to never stop pedaling once you reach that side. The climb consists of fairly loose gravel and requires a certain amount of speed combined with continued pedaling to make it up the other side. Again, if you don't feel comfortable riding, you can easily walk this part.

As you make your way down the trail, you arrive at a fork in the road. Keep to the right and begin a short, easy downhill section. The trail to the left is the Upper Lake View Trail. This trail is fairly technical and, for that reason, is not covered in this guide. The downhill section leads to a slight climb that, once completed, offers magnificent views of Lake Mead. Before the climb, the trail crosses the River Mountain Hiking Trail. This trail was created by the Civilian Conservation Corps (CCC) in the 1930s. It is now a hiking trail, not open to bikes, and is clearly marked as such. Once you reach the top of the hill, take the time to pause and enjoy the view of Lake Mead and a portion of Boulder City, which spreads out in the valley below.

As the trail goes down the hill, it becomes the Lower Lake View Trail. This lower trail is a relatively easy but steady climb out of the desert valley back up to the canyon. There are a couple of dips in this section, but they are nothing like the dips on the Middle Lake View Trail. Just as with the Middle Lake View, other trails frequently cross the main trail, and it is easy to tell which trail is which. Because the Lower Lake View Trail is relatively easy to ride, it provides an opportunity to take in the views of the desert fauna and the unique rock colors of red, purple, and orange that make up the canyon floor and walls.

As the trail progresses it crosses the River Mountains Loop. This trail is easily recognized because it is asphalt. Crossing the asphalt takes you to a bit of a climb on some dark red clay. Once you complete the first part of the climb, turn to the right and keep climbing. Here the trails splits into two and you can take either trail (though the trail to the right is a bit easier), as they join up again in about 20 feet. Staying on the main trail brings you close to the main dirt road leading into the canyon. This portion of the trail offers great views of the lower portion of the canyon. As the trail continues, it climbs until it eventually meets, once again, with the Middle Lake View Trail. Keep to the left and follow the trail back to the restrooms.

The view of Lake Mead that gives the Middle and Lower Lake View Loop its name

Lake Mead

When the first pioneers came upon the grassy meadows that made up Las Vegas in 1855, they found little more than a river meandering through the valley. It was a river that had traveled for thousands of miles, forming a "grand" American landmark on its way to Mexico. What those pioneers didn't find in 1855 was a lake. That body of water wouldn't appear in the valley until almost eighty years later.

In the early 1930s the US Department of the Interior built the first major dam to span the mighty Colorado River. Named Hoover Dam after President Herbert Hoover, it was placed in the Black Mountains just outside of Las Vegas. The creation of the dam formed Lake Mead, the largest man-made lake in the United States. The lake, which is part of the Lake Mead National Recreation Area, has more than 550 miles of shoreline, a large portion of which is viewable by riders of both road and mountain bikes. Modern Lake Mead is a popular destination for all types of water sports. It is used by jet-skiers, boaters, water-skiers, kayakers, windsurfers, sailboaters, kite-surfers, anglers, and people with both party boats and houseboats. The lake is even home to a large, old-fashioned paddleboat that gives tours daily.

Because it is positioned along the north–south migration route, Lake Mead is home to more than 240 different kinds of birds, including the American coot, black-tailed gnatcatcher, burrowing owl, barn owl, great horned owl, common merganser, mallard duck, western grebe, western tanager, rock wren, least sandpiper, yellow-headed blackbird, roadrunner, and various species of hummingbirds. In addition to birds, many other animals and reptiles call Lake Mead, and the area surrounding it, home, including bighorn sheep, coyotes, rabbits, bats, Gila monsters, desert tortoises, and various snakes—including rattlesnakes.

MILES AND DIRECTIONS

0.0 Start at the trailhead just behind and to the right of the restrooms. Follow the trail as it heads down the first incline to the right. When the trail forks, stay to the left. Going right leads to a jump.

0.1 The trail splits into the Middle Lake View and the Lower Lake View. Stay to the left, taking the Middle Lake View Trail. Both trails are clearly marked.

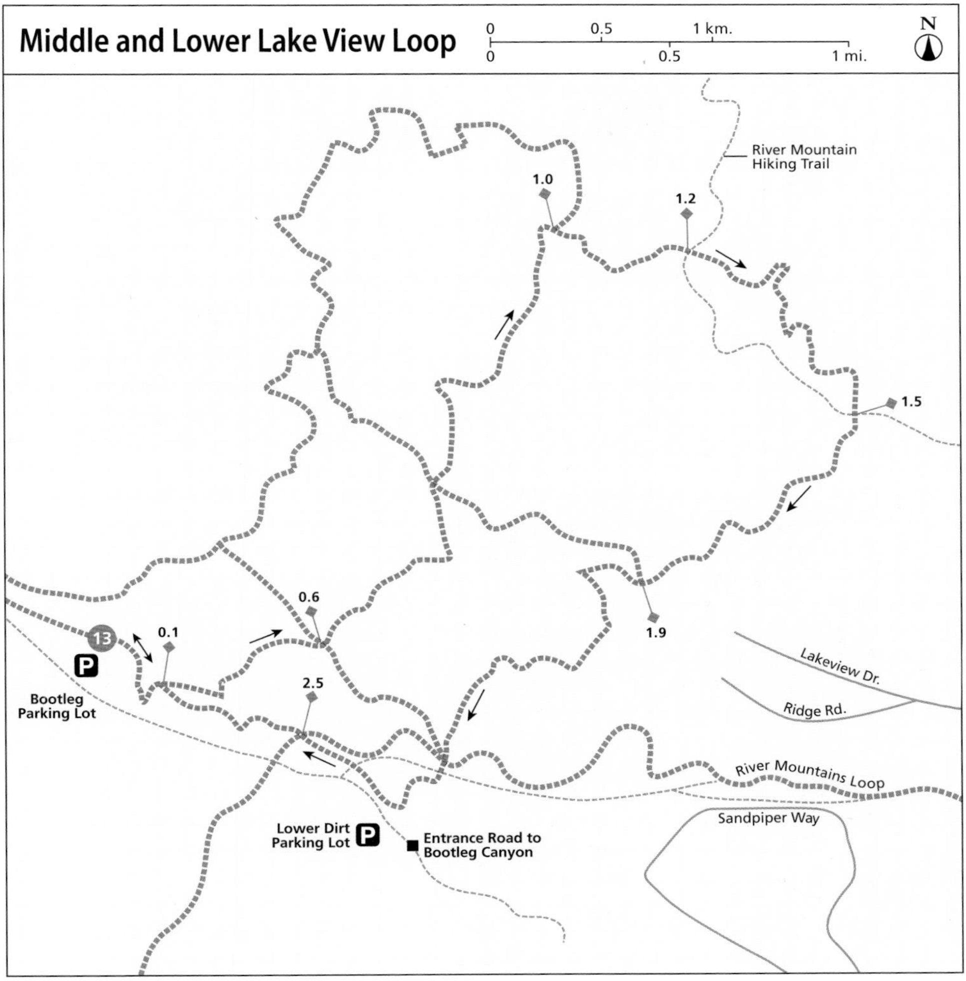

0.2 Takes a sharp turn to the left. A downhill trail crosses the main trail and goes to the right. Stay on the left trail and go up the slight climb. Remember to yield to downhillers.

0.3 Go down the second big dip. An easier trail leading down the dip is located to the right. A little farther along the trail another downhill trail crosses the main trail to the right. Stay on the main trail.

0.6 The trail meets another downhill trail on the left. Stay to the right and make the slight climb.

0.7 Go down the big dip. You'll need momentum to get up the other side. After the dip, another downhill trail crosses the main trail. Keep straight on the main trail.

0.8 This is one of the biggest dips on the trail. You will need a fair amount of momentum to get up the other side. Shortly after the dip, another downhill trail crosses the main trail. Keep going straight.

1.0 The trail forks. Stay to the right and begin a slight descent before another climb.

1.2 The trail crosses the River Mountain Hiking Trail (no bikes allowed). Stay straight on the main trail and begin the climb up the hill.

1.3 Lake Mead comes into view as you travel around the back of the hill, beginning your decent. In 0.1 mile, make a sharp left turn at the end of the steep section and then make a sharp right turn after a short, more gradual, downhill section.

1.5 Take the trail to the right. Do not follow the sign indicating Malaga and Marina Drives. Shortly after this the trail again crosses the River Mountain Hiking Trail. Continue straight.

1.6 The trail crosses the bottom portion of one of the downhill trails crossed previously. Stay straight.

1.8 The trail again crosses a downhill trail and then does so again in about 6 feet. Take the turn to the left into the dip, then cross the dirt road.

1.9 Take the quick climb up and to the right. Stay on the left side of the trail to avoid the loose gravel in the ditch. The trail meets up with a downhill trail. Stay to the right and continue climbing. You will be sharing the downhill trail for a few feet.

2.0 Take the short drop to the left into a wide dip. You will need to keep up your momentum to make it up to the top. Once you take the drop, you are no longer sharing the trail with the downhillers.

2.1 The trail goes over a small wooden bridge. In 0.1 mile, go down the big dip. Again, maintain your momentum to get up the other side.

2.3 The trail crosses another downhill trail. Stay straight and then cross the asphalt road that is part of the River Mountains Loop. Afterward go straight and climb up the other side. This climb is very steep. The key is to keep pedaling. The trail splits for a short distance. You can take either trail, but the trail on the right is slightly easier. The two trails meet back up in about 20 feet.

2.4 Cross the dirt road and begin to climb.

2.5 Cross the River Mountains Loop a second time. In 0.1 mile, go down the small dip and then start a gradual climb.

2.7 The Middle Lake View and the Lower Lake View trails meet. Take the trail to the left and follow it back to the restrooms.

RIDE INFORMATION

Local Events and Attractions

Art in the Park: During this early-October event, more than 300 artists and crafters display and sell their work; bchcares.org/foundation.

Nevada Southern Railway: Visitors sit in a passenger train riding the rails used to build the Hoover Dam on a free ten-minute ride; nevadasouthern.com.

Zipline Bootleg Canyon: If you don't want to see the canyon by trail, you might want to see it by air. This can be done through a series of ziplines positioned on the east side of the canyon; flightlinezbootleg.com.

Restaurants

Boulder Dam Brewing Company: 453 Nevada Way, Boulder City; (702) 243-2739; boulderdambrewing.com. Local brewery and restaurant started by Seattle native Todd Cook.

Boulder Pit Stop: 802 Buchanan Blvd., Boulder City; (720) 293-7080; boulderpitstop.com. Best hamburgers in town, located a short distance from the trail.

Milo's Cellar: 538 Nevada Way, Boulder City; (702) 293-9540; miloswinebar.com. Sidewalk cafe and wine bar.

Restrooms

Mile 0.0: At the trailhead

14

POW/Par None/IMBA Loop

This is a popular trail for beginners because it is not as technical as some of the other trails. The first part of the trail is a steady, continuous climb, but once the halfway point is reached, you're rewarded by a fun, fast downhill section.

Start: Large rocks just off Veterans Drive

Length: 3.7 miles

Approximate riding time: 45 minutes to 1.5 hours

Best bike: Mountain bike with suspension (either front or full)

Terrain and trail surface: Mostly dirt, some large rocks, and loose gravel—asphalt trail crossed once

Traffic and hazards: These trails are only open to human power and are mostly used by mountain bikers. However, hikers and runners also use the trail, and it is best to be courteous and give way to them when encountered.

Things to see: Bootleg Canyon, desert plants and animals

Getting there: **By car:** Take US 93 toward the Hoover Dam (Boulder City). Bootleg Canyon is easily visible on left-hand side of the road. It is marked by a large white BC, which actually stands for Boulder City, not Bootleg Canyon. Turn left on Veterans Memorial Drive and take the first left onto Veterans Drive. Drive down to the large rock formation, which is the trailhead. **GPS:** N35 58.185' / W114 52.489'

THE RIDE

The POW/Par None/IMBA Loop is actually a combination of three trails which together form a loop through the outskirts of Bootleg Canyon. Because this trail is not in the canyon area, the terrain is mainly flat with only small hilly areas. This singletrack trail is not filled with many of the rock obstacles found on most of the other trails in Bootleg Canyon. It is a good intermediate to beginner trail, marked intermediate only because the climb is steady and the downhill portion has some tricky parts. It is a good training trail for anyone looking to build their mountain-biking skills.

Most of the ride is a gradual climb to the top of the loop, where a fun, fast downhill section finishes the ride. The International Mountain Bike Association (IMBA) portion of the trail requires a little more skill than does the rest of the ride, but not advanced skills. Although the trail isn't in the canyon area of Bootleg Canyon, it still showcases the beauty of the Nevada desert. On one portion of the ride, desert tortoises often cross the trail and bats commonly follow bicyclists who ride at dusk—probably because there are more bugs stirred up by the bike.

The trail starts at an area often called "Stonehenge," a formation of large rocks that have been arranged in a big circle and stood on their ends, giving them height. The rocks surround a kiosk that has a map of the trail and advertisements for upcoming events—usually mountain bike races. The map is a little old and can be confusing, so it is best to follow the map provided in this guide. The dirt area in front of and just to the right of the rocks is for parking. The River Mountains Loop is visible to the right and behind the Stonehenge trailhead. This asphalt road is crossed briefly on both the climb and the downhill portions of the ride.

Start the POW/Par None/IMBA Loop by taking the trail just to the right of the rock formation. The first climb is the POW Trail, and it is steeper than it looks. About halfway up the trail, you'll cross an asphalt road that is the River Mountains Loop. Watch for hikers or road bikes on the trail when you cross. When you reach the foot of the hill, you'll travel through a section of lava rocks as you wind around the small hill. Behind that hill the trail splits and the climb continues on the Par None section of the loop. Stay to the right and continue straight. The trail to the left is actually the POW Trail and will be used for the downhill section of the loop.

Follow the Par None Trail for quite a while, as you make your way upward towards the mouth of Bootleg Canyon, but not into the canyon. The loop is singletrack the entire way, and it is nearly impossible to get lost. About 1.2 miles into the ride, you'll enter a gravely area that looks like a large wash. It is in this area where desert tortoises are often seen crossing the road. If you encounter one of these

Bike Shop

All Mountain Cyclery: 1404 Nevada Hwy., Ste. C, Boulder City; (702) 453-2453; allmountaincyclery.com. Rents mountain bikes and gives guided mountain bike tours of all Bootleg Canyon trails.

animals, do not move or touch it—doing so can cause the tortoise to urinate, releasing precious water that it may not be able to get back, and an animal in the desert without water will die.

About 1.3 miles into the ride, there is a steep hill that you navigate through a series of switchbacks. This is one of the more difficult sections of the climb. The hill is steep and the switchbacks are sharp. On the other side of the hill, the loop leaves Par None and goes onto the IMBA Trail to the left. Both the Par None and the IMBA are marked with small wooden signs. The IMBA portion of the loop is still a gradual climb for the first half, after which it is made up of small hills and valleys as it winds its way to the downhill section. Most of the obstacles are easily navigated, but the rock obstacle 2.0 miles into the ride is a bit tricky and you may want to navigate it on foot.

Riding this section, it is not uncommon to see bighorn sheep, rabbits, ground squirrels, and many, many lizards—which love to run across the road in front of you. It is also not uncommon to see or hear rattlesnakes in this area. While they typically do not go on the trail, they can, and it is wise to keep an eye open for these reptiles. When riding, try to keep an eye on the scenery. This area of Bootleg Canyon is filled with a kaleidoscope of some of the most beautiful rocks in the entire valley. You can see black lava rocks as well as rocks in colors of purple, pink, yellow, orange, red, brown, and even blue. The colors are stunning!

Rider making his way down the POW section of the trail

You begin the downhill section by taking the POW Trail to the left about 2.2 miles into the ride. The trail is clearly marked with a wooden sign. After taking the trail to the left, you'll go down two series of drops, with the second more gradual than the first. This portion of the loop has some tricky areas at the beginning, but nothing that can't be navigated by simply slowing down. However, if you're more experienced, you may want to let go and enjoy a fun, fast ride that can take as little as ten minutes to complete. It is easy to pick up speed here, so be careful.

As you get to the end of the hilly portion of the downhill, you go between two large rocks. Shortly after the rock obstacle, the trail again meets Par None. Stay to the right and continue down the trail you climbed at the beginning of the ride. If you want to make another loop, you can take the trail to the left

Bats and Tarantulas

The trails in Bootleg Canyon are accessible for both day and evening rides, although evening rides require bike-mounted lights. When riding at dusk it is not uncommon to see bats flying around, following you as you ride. There are many species of bats in the canyon, and they tend to stay high in the air. This is because they are insectivorous, meaning they only eat insects, something they typically do while in flight—right above your head. While the bats most likely follow cyclists because the bike stirs up insects, it is an interesting experience being followed by bats as one rides.

The bats in Bootleg Canyon are small—with bodies typically 3 to 4 inches long. They fly around in what seems to be erratic patterns as they use echolocation to receive signals that paint a picture of their environment. Bats live a long time, usually giving birth to one or two offspring per year. Because they're mammals, mothers produce milk for their young. The mothers also raise their young alone. Fathers play no part in their children's upbringing.

Once the sun goes down, it is not uncommon to see desert tarantulas on the trail, and while they are relatively harmless, it is best to avoid contact with these furry insects. Most females are brown, while males have black legs. These critters are relatively large—5 inches in some cases—and are very fast. While they'll usually leave you alone, they will passionately defend their territory if disturbed. Although desert spiders are venomous, their bite is most often compared to that of a bee sting. Just be thankful you're not a male tarantula. After mating, the female sometimes catches and eats the male. Maybe he should have brought chocolates.

and trace the path you followed to the IMBA Trail and eventually the POW Trail. If you go to the right, the loop will conclude exactly where it started at the Stonehenge rock formation.

MILES AND DIRECTIONS

0.0 Start at the trailhead just to the right of the rock formation. Follow the trail as it climbs up into the valley.

0.3 Follow the trail to the left, going into a section of lava rocks. The trail weaves around the rocks. In 0.1 mile, take the quick drop into a short gradual climb.

0.5 Follow the trail to the right. As you follow the trail, you can see the outer boundary of Bootleg Canyon. The palm trees in the distance are on a nearby golf course.

0.6 The trail splits. Take the Par None Trail to the right.

0.7 The climb stops and level riding begins. This is a fun section that goes over some small hills and switchbacks. In 0.1 mile, cross the dirt road and keep straight.

0.9 Take the quick drop leading to a steep climb. If you're able to maintain your speed, you'll make the climb to the left. If you don't maintain your speed, take the trail to the right. The trails meet up again in about 20 feet.

1.0 Follow the trail into a short downhill section. Stay on the trail to the left when it splits in 0.1 mile and keep climbing.

1.2 Follow the trail into a level section where desert tortoises can sometimes be found.

1.3 Follow the trail into a steep climb up a hill. This climb has switchbacks with sharp turns.

1.5 Follow the trail onto a short downhill section on the other side of the hill. In a short distance the trail will split. Take the IMBA Trail to the left.

1.8 Follow the trail as it climbs. There are great views of Boulder City at the top of the hill.

2.0 The climb is mostly finished. The next section is partially level and partially downhill. At the beginning of the downhill is a tricky drop with a large bump. Beginners should walk this section.

2.1 Follow the trail into a series of drops and quick climbs. Be careful because this section has lots of loose dirt and small rocks.

POW/Par None/IMBA Loop

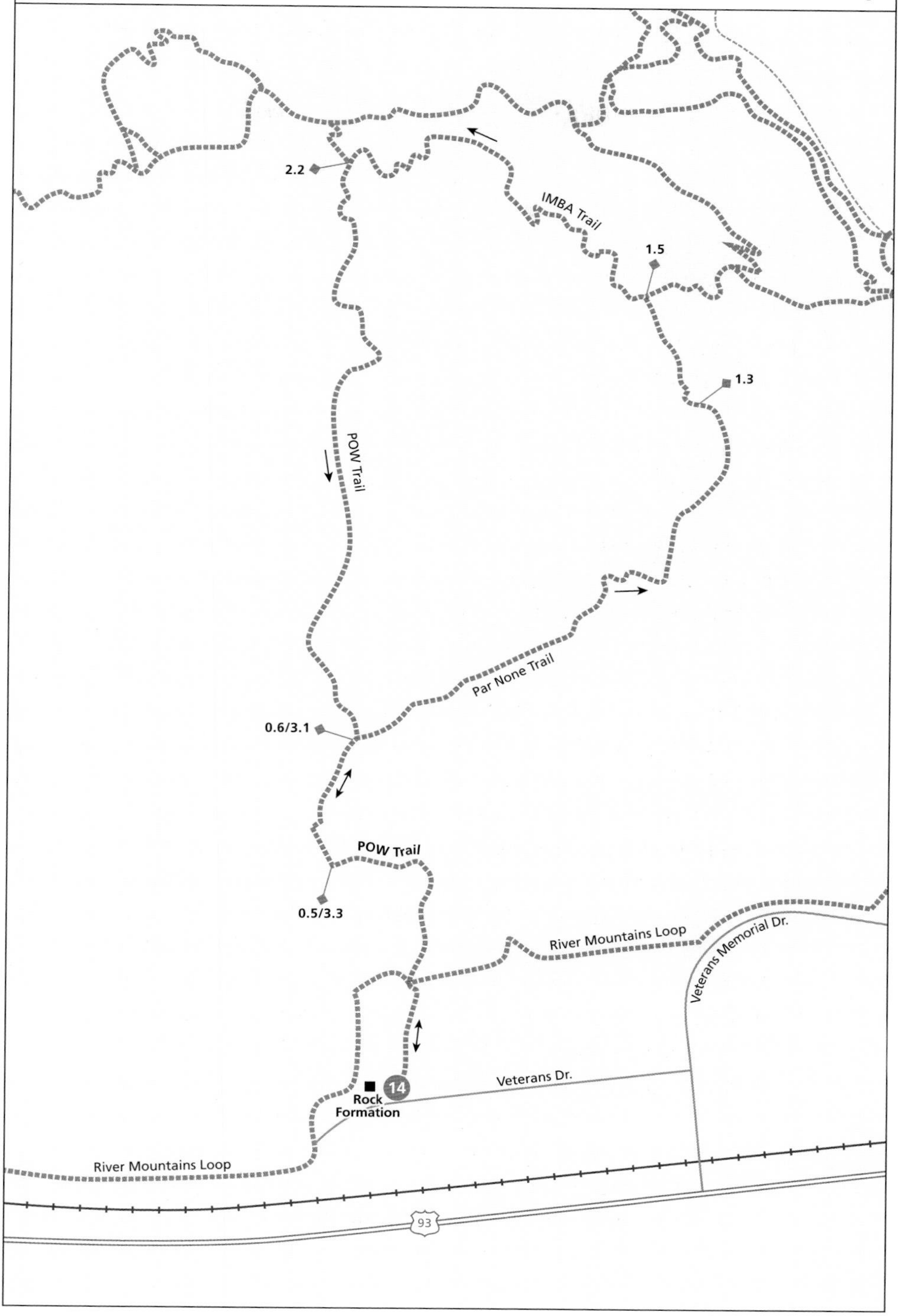

2.2 Take the left onto the POW Trail and two quick drops into the downhill section. Here you can build up quite a bit of speed, so be careful.

2.4 Take the short drop, followed by a much steeper drop and climb. At 2.5 miles, follow the deep grooves in the trail as it curves to the left and then right into a sidetrack on a hill.

2.7 This portion of the trail is a bit of an optical illusion. It looks as if you are going uphill, but you're still going downhill.

2.8 Follow the descent along the side of a hill. There are some tricky rock sections here.

2.9 Keep to the right as the trail splits. The trail to the left is the older trail and is more difficult to ride. The trails will connect again in 25 feet. Cross the dry riverbed and follow the trail up the side of the hill. This section is rocky and has some tricky parts.

3.0 Follow the trail over a small rock section. Inexperienced riders may want to walk this section. Follow the trail along the side of the hill, eventually going between two large rocks.

3.1 Take the trail to the right, following the POW Trail. The trail to the left is Par None.

3.3 Follow the trail into the lava rock section again, and in 0.1 mile start the final descent to the end of the trail.

3.5 Cross the River Mountains Loop and follow the POW Trail to the rock formation.

3.7 Arrive back at the trailhead.

RIDE INFORMATION

Local Events and Attractions

Art in the Park: During this early-October event, more than 300 artists and crafters display and sell their work; bchcares.org/foundation.

Boulder City–Hoover Dam Museum: Located in the historic Boulder Dam Hotel, this museum tells the story of the dam and the city it created; bcmha.org.

Ironman 70.3 Silverman Triathlon: An annual race in October where competitors swim, bike, and run. The event starts at Lake Mead and finishes in Henderson; ironman.com.

Restaurants

Boulder Pit Stop: 802 Buchanan Blvd., Boulder City; (720) 293-7080; boulderpitstop.com. Best hamburgers in town, located a short distance from the trail.

Grandma Daisy's: 530 Nevada Way, Boulder City; (702) 294-6639; grandmadaisys.com. Candy and ice-cream parlor, featuring candy made on the premises.

Jack's Place: 544 Nevada Way, Boulder City; (702) 293-2200; jacksplacebc.com. Sidewalk cafe and sports bar.

Restrooms

There are no restrooms along this trail. The closest restroom is on Canyon Road at the end of the asphalt road.

15

Girl Scout/West Leg/Mother Loop

This is one of the most popular trails in all of Bootleg Canyon. It offers wonderful views of the canyon as well as many of the bootlegging artifacts that gave the canyon its name. The first part of the ride requires a bit of climbing over one of the most technical trails in the canyon. The second portion is high on the canyon walls, providing some great scenic views. Make sure to take the time to explore some of the bootlegging artifacts purposely left in the canyon.

Start: Parking lot below the restrooms at the entrance to Bootleg Canyon

Length: 3.7 miles

Approximate riding time: 1 to 1.5 hours

Best bike: Mountain bike with suspension (either front or full)

Terrain and trail surface: Mostly dirt, large rocks, and loose gravel

Traffic and hazards: These trails are only open to human power and are mostly used by mountain bikers. However, hikers and runners also use the trail, and it is best to be courteous and give way to them when encountered. Rocks can be hazards on this trail, and shin guards are a valuable accessory.

Things to see: Bootleg Canyon, some old remnants of bygone bootlegging, desert plants and animals

Getting there: By car: Take US 93 toward the Hoover Dam (Boulder City). Bootleg Canyon is easily visible on left-hand side of the road. It is marked by a large white BC, which actually stands for Boulder City, not Bootleg Canyon. Turn left on Veterans Memorial Drive and follow the road around to Canyon Road. Turn left on Canyon Road and follow it all the way to the restrooms. There is a parking lot just below the restrooms. You'll know you are in the correct place because you'll see the parking lot, restrooms, and covered picnic tables. If you go far enough to hit another dirt road, you will have gone too far. Park here and then take the bike up that dirt road to the first telephone pole on the left. You'll see the trailhead by the telephone pole. ***Note:*** If the parking lot is full, you can park in the dirt lot just below the asphalt lot. **GPS:** N35 59.119' / W114 51.882'

THE RIDE

Like many of the rides in Bootleg Canyon, the Girl Scout/West Leg/Mother Loop is actually made up of three different trails that connect to form the loop. The first part of the loop, Girl Scout, is one of the most popular trails in Bootleg Canyon for two reasons: First, it has some very technical sections that test the skill of even the most experienced rider, and second, it is just a fun downhill trail. The second portion of the loop, the West Leg Trail, parallels Girl Scout for much of the way as it winds through the side of the canyon. The difference is, this trail is much higher up on the canyon wall. The last portion of the loop, the Mother Trail, is so named because it was the first trail that Brent Thomson and Dan Haskin created in Bootleg Canyon.

The Girl Scout/West Leg/Mother Loop is a fairly technical ride, although more so in some spots than others. For this reason it requires intermediate to advanced mountain bike skills. That said, a beginner could ride the loop but may have to navigate some of the obstacles on foot. The loop starts at the bottom of the Girl Scout Trail and is a long, steady climb, with some fairly steep spots. The beginning of the trail is often called the "rock garden" because it is filled with all manner of rock obstacles, some small, some fairly large. Once you make your way out of the rock garden, the singletrack trail is mostly dirt, with some large rock obstacles at key positions.

The Girl Scout Trail is also one of the best places to see some of the old remnants of a time when bootleg alcohol was stilled in rocky crevices, giving the canyon its name. A little more than half a mile into the ride, you can see a cave-like formation with a rusted stovepipe protruding upward through the rock. Seeing this formation in the rock, it's easy to image the still that once occupied the man-made crevice at the mouth of the canyon. The formation is just off a dirt road that runs the entire length of the

Bike Shop

All Mountain Cyclery: 1404 Nevada Hwy., Ste. C, Boulder City; (702) 453-2453; allmountaincyclery.com. Rents mountain bikes and gives guided mountain bike tours of all Bootleg Canyon trails.

canyon. It's the same road that was once used by bootleggers to transport their illegal brew to their eagerly waiting clients back in Las Vegas.

As you ride along Girl Scout, a look up and to the left will reveal the West Leg Trail, which you will ride on the way down the loop. But first you must navigate some steep climbs and tricky rock obstacles which bring you to the switchbacks at the top of the canyon. Once you've navigated the switchbacks, you'll come to a convergence of trails. Going straight will take you to the Inner Caldera Loop, while taking the trail to the left will take you to the Caldera and West Leg Trails. Take the trail to the left and then the offshoot to the left a short way up the trail. This offshoot is the West Leg Trail. The trail is marked with a small wooden sign off to the side of the trail.

The West Leg Trail will take you back down the canyon you just climbed, only this time you'll be higher on the canyon wall. Not long after you get onto the West Leg Trail, you'll encounter a small but steep drop. This drop takes a certain amount of skill, and you may want to navigate it on foot. After you climb up the hill on the other side of the drop, you'll encounter a series of

A cave and a stovepipe are all that remain from a once-thriving bootlegging era.

tight switchbacks. About 2 miles into the ride, you'll pass a park bench a little ways above the trail. This is a great rest spot that offers wonderful views of the canyon. About a half mile past the park bench, you'll encounter another large drop. If the drop looks too steep, you can take the trail to the left, which is a less steep decline. At the bottom of the drop, take the trail to the right for a more gradual climb out.

As you climb to the top of the canyon wall, you pass many offshoot trails on your left. Any of these trails can be taken to return to the lower trail, but if you want to finish the loop, you should stay on the main trail. At 2.9 miles the West Leg Trail goes off to the left. Stay on the trail to the right, which becomes Mother. The trail takes a long, steep decline and is filled with lots of small loose rocks. Inexperienced riders will want to navigate this obstacle on foot. Towards the bottom of the decline, take the offshoot trail to the left. The trail is a fairly steep downhill with a couple of large drops. At each drop, an alternate trail is available that will allow you to bypass the drop and still remain on the trail.

Follow this trail downward until it meets up with the International Mountain Bike Association (IMBA) Trail about 3.4 miles into the ride. Take that trail to the left and follow it back towards the trailhead. This section is fairly rocky,

Bootleg Canyon Origins

Bootleg Canyon received its Prohibition-era name when the eighteenth amendment to the Constitution forbade the manufacture, sale, and transportation of intoxicating liquors in the United States. Instead of giving in to the new law, some residents of Las Vegas simply moved to the then-unnamed canyon and began the production of bootleg alcohol. They blew holes in the rocks, set up stills, and sold alcohol right out of the canyon until 1933 when the twenty-first amendment overturned the eighteenth amendment, again making the manufacture, sale, and transportation of intoxicating liquors legal.

Once the residents of Las Vegas could again buy and sell alcohol out in the open, they abandoned the canyon, leaving behind their tools of the trade. Riding a bike through the canyon, it is possible to see smokestacks protruding out of rocks, cans, bottles, mattress springs, and even an old car, all rusted and all the remnants of a bygone era when outlaws took over the canyon in defiance of a national law. The freedom the canyon afforded the bootleggers of the 1920s and '30s is still felt today by mountain bikers who follow the 35-plus miles of trails located in and around the canyon.

and there are a couple of difficult rock obstacles that inexperienced riders may walk to navigate on foot. At the top of the small hill, the trail splits. Stay straight. The trail to the left is the West Leg Trail, and the trail to the right is a downhill section that isn't an official trail. Keep straight and follow the trail to the point where the loop began. You can then ride down the dirt road back to the parking lot.

MILES AND DIRECTIONS

0.0 Start at the trailhead just to the left of the telephone pole. Follow the trail as it climbs up into the canyon. You'll almost immediately enter the rock garden.

0.1 One large rock obstacle followed by another. Stay between the rocks on the second obstacle. You reach the last rock obstacle in the rock garden at 0.2 mile.

0.3 Take the large dip and prepare for a steep, steady climb. In 0.1 mile, follow the trail through a short downhill section and then across a gravel/dirt road.

0.5 Large and difficult rock obstacle, which inexperienced riders may want to navigate on foot. This large obstacle is followed by a climb and a series of smaller rock obstacles.

0.6 Follow the trail between two large rocks. Take the sharp left turn after passing the rocks. The climb is rather steep and there are large flat rocks that must be navigated. Look off to the right to see the remnants of an old still.

0.9 Take the large dip and continue on with the small climb on the other side. Stay on the main trail at 1.0 mile, crossing a type of road. Continue on with a small downhill section, crossing a second dirt road and then a large, difficult rock obstacle. After this there is a series of small mogul-like hills, followed by another climb.

1.1 Take the large drop followed by a very steep climb and a sharp turn to the right. Follow the trails through a series of tight switchbacks at 1.3 miles.

1.5 The Girl Scout Trail ends. Take the trail to the left and then the offshoot trail on the left a short distance up. Look for a small wooden sign to the left of the trail that marks the West Leg Trail. The trail takes a gradual drop followed by a steep drop, which may be best to walk.

1.7 Follow the trail through a series of switchbacks.

Girl Scout/West Leg/Mother Loop

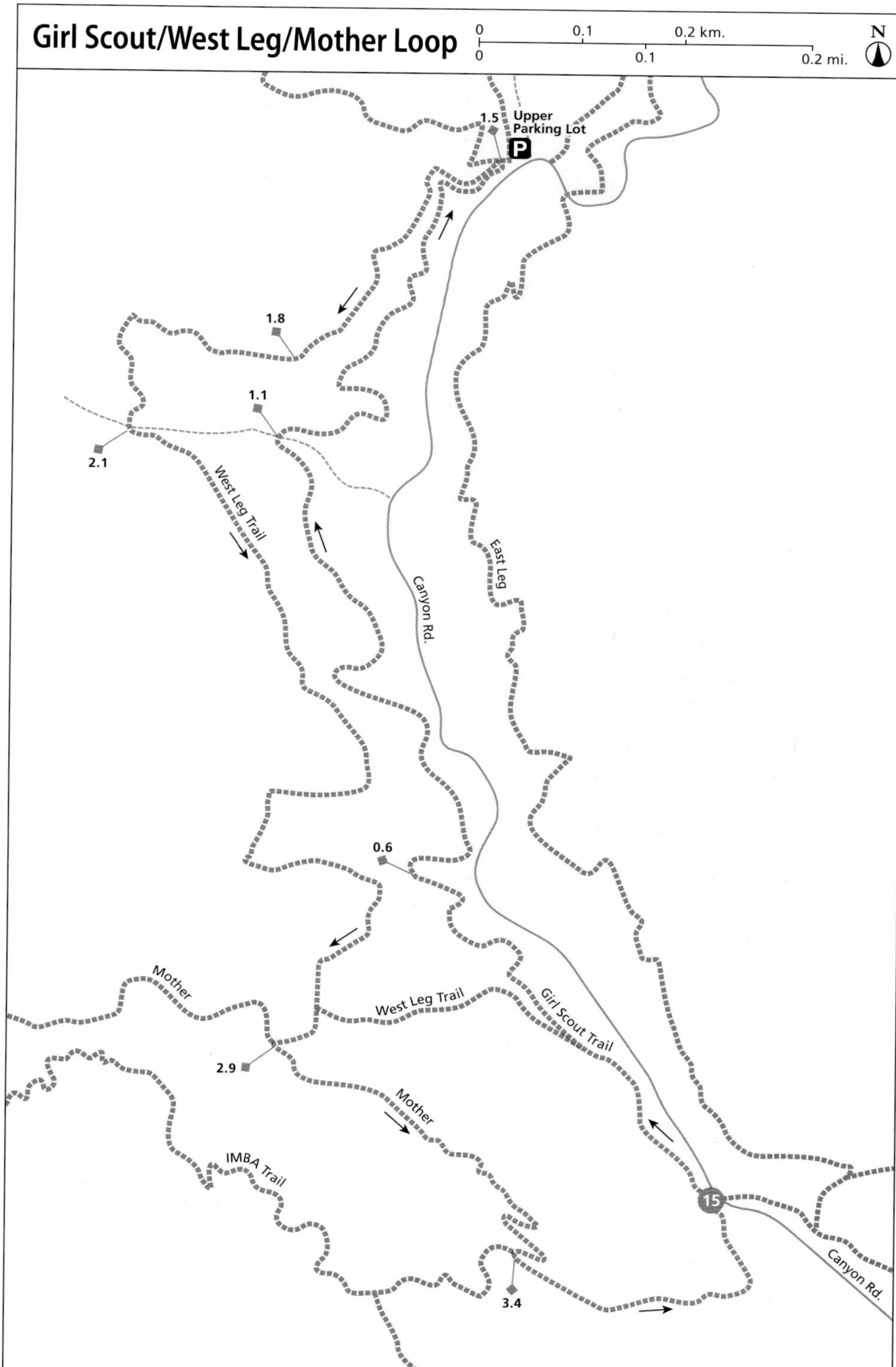

1.8 Turn to the right and start a small downhill section. The trail splits at mile 2.0 and you can take either trail, as they meet up again a short distance ahead. This guide follows the trail to the right.

2.1 Follow the trail to the right around a massive rock, after crossing the remnants of an old road. Just to the right and above the trail is a park bench that makes a good resting spot. Follow the trail into a rocky area at 2.3 miles that offers great views of the canyon.

2.6 Take the big drop. You can also take the trail to the left, which is a more gradual drop. At the bottom of the drop, take the trail to the right for a more gradual climb. A series of offshoot trails can be found on the left at mile 2.8. Stay to the right on the main trail.

2.9 Follow the trail to the right, entering a steep downhill section. The West Leg Trail continues to the left. Taking the trail to the right puts you on Mother. This downhill section is steep with lots of loose rocks. Inexperienced riders should walk this section.

3.0 Take the sharp turn to the left and enter a difficult rock area that may be best navigated on foot. In 0.1 mile, take the drop or the trail to the left to avoid the drop. The trails meet on the other side of the drop. A larger drop follows. Take the trail to the left to avoid the larger drop.

3.2 After a series of switchbacks, take the climb, followed by a quick right-hand turn into a downhill section.

3.4 The Mother Trail merges with the IMBA Trail. Take the trail to the left.

3.6 Follow the trail though a couple of tricky rock sections, the second of which might be best navigated on foot. When the trail splits at the top of the hill, follow the trail straight. Do not take the turnoff to the left or the right.

3.7 The trail ends where it began.

RIDE INFORMATION

Local Events and Attractions

Boulder City Antiques Shops: Boulder City is full of antiques stores, all within walking distance of each other. Many of these places have even been featured on national television shows. They can all be easily found in *The Country Register*, a free guide to specialty shops and events available from most businesses in downtown Boulder City.

Restaurants

Boulder Dam Brewing Company: 453 Nevada Way, Boulder City; (702) 243-2739; boulderdambrewing.com. Local brewery and restaurant started by Seattle native Todd Cook.

Boulder Pit Stop: 802 Buchanan Blvd., Boulder City; (720) 293-7080; boulderpitstop.com. Best hamburgers in town, located a short distance from the trail.

Milo's Cellar: 538 Nevada Way, Boulder City; (702) 293-9540; miloswinebar.com. Sidewalk cafe and wine bar.

Restrooms

There are no restrooms along this trail. The closest restroom is on Canyon Road at the end of the asphalt road at the top of the parking lot.

16

Caldera Loop

Caldera is a ride just outside the confines of Bootleg Canyon. This ride offers great views of the Las Vegas valley as well as some of the most interesting desert scenery around. Here the terrain can differ dramatically in only a few short feet.

Start: To the left of the dirt parking lot located at the top of the dirt road before it climbs the last hill

Length: 4.3 miles

Approximate riding time: 1.5 to 2.5 hours

Best bike: Mountain bike with suspension (either front or full)

Terrain and trail surface: Mostly dirt, some large rocks, and loose gravel

Traffic and hazards: These trails are only open to human power and are mostly used by mountain bikers. However, hikers and runners also use the trail, and it is best to be courteous and give way to them when encountered.

Things to see: Bootleg Canyon, Las Vegas valley, desert plants and animals

Getting there: **By car:** Take US 93 toward the Hoover Dam (Boulder City). Bootleg Canyon is easily visible on left-hand side of the road. It is marked by a large white BC, which actually stands for Boulder City, not Bootleg Canyon. Turn left on Veterans Memorial Drive and follow the road around to Canyon Road. Turn left on Canyon Road and follow it all the way to the restrooms. There is a parking lot just below the restrooms. Keep driving until the road turns to dirt, then follow the road as it winds up the canyon. Drive slow to be courteous and not stir up dust for riders on the trails on either side of the road.

Just to the left of where the dirt road plateaus is a dirt parking lot that is not initially visible. The parking lot is a little lower than the dirt road, making it difficult to see. However, you can find it by driving just a little farther up the road and looking to your left. **GPS:** N35 59.895' / W114 52.049'

THE RIDE

The Caldera Loop, more commonly called Caldera, is one of the few loops in Bootleg Canyon that is not a combination of several trails. It is also not technically in Bootleg Canyon, but instead is located just to the back of the canyon where it levels out into the Las Vegas desert. The ride offers great views of the Las Vegas valley, including the buildings on the famous strip. It also affords some of the greatest desert views in all of Bootleg Canyon. Here you watch as the terrain literally changes right before your eyes. You can start up a hill

One of the many quail that can be spotted along the trail

formed by lava rock only to have those rocks change into ones covered with multicolored lichen.

The trail also passes some areas where massive rocks have slid from the top of the hill right down to the edge of the trail itself. This portion of the desert is rich in colors. There are browns, reds, purples, blacks, yellows, oranges, and, of course, greens. Here you can find jackrabbits the size of small dogs, as well as lizards of all shapes and sizes. You can also find birds, snakes, and desert tortoises.

The trail is also one of the longest in Bootleg Canyon at a little over 4 miles. It is mostly smooth singletrack with some rocky areas and some areas filled with loose dirt and small loose rocks. The start of the trail is fairly technical, but shortly into the ride the trail turns much less technical and is a very enjoyable ride. The trailhead is actually a confluence of three trails: the Girl Scout, the Caldera, and the Inner Caldera Loop. Going straight up the hill will lead to Caldera. Going to the left leads to Girl Scout and to the right leads to the Inner Caldera Loop. Shortly into the ride you will see another trail breaking off to the left, above Girl Scout. This is the West Leg Trail. All these trails are clearly marked with small wooden signs.

The trail starts by climbing up the canyon wall, but takes a turn to the right before the top of the hill is reached. The trail can be a little tricky to spot here, so make sure you don't go over the crest of the hill. If you do, it won't take long for you to realize you've gone too far. It's not dangerous, but it's also not a trail. Caldera is very easy to follow. There are few other trails in the area and each requires you to turn off the main trail, so as long as you stay on the main trail, you won't get lost. With the exception of the first half mile, the terrain is relatively flat. There are some small climbs, but almost all of them are very gradual and there are only a couple of drops. The trail would actually work for a rider with beginner skills if it wasn't so long. Also, once you start down the trail, you're kind of committed, as there are no turnoffs.

Bike Shop

All Mountain Cyclery: 1404 Nevada Hwy., Ste. C, Boulder City; (702) 453-2453; allmountaincyclery.com. Rents mountain bikes and gives guided mountain bike tours of all Bootleg Canyon trails.

As the trail begins, it follows the side of several hills, making its way down to the flatter desert. The trail can be ridden clockwise or counterclockwise, but the originators of the trail meant for it to be ridden clockwise. It also makes the first part of the trail much easier, as it is mainly downhill with a few rock obstacles. That said, however, you should allow yourself to ride this trail either way because it provides a bit of a different experience with each direction.

At 1.4 miles into the ride, another trail meets up with Caldera. This is a portion of the Bootlegger Loop. Stay to the right and do not take this offshoot trail. Shortly after this another trail shoots off to the right. Do not take this trail either—it is a connector trail between Caldera and the Inner Caldera Loop. From this point there are no other offshoot trails until Caldera meets up with the Boy Scout Trail at 3.9 miles into the ride. The trail is mostly dirt; however, there are a few places where you have to cross a rock-filled wash and there is a little climbing involved. At the end of the trail, you'll be able to see some old man-made caves that were once used to hide the alcohol bootleggers made in the canyon during Prohibition. The trail ends on the opposite side of the parking lot where it began.

MILES AND DIRECTIONS

0.0 Start at the trailhead just to the left of the upper parking lot. Head straight up the hill. Do not take the trail to the right or the left, and do not take the West Leg Trail that breaks off to the left a short distance up the hill. Turn right just before you reach the crest of the hill. Several rock obstacles follow, and you may want to navigate them on foot.

0.1 There are two large rock obstacles at the top of the hill. You may want to navigate them on foot. In 0.1 mile, the trail turns into well-groomed singletrack.

0.3 Follow the trail on the hillside singletrack. Notice the beautiful black rocks. Much of the trail system is easily visible at this point.

0.6 Follow the trail into a steep downhill section. This section of the trail offers wonderful views of the Las Vegas valley.

0.7 Take the steep drop and continue on with a series of hillside moguls. In 0.1 mile, take the quick drop, which is followed by a tricky rock obstacle.

1.1 Stay straight on the trail. Do not take the offshoot trail to the left.

1.4 Bear to the right. Do not take the offshoot trail to the left.

1.6 Stay straight as two trails merge into one. In 0.2 mile, the trail turns to the left.

1.9 Take the little drop and then the quick, easy climb.

2.0 Start an easy, fun, level section, going across the dirt road and heading into a smooth rock area. The trail seems to disappear, but can easily be seen to the right.

2.4 Follow the trail as it runs along a barbed wire fence, marking the outskirts of Bootleg Canyon.

2.6 Enter an area of rocky shale. Follow the trail until it turns back into dirt singletrack.

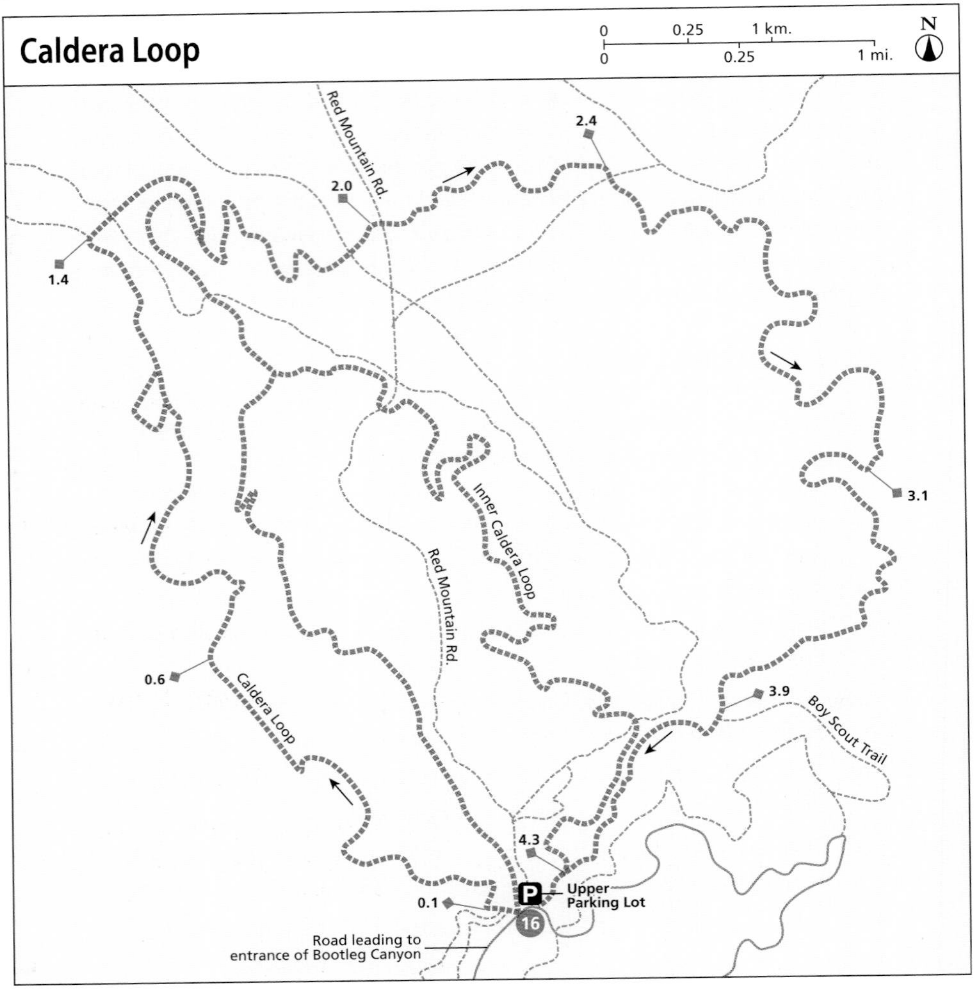

3.1 Follow the trail as it turns to the left and heads out of the canyon before eventually going to the right, back in. In 0.1 mile, the trail passed through a section of lava rocks. Be careful in this section, as the rocks can be sharp. The rocks are followed by a tricky rock obstacle which is part of a short, steep climb. It may be easier to walk.

3.3 Take the gradual drop, followed by a steep climb. At 3.6 miles, take another steep drop, followed by another steep climb, and then a more gradual climb out of the valley back into the canyon.

3.9 Caldera merges briefly with the Boy Scout Trail. Stay straight.

4.3 Caldera merges briefly with Inner Caldera. Stay to the right when the trail splits a short distance away. Follow the trail and take the right into the parking lot to finish the ride.

RIDE INFORMATION

Local Events and Attractions

Art in the Park: During this early-October event, more than 300 artists and crafters display and sell their work; bchcares.org/foundation.

Ironman 70.3 Silverman Triathlon: An annual race in October where competitors swim, bike, and run. The event starts at Lake Mead and finishes in Henderson; ironman.com.

Nevada Southern Railway: Visitors sit in a passenger train riding the rails used to build the Hoover Dam on a free ten-minute ride; nevadasouthern.com.

Restaurants

Boulder Pit Stop: 802 Buchanan Blvd., Boulder City; (720) 293-7080; boulderpitstop.com. Best hamburgers in town, located a short distance from the trail.

Jack's Place: 544 Nevada Way, Boulder City; (702) 293-2200; jacksplacebc.com. Sidewalk cafe and sports bar.

Milo's Cellar: 538 Nevada Way, Boulder City; (702) 293-9540; miloswinebar.com. Sidewalk cafe and wine bar.

Restrooms

There are no restrooms along this trail. The closest restroom is on Canyon Road at the end of the asphalt road at the top of the parking lot.

17

Inner Caldera Loop

Following much the same terrain as the Caldera Loop, this shorter, easier trail offers some of the same views of the colorful Nevada desert. Be sure to take the time to notice the terrain and the rocks of red, orange, yellow, green, brown, and blue.

Start: To the left of the dirt parking lot located at the top of the dirt road before it climbs the last hill

Length: 2.5 miles

Approximate riding time: 1 to 2 hours

Best bike: Mountain bike with suspension (either front or full)

Terrain and trail surface: Mostly dirt, some large rocks, and loose gravel

Traffic and hazards: These trails are only open to human power and are mostly used by mountain bikers. However, hikers and runners also use the trail, and it is best to be courteous and give way to them when encountered. Rocks can be hazards on this trail, and shin guards are a valuable accessory.

Things to see: Bootleg Canyon, Las Vegas valley, desert plants and animals

Getting there: By car: Take US 93 toward the Hoover Dam (Boulder City). Bootleg Canyon is easily visible on left-hand side of the road. It is marked by a large white BC, which actually stands for Boulder City, not Bootleg Canyon. Turn left on Veterans Memorial Drive and follow the road around to Canyon Road. Turn left on Canyon Road and follow it all the way to the restrooms. There is a parking lot just below the restrooms. Keep driving until the road turns to dirt, then follow the road as it winds up the canyon. Drive slow to be courteous and not stir up dust for riders on the trails on either side of the road.

Just to the left of where the dirt road plateaus is a dirt road that is not initially visible. The parking lot is a little lower than the dirt road, making it difficult to see. However, you can find it by driving just a little farther up the road and looking to your left. **GPS:** N35 59.895' / W114 52.049'

THE RIDE

Like the Caldera Loop, the Inner Caldera Loop is one of the few loops in Bootleg Canyon that is not a combination of several trails. While it covers much of the same area as does the Caldera Loop, the Inner Caldera Loop is a distinctly different ride. The Inner Caldera Loop, commonly referred to as Inner Caldera, starts at the edge of Bootleg Canyon and heads into the valley just to the back of the canyon, before making its way back to the trailhead. The ride is entirely singletrack, although it does cross several dirt roads used for motor vehicle travel. The trail crosses these types of roads many times, and for this reason, it can be a little difficult to see at times. However, even when the trail is difficult to spot, it can easily be picked up again by simply looking ahead or, as they say, down the road.

Inner Caldera has a difficult beginning, especially the first part, where there is a large and difficult drop. While the drop can be walked, even doing that requires a bit of skill. Still, this obstacle shouldn't sway you from the trail, because once it is successfully navigated, the rest of the ride is relatively easy. Like Caldera, Inner Caldera offers great views of the Las Vegas valley, including the buildings on the famous Strip. The ride also affords some of the greatest desert views in all of Bootleg Canyon. Here you watch as the terrain literally changes right before your eyes. You can start up a hill formed by lava rock only to have those rocks change into ones covered with multicolored lichen.

Bike Shop

All Mountain Cyclery: 1404 Nevada Hwy., Ste. C, Boulder City; (702) 453-2453; allmountaincyclery.com. Rents mountain bikes and gives guided mountain bike tours of all Bootleg Canyon trails.

The trailhead is actually a confluence of three trails: the Girl Scout, the Caldera, and the Inner Caldera Loop. Going straight up the hill leads to Caldera. Going to the left leads to Girl Scout and to the right leads to the Inner Caldera Loop. All these trails are clearly marked with small wooden signs. The trail starts to the right, before eventually making its way around the hill to the left. Not far into the ride you'll encounter the large drop-off described above. It is best to walk this obstacle unless your mountain-biking skills are more advanced. Shortly after that you'll encounter a more gradual drop with a tricky rock obstacle at the bottom. It may be best to walk this obstacle as well. Inexperienced riders may choose to walk this section because the grade is steep and the trail is a bit slippery. This only lasts about 0.1 mile before the terrain becomes much easier.

Rock formations high up in the hills above the trail

As the trail starts to wind its way down from the outer canyon walls into the valley through a series of switchbacks and short downhill sections, the ride offers great views of the Las Vegas valley and the beautiful southern Nevada desert. Take time to notice the hundreds of lizards scurrying along the trail, and don't forget to look out into the hills to spot various forms of wildlife. About a mile into the trail, a large rock formation can be seen to the right. Numerous crevices have developed in this rock over the years, and these are home to many types of wildlife. This trail can be ridden at night, as long as you have the proper lighting on your bike. Doing so allows you views of different wildlife, such as bats and tarantulas. As always, when wildlife is spotted, it should be viewed from a distance and left alone.

Shortly after the rock formation, you'll encounter a large rock obstacle that inexperienced riders may want to walk. The trail heads over the rocks to the right, and immediately following this obstacle is a similar one that, like the first, may be best to walk. Here the rocks are covered by multicolored lichen. The trail makes its way down into the valley floor before starting its climb back up into the canyon and eventually to the parking lot at the trailhead.

The trail is meant to be ridden clockwise—how it is described in this guide—but it can also be ridden counterclockwise. Riding the trail in a different direction presents different obstacles. For examples, an uphill section now becomes a downhill section and vice versa. It also requires you to look at the obstacles in a different may, as it may take a different approach to ride the obstacle going one way than it took going the other. But doing this can turn a well-worn ride into a new and exciting experience and is often well worth the effort.

MILES AND DIRECTIONS

0.0 Start at the trailhead just to the left of the upper parking lot. Take the trail to the right. Do not head straight up the hill or take the trail to the left.

0.1 Follow the trail to the large drop-off. This is a difficult drop, and it may be best to walk it because there is a steep climb on the other side. In 0.1 mile, take the gradual drop, noting the tricky rock obstacle at the bottom of the drop and the quick but steep climb on the other side. This obstacle may be best to walk as well.

0.3 Start a nice downhill section. Follow the trail as it takes a gradual drop in 0.2 mile, followed by a steep climb. Here the views of the Las Vegas valley start.

0.7 Enter a series of tight but easy switchbacks.

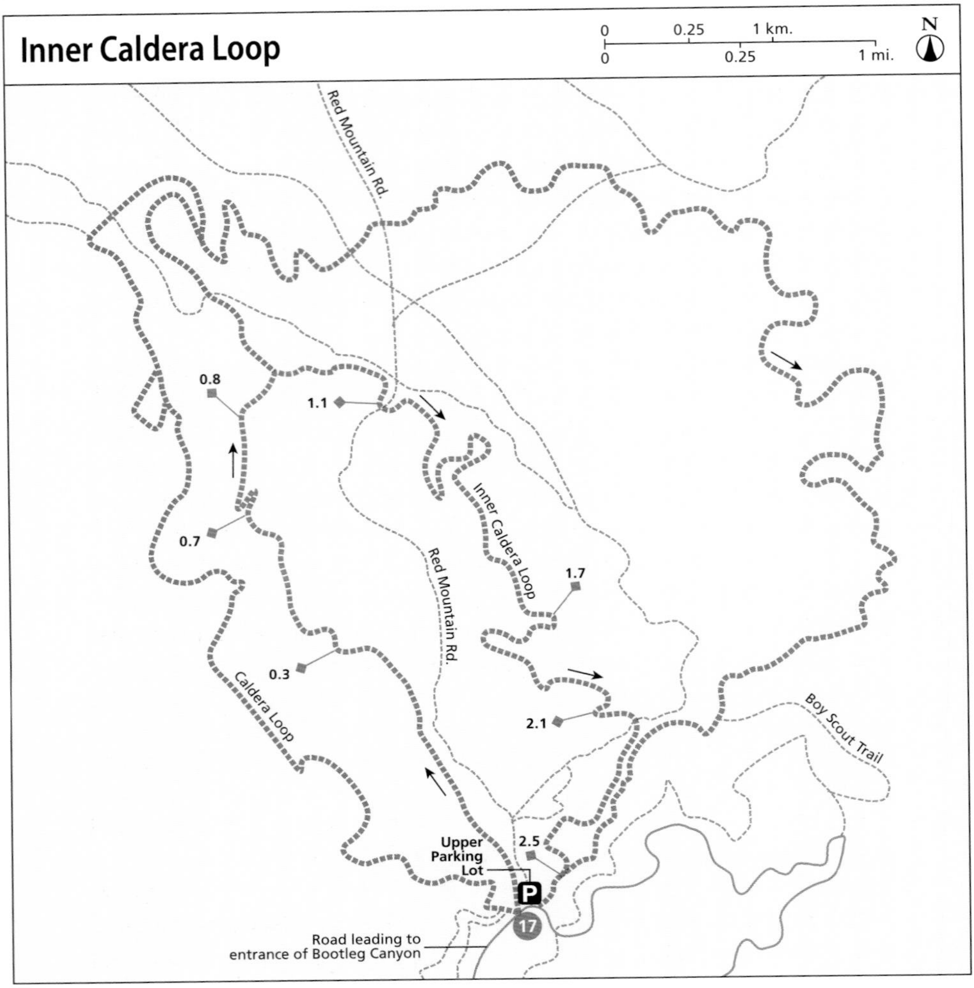

0.8 The trail takes a steep drop across a dry riverbed and is followed by a steep climb. There are some tricky spots as the trail makes its way around the side of the hill. Some sections may be easier to walk.

0.9 The trail splits; take the trail to the right. The trail to the left is a connector to the Caldera trail. In 0.1 mile the trail splits again for a short distance, but then meets back up again. Going straight requires navigating some tricky rock obstacles. Going to the left avoids those obstacles.

1.1 Follow the trail over a large rock and to the right. Another large rock is encountered quickly afterward. It may be best to walk these two obstacles. After navigating them, follow the trail across the dirt road and then turn to the left.

1.2 Take the short climb, then follow the trail to a short drop, followed by a series of hillside moguls. In 0.1 mile, follow the trail as it curves to the left then climbs.

1.6 Take the short drop, followed by a short climb on the other side.

1.7 Follow the trail over a series of small hills over fairly level ground. Afterwards take a quick little climb, followed by a small drop. Follow the trail to the right after the drop.

2.0 Follow the trail over a small rock obstacle.

2.1 Follow the trail as it turns to the right then cuts back to the left. There is a big drop a short distance ahead. Take the drop and follow the trail to the right, crossing the dirt road.

2.4 The trail goes over a series of large, flat rocks. Go over each rock obstacle, eventually taking the trail to the left once you've navigated the last rock. The rock formation—which looks like large clumps of mud—is unique to this area.

2.5 Inner Caldera meets up with Caldera. When the trail splits again, take the trail to the right to arrive at the parking lot.

RIDE INFORMATION

Local Events and Attractions

Art in the Park: During this early-October event, more than 300 artists and crafters display and sell their work; bchcares.org/foundation.

Boulder City–Hoover Dam Museum: Located in the historic Boulder Dam Hotel, this museum tells the story of the dam and the city it created; bcmha.org.

Nevada Southern Railway: Visitors sit in a passenger train riding the rails used to build the Hoover Dam on a free ten-minute ride; nevadasouthern.com.

Restaurants

Boulder Dam Brewing Company: 453 Nevada Way, Boulder City; (702) 243-2739; boulderdambrewing.com. Local brewery and restaurant started by Seattle native Todd Cook.

Grandma Daisy's: 530 Nevada Way, Boulder City; (702) 294-6639; grandmadaisys.com. Candy and ice-cream parlor, featuring candy made on the premises.

Jack's Place: 544 Nevada Way, Boulder City; (702) 293-2200; jacksplacebc.com. Sidewalk cafe and sports bar.

Restrooms

There are no restrooms along this trail. The closest restroom is on Canyon Road at the end of the asphalt road at the top of the parking lot.

18

Valley of Fire: White Domes

This lengthy trail heads into the Valley of Fire State Park, home to some of the most amazing rock formations and color combinations in all of Nevada. Valley of Fire is the oldest and largest state park in Nevada. Along with beautiful rock formations, it is home to petrified wood and 3,000-year-old petroglyphs.

Start: Moapa Paiute Travel Plaza and Casino

Length: 47.6 miles

Approximate riding time: 2 to 4 hours

Best bike: Road bike

Terrain and trail surface: Asphalt road

Traffic and hazards: The roads on this ride are heavily traveled by cars and there is no bike lane.

Things to see: Desert plants and animals, interesting rock formations and colors

Getting there: **By car:** Take I-15 east to the Moapa Paiute exit. Turn right and park in the parking lot outside the travel plaza and casino. **GPS:** N36 29.912' / W114 45.586'

An alternate parking spot is the visitor center inside the park. This will eliminate a little over 36 miles from the entire ride. Take I-15 east to the Moapa Paiute exit. Turn right and follow the road into the Valley of Fire State Park. Turn on Mouse's Tank Road and park in the visitor center parking lot.

Fees: Entering the Valley of Fire State Park by car will cost $10 per day. If you only ride your bike, the cost is $1 per day. Yearly passes are $65. National Park passes are not accepted in state parks. Payments are made at the ranger booth at the entrance to the park.

THE RIDE

Take one trip into the Valley of Fire State Park, and you'll easily see how it got its name. Its bright red Aztec sandstone formations towering above the road were formed 150 million years ago, during the time of the dinosaurs, from shifting sands, complex uplifting, and extensive erosion. All of this combined to form some of the most breathtaking rock formations in all of Nevada. As you enter the park, the typical desert landscape changes dramatically. Large red rock formations appear to have been dropped in place by some unseen deity who then used sand and wind as a paintbrush on a rock canvas.

This ride heads into the heart of the Valley of Fire, providing some of the best views of these amazing rock formations. As you ride, red sandstone changes to limestone, shale, and conglomerates, creating interesting and intriguing color combinations, many of which appear as if a painter spilled his palette of pastels onto the land.

The ride can be completed in one of two ways. Most riders start at the Moapa Paiute Travel Plaza and Casino, riding through the desert to the entrance of the state park. If you choose to take this route, the entrance fee to the park is lessened for a bike; however, the scenery on the ride itself pales in comparison to the scenery in the Valley of Fire State Park, and there is no bike lane on the road. The other option is to enter the Valley of Fire by car and park at the visitor center off Mouse's Tank Road. This will cut a little over 36 miles off the ride, avoiding the less appealing scenery; however, the fee is greater for a vehicle than it is for a bike. This guide follows the ride from the Moapa Paiute Travel Plaza and Casino, which is the most popular route for people who do this ride regularly.

Park in the parking lot at the travel plaza and casino, then head down the Valley of Fire Highway. This is a winding road with many small dips and climbs, and there is no bike lane on any portion of the ride. The road is also heavily traveled, especially on weekends and holidays. For this reason, it is best to plan your ride so it is not taken during these high-traffic times. Because there is no bike lane, it is best to draw as much attention to yourself as possible. This can be done with bright clothing and blinking lights—which work well even during daylight hours.

There are several offshoot roads, many of which are dirt, that should not be taken. A little over 14 miles into the ride is the ranger pay station for the park. Pay your fee and continue straight down the road. Here the road turns into a scenic byway. In a little over 1 mile after the pay station is the Beehives Scenic Overlook, so named because the rocks in the area resemble beehives. (If you prefer, you can drive to this overlook, park, and bike the rest of the ride.) Follow the main road to Mouse's Tank Road and turn left. Pass the visitor

The colorful rock formations in the Valley of Fire

center and follow the trail as it makes a rather steep climb. Take time to look at the rock formations and take in the natural beauty of your surroundings.

This section of the road has some larger dips and climbs. It is important to watch for cars traveling on the road, as drivers may be paying more attention to the scenery than the road itself. Additionally, Pink Jeep Tours takes customers on this road, and they make frequent stops to show and explain the scenery. Follow the trail back the way you came, passing Mouse's Tank on the right.

As you continue on the road, the color of the rocks change from bright red, to white, to pastels of yellow, purple, and red, earning the name Rainbow Vista. This area is a maze of canyons, ridges, domes, and valleys that form a

Mouse's Tank

The legend of Mouse's Tank is well-known in Las Vegas. Back in the days before casinos and neon lights, the Paiute Indians settled the area known as The Meadows (Las Vegas). This included the area that would eventually be made into the Valley of Fire State Park. As settlers moved into the area, the Paiutes, for the most part, welcomed them, even showing them how to make adobe bricks for their structures. While most of the Paiutes were welcoming and friendly to the settlers, at least one Paiute viewed them in a different light—as a threat.

Mouse was a Paiute who didn't want settlers moving onto the sacred land his tribe had been using for hundreds of years. In fact, his ancestors were hunting and gathering food in the area as far back as 300 BCE. They also used the area currently known as the Valley of Fire for religious ceremonies. Mouse terrorized the settlers who moved into the valley, stealing supplies from them and just becoming a general nuisance. Every time the settlers chased Mouse into the bright red rocks where his ancestors performed religious ceremonies, they were unable to catch or even to find him. The erosion in one of the rocks created two bowl-like crevasses that allowed water to be caught and retained. Because these crevasses were mostly shaded, water would last in them for months. This, combined with the supplies Mouse stole from the settlers, allowed him to hide out for days, weeks, and even months at a time. Mouse was able to elude all his chasers and hide so well that the area he hid in became known as Mouse's Tank. The word *tank* came from lingo the settlers used to indicate a place that holds water.

Mouse's Tank is now a popular hiking trail. Not only are the two bowl-shaped crevasses still there, but the area is also filled with extensive and varied petroglyphs in a place known as Petroglyph Canyon. If you hike this trail, please remember that petroglyphs are national treasures and, like wildlife, should only be viewed from afar. Take as many photos as you'd like, but please do not touch.

virtually untouched wilderness. The road eventually winds its way to rock formations known as White Domes, so named because the white rocks shoot upward into the sky, forming towers—or domes. Take the road to the White Domes, which is marked with a sign. The road ends at a parking lot, and a 1.25-mile hiking trail goes between the domes. From here you turn around and follow the roads back to the Moapa Paiute Travel Plaza and Casino.

Valley of Fire: White Domes

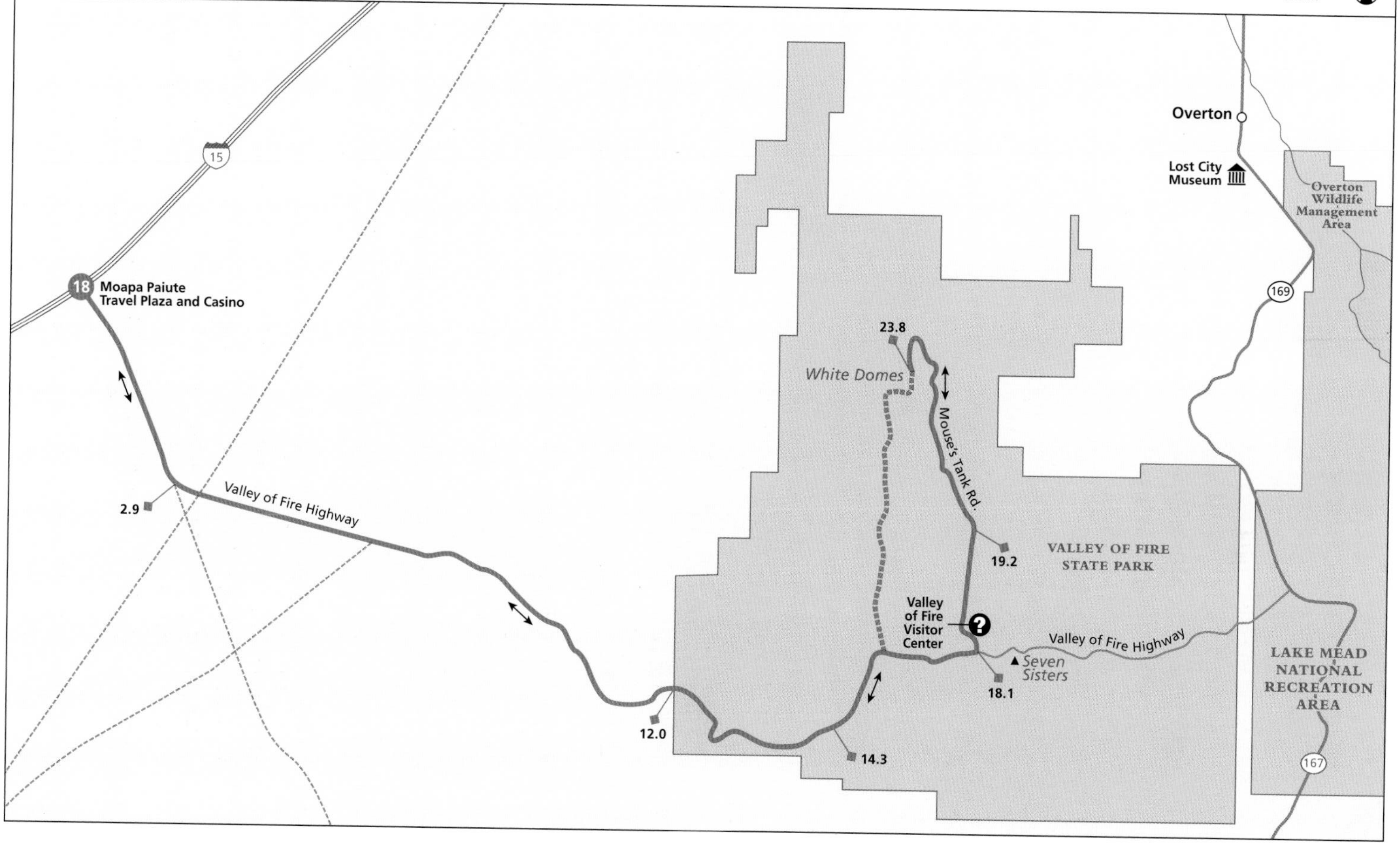

MILES AND DIRECTIONS

0.0 Park at the Moapa Paiute Travel Plaza and Casino parking lot. Pull out of the parking lot and head down the Valley of Fire Highway. Be careful, there is no bike lane.

0.7 Follow the road as it curves to the right. Do not take the road to the left heading to the gravel pit.

2.5 Follow the road through the wash. This road consists of many small dips and climbs.

2.9 Follow the road as it curves to the left, entering the area known as Muddy Mountains. Do not take the road that is straight.

6.3 Stay straight; do not take the dirt road to the right. In 1.0 mile, climb the hill.

12.0 Enter the Valley of Fire State Park. In 1.0 mile, start a downhill section.

14.3 Pay the fee at the pay station. Stay straight at 14.4 miles; do not take the road to the left.

15.4 Pass Beehives Scenic Overlook, then pass the road to Atlatl Rock and Arch Rock on the left at mile 16.1.

18.1 Take Mouse's Tank Road, pass the visitor center, and start a rather steep climb.

18.7 Follow the curvy road into a downhill section.

19.2 Pass the entrance to Mouse's Tank on the right. In 0.3 mile, begin a climb up a hill.

19.9 Pass Rainbow Vista on the right. Stay to the left in 0.1 mile and begin a downhill section. Follow the sign to White Domes. Do not take the road to the right.

20.6 Cross the cement wash and make the steep climb up the other side. In 0.2 mile, pass the scenic overlook on the left.

21.2 Cross another cement wash and make the steep climb up the other side. Pass a scenic overlook on the left at mile 21.7.

22.9 Pass another scenic overlook on the left.

23.8 Reach the White Domes parking lot. Turn around and head back to the parking lot.

47.6 Arrive at the Moapa Paiute Travel Plaza and Casino parking lot.

RIDE INFORMATION

Local Events and Attractions

Valley of Fire State Park: Founded in 1935, Valley of Fire State Park is filled with many different hiking trails. Each of these offer outstanding views of this amazing park and the rock formations contained within. If you keep your receipt, you can return to the park the same day and hike any of these trails. Additionally, the visitor center provides a great deal of information about the state park and is well worth a visit.

Restrooms

Mile 0.0: Moapa Paiute Travel Plaza and Casino
Mile 14.3: Ranger pay station
Mile 15.4: Beehives Scenic Overlook
Mile 18.1: Valley of Fire Visitor Center
Mile 19.2: Mouse's Tank
Mile 19.9: Rainbow Vista
Mile 23.8: White Domes

19

Valley of Fire: Overton

This ride travels through the Valley of Fire State Park, home to some of the most amazing sandstone formations in all of Nevada. The ride follows Valley of Fire Highway, winding its way through the park and eventually making its way to the neighboring town of Overton.

Start: Moapa Paiute Travel Plaza and Casino

Length: 63.8 miles

Approximate riding time: 3 to 5 hours

Best bike: Road bike

Terrain and trail surface: Asphalt road

Traffic and hazards: This road is heavily traveled by cars and there is no bike lane.

Things to see: Desert plants and animals, interesting rock formations and colors

Getting there: By car: Take I-15 east to the Moapa Paiute exit. Turn right and park in the parking lot outside the travel plaza and casino. **GPS:** N36 29.912' / W114 45.586'

An alternate parking spot is the visitor center inside the park. This will eliminate a little over 36 miles from the entire ride. Take I-15 east to the Moapa Paiute exit. Turn right and follow the trail into the Valley of Fire State Park. Turn on Mouse's Tank Road and park in the visitor center parking lot.

Fees: Entering the Valley of Fire State Park by car will cost $10 per day. If you only ride your bike, the cost is $1 per day. Yearly passes are $65. National Park passes are not accepted in state parks. Payments are made at the ranger booth at the entrance to the park.

THE RIDE

Dedicated in 1935, the Valley of Fire is the oldest park in the state of Nevada. It is home to formations of bright red Aztec sandstone that were created during the Jurassic period 150 million years ago. Because these bright red rocks stand out in the otherwise muted desert, it gives the rocks the appearance of being on fire—giving the area its name. The park, which is not far from Lake Mead, covers 42,000 acres. The sandstone formations are the result of giant sand dunes—estimated to be 3,000 feet deep—that stretched across the area during the time of the dinosaurs. Over time, the grains in the sand cemented together, forming petrified sandstone, which was then shaped by wind and erosion. The red in the sandstone is a result of iron oxide, although experts are unable to explain how the iron oxide got into the petrified sandstone in the first place.

Valley of Fire State Park has become a popular shooting location for professional filmmakers. It has been featured in hundreds of commercials and has appeared in music videos and educational films. Even Hollywood has gotten into the act, filming such movies as *The Good Son, Breakdown, Star Trek—Generations, The Beastmaster, When Fools Rush In, 1,000,000 Years B.C., The Stand, Kill Me Again, Father Hood, The Ballad of Cable Hogue*, and *The Professionals*.

The ride can be completed in one of two ways. Most riders start at the Moapa Paiute Travel Plaza and Casino, riding through the desert to the entrance of the state park. If you choose to take this route, the entrance fee to the park is lessened for a bike; however, the scenery on the ride itself pales in comparison to the scenery in the Valley of Fire State Park, and there is no bike lane on the road. The other option is to enter the Valley of Fire by car and park at the visitor center off Mouse's Tank Road. This will cut a little over 36 miles off the trail, avoiding the less appealing scenery; however, the fee is greater for a vehicle than it is for a bike. This guide follows the ride from the Moapa Paiute Travel Plaza and Casino, which is the most popular route for people who do this ride regularly.

Park in the parking lot at the travel plaza and casino, then head down the Valley of Fire Highway. This is a winding road with many small dips and climbs, and there is no bike lane. The road is also heavily traveled, especially on weekends and holidays. For this reason, it is best to plan your ride so it is not taken during these high-traffic times. Because there is no bike lane, it is best to draw as much attention to yourself as possible. This can be done with bright clothing and blinking lights—which work well even during daylight hours.

There are several offshoot roads, many of which are dirt, that should not be taken. A little over 14 miles into the ride is the ranger pay station for the park. Pay your fee and continue straight down the road. Here the road turns into a scenic byway. A little over 1 mile after the pay station is the Beehives Scenic Overlook, so named because the rocks in the area resemble beehives. (If you prefer, you can drive to this overlook, park, and bike the rest of the ride.) Follow the trail past the visitor center off Mouse's Tank Road on the left, then pass Seven Sisters on the right. Seven Sisters is a group of rocks that form seven towers of varying sizes. There are seating areas where you can stop, take a break, and enjoy the scenery.

About 1.8 miles after Seven Sisters, there is a large drop in the road. At the top of the climb is a memorial to Sergeant John J. Clark on the right. Clark, a Civil War officer, immigrated to Southern California after the war. On one of his trips to Salt Lake City, he stopped near the marker, tied his horse to the back of the wagon, and began looking for water. Unfortunately, Clark chose a bad place to run out of water. His dead body was found under his buckboard on June 30, 1915.

Pass the east entrance at Elephant Rocks and exit the Valley of Fire State Park, entering Lake Mead National Recreation Area. When the Valley of Fire

A portion of the Seven Sisters rock formation in the Valley of Fire

Lost City Museum

In the mid-1920s, brothers and Overton natives John and Fay Perkins reported what appeared to be the ruins of an ancient civilization to Nevada governor James Scrugham. The find drew in noted archaeologist Mark. R. Harrington, who had become famous for penning a series of adventures with Native Americans called ***Raymond de la Cuevas*** (***Raymond of the Caves***). Harrington found valuable artifacts, including pottery and arrow shafts, as well as other evidence of the Anasazi civilization.

In 1935 Congress allocated $5,900 to the construction of a museum in Overton. The museum's Pueblo Revival–style main building, constructed of sun-dried adobe brick, was built by the Civilian Conservation Corps—a public relief organization. The museum is now home to many of the artifacts found on the site originally reported by the Perkins brothers, as well as replicas of the adobe structures these people lived in, all of this giving insight into the people who once populated the Mojave Desert.

Highway dead-ends, turn left on Northshore Road. Once you turn onto Northshore, there will be a bike lane to ride in. Pass the Overton Wildlife Management Area on the right and the Lost City Museum on the left. When you reach the town of Overton, pull into the parking lot at McDonald's before turning and heading back.

MILES AND DIRECTIONS

0.0 Park at the Moapa Paiute Travel Plaza and Casino parking lot. Pull out of the parking lot and head down the Valley of Fire Highway. Be careful, there is no bike lane.

0.7 Follow the road as it curves to the right. Do not take the road to the left heading to the gravel pit.

2.5 Follow the road through the wash. This road consists of many small dips and climbs.

2.9 Follow the road as it curves to the left, entering the area known as Muddy Mountains. Do not take the road that is straight.

6.3 Stay straight; do not take the dirt road to the right. In 1.0 mile, climb the hill.

12.0 Enter the Valley of Fire State Park. In 1.0 mile, start a downhill section.

Valley of Fire: Overton

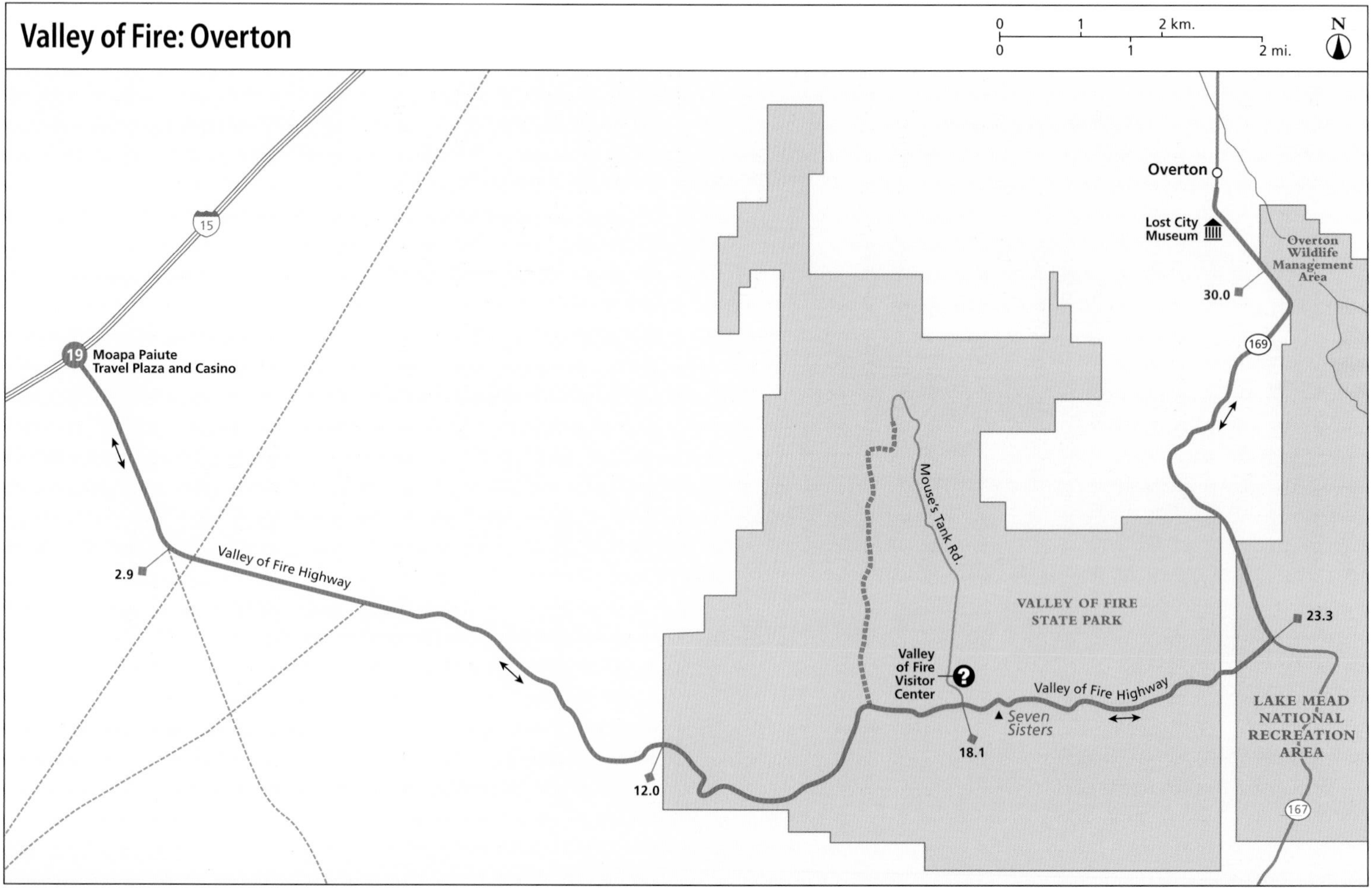

14.3 Pay the fee at the pay station. Stay straight at 14.4 miles; do not take the road to the left.

15.4 Pass Beehives Scenic Overlook, then pass the road to Atlatl Rock and Arch Rock on the left at 16.1 miles.

18.1 Pass Mouse's Tank Road on the left. In 0.6 mile, pass Seven Sisters on the right.

19.9 Stay straight. Do not take the cabins road on the left.

20.5 Take the big dip in the road, followed by a gradual climb. Pass the memorial to John J. Clark on the right at mile 20.7.

21.3 Pass the east entrance to the Valley of Fire State Park. In 0.2 mile, enter Lake Mead National Recreation Area. There is no fee at this point.

23.3 Turn left at the stop sign onto Northshore Road. Ride in the bike lane.

30.0 Pass the Overton Wildlife Management Area on the right. In 1.3 miles, pass the Lost City Museum on the left.

31.9 Turn into the McDonald's parking lot. Rest before heading back.

63.8 Arrive at the Moapa Paiute Travel Plaza and Casino parking lot.

RIDE INFORMATION

Local Events and Attractions

Valley of Fire State Park: Valley of Fire State Park is filled with many different hiking trails. Each of these offer outstanding views of this amazing park and the rock formations contained within. If you keep your receipt, you can return to the park the same day and hike any of these trails. Additionally, the visitor center provides a great deal of information about the state park.

Lost City Museum: Built in 1935, this museum displays artifacts and recreated housing from the time period when Anasazi Indians lived in the Grande de Nevada. Open daily 8:30 a.m. to 4:30 p.m. Admission: $5 per person, children free. Visit museums.nevadaculture.org.

Restrooms

Mile 0.0: Moapa Paiute Travel Plaza and Casino
Mile 14.3: Ranger pay station
Mile 15.4: Beehives Scenic Overlook
Mile 18.1: Valley of Fire Visitor Center
Mile 21.3: East entrance to Valley of Fire State Park
Mile 31.9: McDonald's

20

Hoover Dam

Built in only five years, the Hoover Dam is not just an engineering marvel, it's an American icon. This trail follows the road that once took workers down the steep inclines to the dam construction site. You'll pass rock walls constructed in 1932 and see the dam from a unique perspective. This road is heavily traveled by vehicles and has a steep climb to get back out. But it is a one-of-a-kind trail that just shouldn't be missed.

Start: Parking lot just below the Alan Bible Visitor Center

Length: 10.5 miles

Approximate riding time: 2 to 3.5 hours

Best bike: Road bike

Terrain and trail surface: Asphalt

Traffic and hazards: This road is heavily traveled by cars and there is no bike lane.

Things to see: Lake Mead, desert scenery, wildlife, the Hoover Dam, Mike O'Callaghan–Pat Tillman Memorial Bridge.

Getting there: By car: Take US 93 toward the Hoover Dam (Boulder City). Turn onto Lakeshore Road and follow it to the parking lot just below the Alan Bible Visitor Center. **GPS:** N36 00.707' / W114 47.609'

THE RIDE

Built in just five short years, the Hoover Dam is a modern Art Deco masterpiece. The structure is not simply functional, it is truly a work of art, created by craftsmen who took immense pride in their work and who were conscious about building a showcase for the world to see. Constructed in the heart of the Great Depression, the dam was an amazing undertaking, one that showed not only America's ingenuity, but also its drive to let nothing stand in the way of progress.

The Hoover Dam has been standing for close to eighty years, and during that time people have run, driven, walked, and biked across it, making the trip from Nevada to Arizona. In fact, for many years the road over the dam was one of the few ways to get to the Grand Canyon State from Las Vegas. After the attacks on the World Trade Center in New York and in an attempt to control the flow of traffic across the dam, a bypass bridge was envisioned and constructed. The nearly 2,000-foot bridge—complete with a 1,060-foot twin-rib concrete arch—was completed in 2010, allowing motorists to travel safely and quickly across the Colorado River, high above the dam. It was named jointly after Mike O'Callaghan—Nevada governor from 1971 to 1979—and Pat Tillman, a member of the Arizona Cardinals who enlisted in the US Army and was killed in Afghanistan in 2004, a result of friendly fire.

Bike Shop

All Mountain Cyclery: 1404 Nevada Hwy., Ste. C, Boulder City; (702) 453-2453; allmountaincyclery.com

With the completion of the Mike O'Callaghan–Pat Tillman Memorial Bridge, the old road to the dam became much less traveled. However, the road is still open and is still the only way to get to the Hoover Dam and the dam's visitor center. This road offers one of the best views of the Hoover Dam and the original construction site. The road, however, is narrow and there is no actual bike lane. This can make the trip a bit treacherous and, for this reason, the trail shouldn't be undertaken on weekends or holidays. In fact, it is best taken early in the morning when the traffic is light.

The trip is well worth the effort. Not only do you get wonderful views of Lake Mead, you can also see the dam from a unique vantage point as you descend into the canyon. While you make your way down the winding road that snakes its way to the dam, you can see the original rock wall, built in 1932, along the side of the road—the same road used by workers to get to the construction site from 1931 to 1935.

Once you reach the dam, you can actually bike across it, or you can get off your bike and walk across the dam. If you choose to take photos, you may want to do the latter, as there are no real places to lock and leave a bike—and there are several photo ops along the top of the dam. A parking garage is located near the visitor center, but it costs $10 to park a vehicle. There are several free parking lots on the Arizona side of the dam, but none of them are set up to receive bikes.

On the Hoover Dam Trail, you can ride across a Nevada icon.

You can start the trip at several different places. This guide starts at the parking lot below the Alan Bible Visitor Center at Lake Mead. This was chosen because it is a convenient, easy place to park a vehicle and leave it while on the trip. However, the trip can also be started at the intersection of Buchanan Boulevard and US 93. There you can park in the shopping center and take US 93 down to the dam. This route offers some of the best views of Lake Mead possible. In fact, the road is, at times, simply breathtaking. However, the road is also very steep, and while it is easy to go down, going back up is quite a different story. Starting at the Alan Bible Visitor Center removes that climb while still offering limited views of Lake Mead.

The trail begins at the parking lot below the visitor center. Leaving the lot, you turn to the left onto Lakeshore Road. Take that road to US 93, also called the Great Basin Highway, and turn left onto US 93. From there you follow US 93 as it climbs up past the Hacienda Hotel & Casino. US 93 eventually makes its way to the Mike O'Callaghan–Pat Tillman Memorial Bridge; however, you'll be taking exit 2 to SR 172—the road leading to Hoover Dam. Turn left at the stop sign and follow the road to the right as it climbs a small hill overlooking Lake Mead. This road is narrow and winding. When you get to the top of the road, it makes its descent, still winding and very narrow.

At the end of the road, you'll have to stop at an inspection station. This is meant mainly for vehicles, so you're usually shuffled through fairly quickly. From here the road snakes its way down into the canyon to the dam. It doesn't take long for the winding road to narrow and again, there is no actual bike lane. As you make your way around the first bend, you'll see a parking lot to the right. This parking lot leads to the Mike O'Callaghan–Pat Tillman Memorial Bridge and you can actually walk across the bridge, though you will not be able to take your bike.

Once you get to the bottom of the canyon, you can go across the dam. From here you can decide how far you want the ride to go. This guide goes to parking lot 13, which is just above the dam on the Arizona side. This is a large parking lot here, making it easier to turn around for the trip back. This lot also offers great views of the dam, the visitor center, and the Mike O'Callaghan–Pat Tillman Memorial Bridge.

The Hoover Dam

On December 30, 1929, in the heart of the Great Depression, President Herbert Hoover took a gamble and decided to build a dam to tame the mighty Colorado River. The project brought thousands of out-of-work Americans to the Las Vegas valley in hopes of finding a job, many of whom lived in tents just outside the dam site. With the construction of the Hoover Dam, the US government employed 21,000 people, with an average of 5,000 men working on the dam at any one time.

The construction of the dam was truly an American project. Every state in the United States furnished supplies and materials. The dam, which was constructed in only five years—ahead of schedule—is 726 feet tall, 660 feet thick at its base, and 45 feet wide at the top. It is constructed of 4,360,000 cubic yards of concrete and weighs more than 6,600,000 tons. At the time it was built, it was the tallest dam in the world and was seen as a model for many dams to follow.

At the peak of construction, 5,000 men labored day and night on the dam, working their way through 7,500 to 10,800 barrels of concrete each and every day. Working conditions were difficult, and the men were in almost constant danger. An estimated ninety-six men lost their lives building the dam, and, contrary to popular legend, none were buried in the concrete. The construction of Hoover Dam also created Lake Mead, the largest man-made lake in the world. Lake Mead has 550 miles of shoreline and contains enough water to flood the entire state of New York to 1 foot.

Hoover Dam

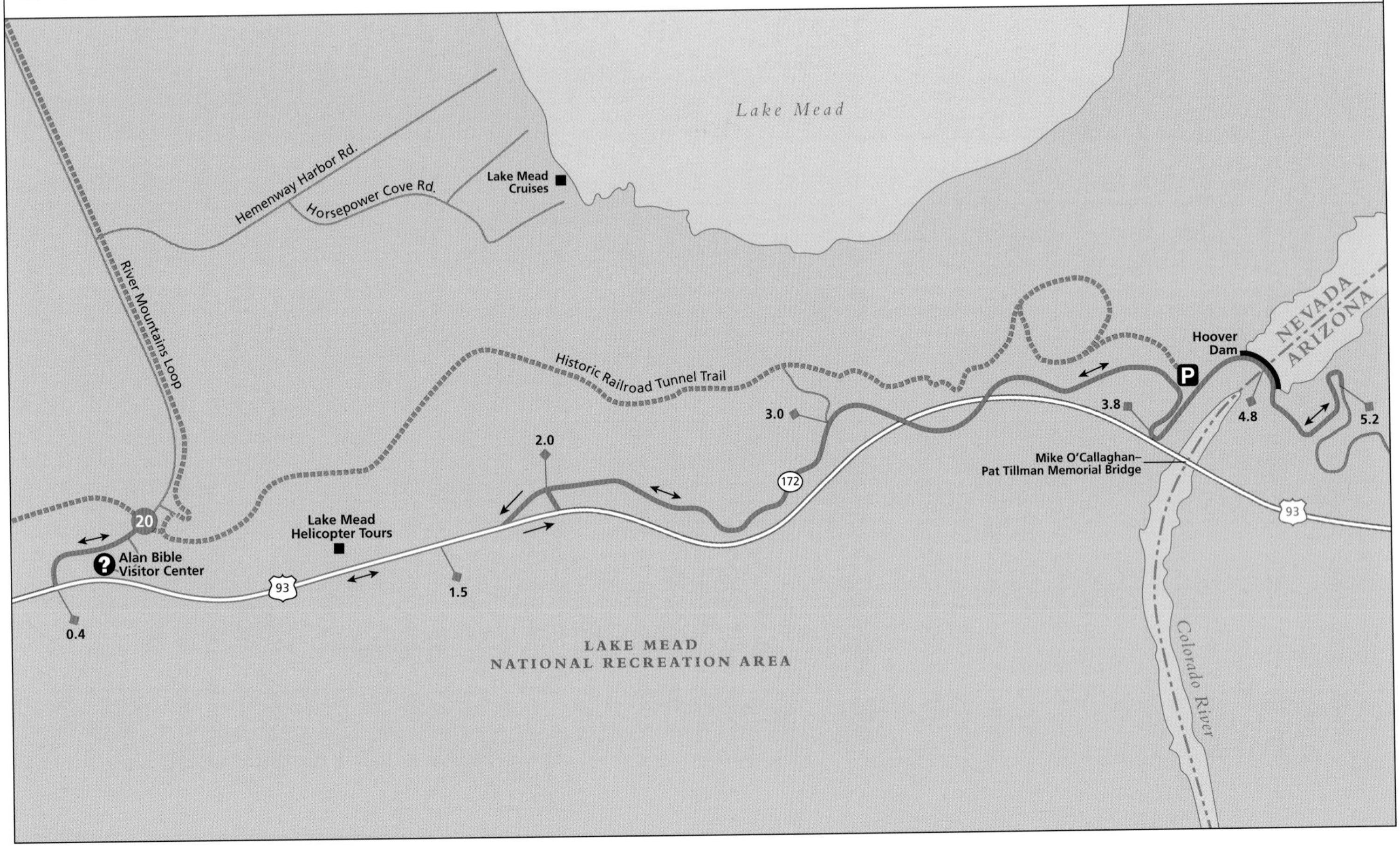

0
0.5
1 km.
0
0.5
1 mi.
N
Lake Mead
Hemenway Harbor Rd.
Horsepower Cove Rd.
Lake Mead Cruises
River Mountains Loop
Historic Railroad Tunnel Trail
20
Alan Bible Visitor Center
Lake Mead Helicopter Tours
93
0.4
1.5
2.0
3.0
172
3.8
Hoover Dam
P
4.8
5.2
NEVADA
ARIZONA
Mike O'Callaghan–Pat Tillman Memorial Bridge
Colorado River
LAKE MEAD NATIONAL RECREATION AREA

MILES AND DIRECTIONS

0.0 Start at the trailhead at the parking lot below the Alan Bible Visitor Center. Turn left onto Lakeshore Road.

0.4 Turn left onto US 93, the Great Basin Highway, and pass the Hacienda Hotel & Casino at 1.2 miles.

1.5 Take exit 2.

1.9 Turn left onto SR 172.

2.0 Follow the road to the right after the stop sign.

2.3 Follow the winding road over the mountain.

3.0 Follow the trail to the right and proceed through the inspection spot in 0.4 mile.

3.8 Pass the Memorial Bridge Plaza and head down the winding road to the dam.

4.5 Pass the parking lot on the left. In 0.2 mile, cross Hoover Dam.

4.8 Cross into Arizona. In 0.1 mile, follow the trail to the left up the hill.

5.0 Follow the road to the left and climb.

5.2 Follow the road to the right and pull into parking lot 13. Turn around and head back down the road. Retrace the original route from here and at mile 8.6 go straight onto US 93.

10.5 Turn into the parking lot below the Alan Bible Visitor Center and the trailhead.

RIDE INFORMATION

Local Events and Attractions

Lake Mead Cruises: A popular attraction on Lake Mead is a cruise on a Mississippi River–style paddleboat; lakemeadcruises.com.

Tour the Hoover Dam: Various tours are available of Hoover Dam, including one that takes you into the bowels of the dam. Or you can simply hang out in the visitor center; usbr.gov/lc/hooverdam/service.

Walk over the Mike O'Callaghan–Pat Tillman Memorial Bridge: For one of the best views of the Hoover Dam, take a walk across the Mike O'Callaghan–Pat Tillman Memorial Bridge, also known as the Hoover Dam bypass; hooverdambypass.org.

Restaurants

Boulder Dam Brewing Company: 453 Nevada Way, Boulder City; (702) 243-2739; boulderdambrewing.com. Local brewery and restaurant started by Seattle native Todd Cook.

Boulder Pit Stop: 802 Buchanan Blvd., Boulder City; (720) 293-7080; boulderpitstop.com. Best hamburgers in town, located a short distance from the trail.

The Harbor House Cafe: 490 Horsepower Cove, Boulder City; (702) 293-3081; boatinglakemead.com. Unique floating restaurant and bar on Lake Mead.

Restrooms

Mile 0.0: Parking lot below the Alan Bible Visitor Center
Mile 1.2: Hacienda Hotel & Casino
Mile 3.4: Inspection spot
Mile 4.7: Hoover Dam Visitor Center

Southwest

Spring Mountain Ranch is one of the southwest valley's attractions.

The southwest section of the valley is arguably the most scenic, encompassing both Cottonwood Valley and the Red Rock Canyon National Conservation Area—Nevada's first national conservation area. The southwest is filled with trails for both road bike and mountain bike enthusiasts. Here you can find petroglyphs, wild burros, and some of the most colorful mountains in all of Nevada.

The southwest portion of the valley is also the most remote. Much of it is owned and controlled by the Bureau of Land Management, meaning there are few housing developments. However, the region is a well-used recreation area, home to such treasures as Spring Mountain Ranch State Park, and is one of the few places where you can actually ride a bike along the same dirt once trodden by settlers making their way along the Old Spanish Trail.

21

Red Rock Scenic Loop

You'd be hard-pressed to find a more scenic ride in all of Las Vegas than the Red Rock Scenic Loop. Here you ride through an area that looks like the personal palette of some artful being. Reds fold into whites, which then become some of the most colorful mountains in all of Las Vegas—so colorful, one is actually called Rainbow Mountain. While riding this loop, take the time to visit the many scenic lookouts along the side of the road.

Start: Red Rock Visitor Center in the Red Rock Canyon National Conservation Area or the entrance booth

Length: 14.6 miles

Approximate riding time: 1.5 to 3 hours

Best bike: Road bike

Terrain and trail surface: Two-lane, one-way asphalt road

Traffic and hazards: This road is open to bikes, runners, and vehicles, but is heavily used by vehicles on holidays and weekends. Watch for drivers paying more attention to the scenery than the road. The winding road has many climbs and downhill sections.

Things to see: Red Rock Canyon, colorful rock formations, desert plants and animals, views of the Las Vegas valley

Getting there: **By car:** Take I-15 south to the Charleston exit. Take Charleston west as it becomes SR 159. Follow SR 159 and turn right onto Scenic Loop Drive. There will be signs identifying Red Rock Canyon. Park in either of the two lots outside the Red Rock Visitor Center. **By bike:** A dirt parking lot is located at the point where the one-way exit of Scenic Loop Drive meets SR 159. You can park in that lot and ride your bike to the entrance of the scenic loop. After parking, turn left onto SR 159 and ride up the road to the entrance of the scenic loop. The entrance is well-marked. If you prefer not to take a vehicle at all, you can ride your bike along Charleston to SR 159 and then to the entrance of Red Rock Canyon. **GPS:** N36 08.117' / W115 25.616'

Fees: Entering the Red Rock Canyon National Conservation Area by car will cost $7 per day. Be sure to take your receipt with you on the bike ride. You will need it to get back through the booth entrance to your car. If you only ride your bike onto the loop, the cost is $3 per day. Yearly passes are $30. National Park passes are also accepted. Payments are made at the ranger booth at the entrance to the canyon.

THE RIDE

This Red Rock Scenic Loop is probably one of the most appealing rides in all of Las Vegas, with much to offer. The formation of colorful rocks giving the canyon its name is unique to this area and is a popular tourist attraction. Red Rock Canyon is a national conservation area, established in 1967, that affords opportunities for road biking, hiking, and rock climbing. Visitors travel along a two-lane, one-way asphalt road that can become very congested, especially holidays and weekends. As you ride this trail, it is important to remember that bikes should stay to the right of the road—that is where cars will expect you to be and it is where the signs on the road direct you to stay. This is also the safest place to ride. Be sure to watch out for runners, as they will be sharing the same portion of road.

Some of the most unique views in the Las Vegas valley are at the start of the trail. Here the rocks seem to have been painted with sweeping bands of red and white that become mixed in many places. These large rock formations, on the right side of the road, are composed of Aztec sandstone created from 190-million-year-old sand dunes. The rock formations, which were carved through millions of years of weathering, offer rock-climbing and hiking opportunities, and there are many scenic overlooks and pullouts that attract motorists. Taking any of these turnouts allows you to stop and really take in the beauty of these unique formations. On the other side of the road, the valley floor is home to both multi-stemmed creosote bushes and Joshua trees, as well as many types of wildlife.

The trail follows the ancient rock formations past an old sand quarry, eventually curving to the left as it winds its way to the high point lookout at 4,771 feet. This lookout is a great place to stop, as it offers wonderful views of the Red Rock Escarpment and the Calico Hills, as well as the Las Vegas valley in the background. The high point lookout is not only at the top of the hill, but also at a curve in the trail. While the trail is one-way, it is best to be careful when pulling in and out of this outlook.

As the trail continues, it snakes down the other side of the hill, for the next 3 miles, back down to the valley floor. You pass a popular turnout called Willow Springs, popular because it offers many types of outdoor activities, including bird-watching, hiking, rock climbing, rappelling, and canyoneering. It is also a great spot to learn about the Native Americans who once made the area their home. Here you can find pictographs and petroglyphs, painted thousands of years ago, on rocks just off the trail.

As the trail continues, the scenery changes from rich red and white sandstone to mountains created by large multicolored jagged rocks. In fact, one of the best things about this ride is that it offers many different views, all showcasing the changing beauty of the Nevada desert. Because this part of the valley is lower, there are more chances to see desert tortoises. These animals are slow and will not get out of your way, so it is your responsibility to get out of theirs. Remember, you should always observe desert tortoises from a distance and never touch these animals if you are lucky enough to see them. Touching a desert tortoise can cause it to urinate, loosing valuable, life-sustaining water—something it may not be able to get back.

As the trail makes its way out of the canyon back toward SR 159, you can see a number of beige cones on the left side of the road. These cones are plant enclosures placed by the Bureau of Land Management. They are used to study how certain plants return to severely burned areas and should not be touched. The study is a result of a 1,600-acre fire that swept through the conservation area in September of 2006.

Bike Shops

Broken Spoke Bikes: 11700 W. Charleston, #190, Las Vegas; (702) 823-1680; brokenspokebikeslv.com. Rents road bikes and sponsors group rides.
Las Vegas Cyclery: 10575 Discovery Dr., Las Vegas; (702) 596-2953; lasvegascyclery.com. Rents road bikes and sponsors group rides.
McGhie's Bike Outpost: 16 Cottonwood, #B, Blue Diamond; (702) 875-4820; mcghies.com
Pro Cyclery: 7034 W. Charleston, Las Vegas; (702) 228-9460; procyclery.com. Rents road bikes.
REI: 710 S. Rampart Blvd., Las Vegas; (702) 951-4488; rei.com
Southern Highlands Cyclery: 10550 Southern Highlands Pkwy., Ste. 130, Las Vegas; (702) 778-7786; southernhighlandscyclery.com

A pair of riders traveling along the scenic loop

Las Vegas Petroglyphs and Pictographs

Long before Las Vegas was ever populated by one-armed bandits and adult-oriented entertainment, a simple group of people made the valley their home. While they didn't make permanent settlements in the Las Vegas valley, the Paiute Indians did come in and out of the valley as the weather changed. While they were here, they left their mark in form of petroglyphs and pictographs. A petroglyph is a prehistoric rock carving made by scraping away a darker portion of the rock to reveal a lighter portion below. A pictograph, on the other hand, is painting on the rock, usually made with plant and mineral spirits.

Both petroglyphs and pictographs are clearly visible and easy to reach in Willow Springs by hiking the Willow Springs Loop trail. This trail is well-marked, and signs along the way point out where the petroglyphs and pictographs can be seen. One of the most famous is the Painted Hands pictograph, which, as the name suggests, is a collection of five hands along the side of a rock. Along this trail you can also see an agave roasting pot, believed to have been used by the same Native Americans.

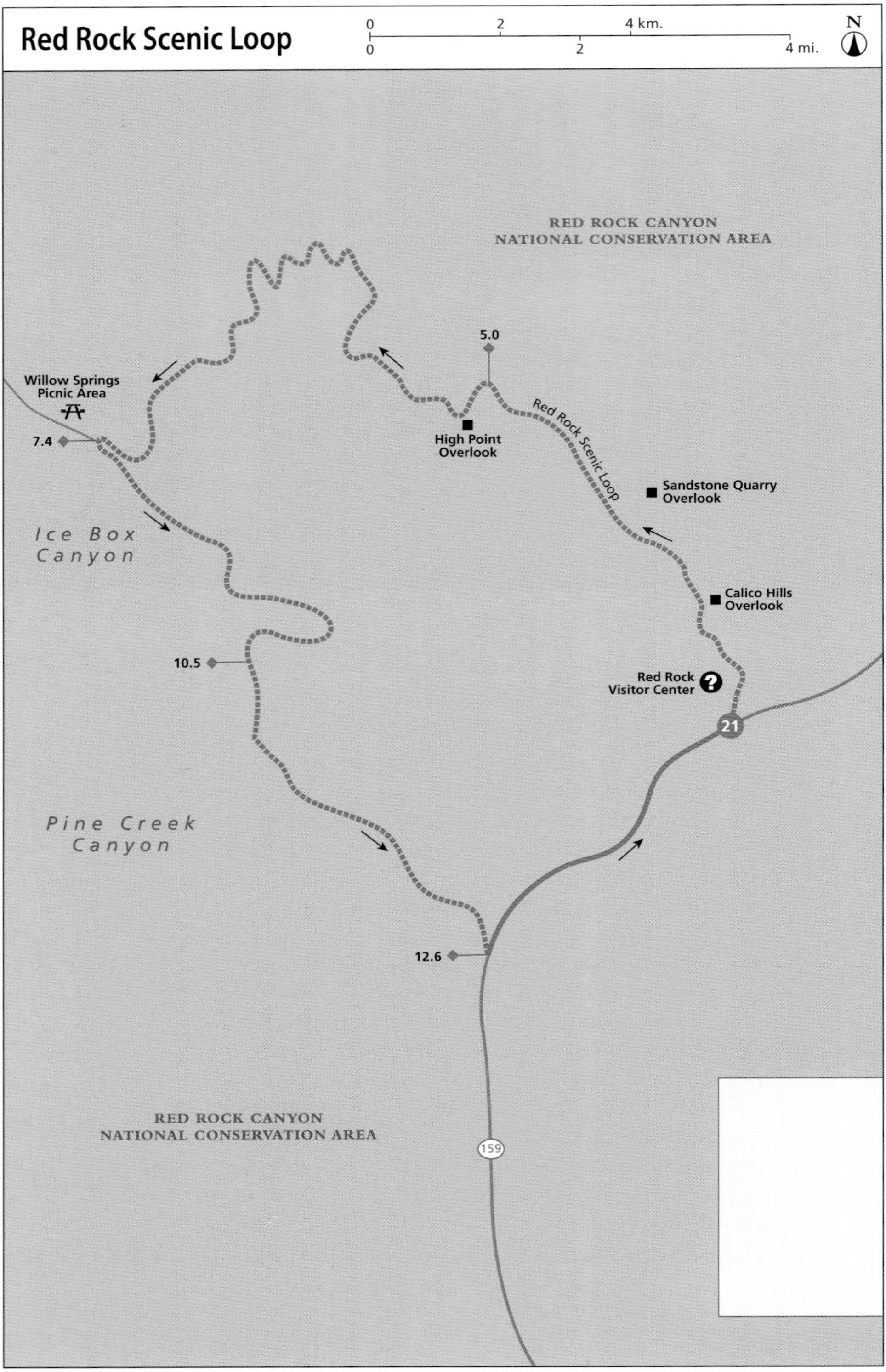
Red Rock Scenic Loop
0 2 4 km.
0 2 4 mi.
N
RED ROCK CANYON
NATIONAL CONSERVATION AREA
5.0
Willow Springs
Picnic Area
7.4
High Point
Overlook
Red Rock Scenic Loop
Sandstone Quarry
Overlook
Ice Box
Canyon
Calico Hills
Overlook
10.5
Red Rock
Visitor Center
21
Pine Creek
Canyon
12.6
RED ROCK CANYON
NATIONAL CONSERVATION AREA
159

The trail ends at the point where it meets SR 159. If you parked your vehicle in the dirt lot next to the end of the trail, the ride is complete. If you parked your vehicle at the Red Rocks Visitor Center, you will need to cross SR 159 and go left back to the entrance to Red Rocks National Conservation Area, approximately 2 miles. Be very careful when crossing this street. The speed limit is 50 mph, and depending on the time of day, there may be many vehicles on the road. When you reach the pay booth, simply show your receipt and you'll be allowed back in without having to repay the fee.

MILES AND DIRECTIONS

0.0 Start at the trailhead just to the right after entering the pay booth.

0.2 Stay to the right through a short downhill section. Continue across the wash in 0.2 mile.

1.0 Pass Calico Hills 1 Overlook on the right. In 0.7 mile, pass Calico Hills 2 Overlook on the right.

2.0 Follow the trail as it continues to climb, passing Sandstone Quarry Overlook in 0.6 mile.

4.6 Pass another scenic overlook.

5.0 Follow the trail as it curves to the left and continues to climb, passing High Point Overlook on the left in 0.5 mile.

5.8 Pass White Rock Trailhead to the right.

7.4 Pass Willow Springs Picnic area, followed by Ice Box Canyon Trailhead in 0.5 mile.

8.5 Follow the trail across the wash. In 0.4 mile, pass Red Rock Wash Overlook to the left.

10.5 Pass Pine Creek Overlook and trailhead on the right.

11.9 Pass Oak Creek Trailhead on the right.

12.6 Official end of trail at SR 159. Ride back to starting point.

14.6 End of ride at pay booth, if this is where you started.

RIDE INFORMATION

Local Events and Attractions

Children's Discovery Trail: Located inside Willow Springs is a trail dedicated specifically to children. To help them understand the significance of the area, the BLM has installed signs along the trail at certain points of interest.

Red Rock Visitor Center: This LEED Gold–certified visitor center demonstrates the wonders of the canyon, including the flora and fauna, through innovative exhibits located both inside and outside the center, 8 a.m. to 4:30 p.m.; redrockcanyonlv.org.

Willow Springs: This multiuse area inside Red Rock Canyon National Conservation Area is a destination in itself, offering riparian areas, bird-watching, picnicking, rock climbing, rappelling, and hiking.

Restaurants

Bonnie Springs Ranch Restaurant: 1 Gunfighter Ln., Bonnie Springs; (702) 875-4400; bonniesprings.com. American-style food located next to Bonnie Springs Ranch.

Lucille's Smokehouse Bar-B-Que: 11011 W. Charleston Blvd., Las Vegas; (702) 220-7427; redrock.sclv.com. A local favorite located inside the Red Rock Casino.

Rocco's NY Pizza: 10860 W. Charleston Blvd., #190, Las Vegas; (702) 796-0111; roccosnypizza.com. Local pizzeria inside the Canyon Pointe shopping center.

Restrooms

Mile 0.0: Red Rock Visitor Center, parking lot and outside the center
Mile 1.7: Calico Hills 2 Overlook
Mile 2.6: Sandstone Quarry Overlook
Mile 5.8: White Rock Trailhead
Mile 7.3: Lost Creek Trail
Mile 7.9: Ice Box Canyon
Mile 10.5: Pine Creek Overlook
Mile 11.9: Oak Creek Trailhead

State Route 159

This trail offers many of the same views as the Red Rock Scenic Loop, only without the entrance fee. It is one of the favorite trails of road bikers, who tend to ride it early in the morning and on the weekends. There is a very good chance to encounter burrows on the road or in the ditch off to the side of the road while riding this trail.

Start: Canyon Pointe shopping center

Length: 32.4 miles

Approximate riding time: 2.5 to 5 hours

Best bike: Road bike

Terrain and trail surface: Two-lane asphalt road

Traffic and hazards: This is an actual state route that makes its way through the Red Rock Escarpment and the Calico Hills. It's a 50 mph two-lane road used by cars, trucks, and motorcycles. It is also heavily traveled by wild burros, which, by law, have the right-of-way. While they typically stick to the side of the road, they do often cross the road to get, as they say, to the other side.

Things to see: Red Rock Canyon, colorful rock formations, desert plants and animals, wild burros

Getting there: **By car:** Take I-15 south to the Charleston exit. Turn onto West Charleston Boulevard and take it all the way up to Canyon Pointe Road. Pull into the Canyon Pointe shopping center and park there. **By bike:** Follow W. Charleston Boulevard until it turns into Red Rock Road. **GPS:** N36 09.034' / W115 19.059'

THE RIDE

This trail follows SR 159 as it makes its way through the Red Rock Escarpment and the Calico Hills—part of the Calico Basin—along the bike lane on each side of the two-lane road that is heavily used by vehicles, all taking the scenic drive. State Route 159 (SR 159) is a Nevada Scenic Byway, meaning it is one of twenty distinct and diverse roads established by the Nevada Department of Transportation. This 32-mile ride is composed of alternating long, gradual climbs and downhill sections. In fact, very little of this road is what one would consider flat and level. Still, the ride is a popular one among road bikers because of the scenery and because the bike lane on either side of the road is relatively wide.

The majority of the trail follows Red Rock Canyon Road, which begins where W. Charleston Boulevard ends. The trail can begin in many places, such as Red Rocks Visitor Center, Spring Mountain Ranch, Blue Diamond, Red Rock Casino, or the Canyon Pointe shopping center. However, many of these places have fees associated with them, and I have found that starting from the Canyon Pointe shopping center is the best place because it has ample parking and there is a gas station with a restroom and water.

Turn right onto W. Charleston Boulevard and follow it past the Bruce Woodbury Beltway, Vista Center Drive, Desert Foothills Drive, and Sky Vista Drive as W. Charleston Boulevard turns into Red Rock Canyon Road. From here there are several turnoffs on the road, but you will not be taking any of them, unless, of course, you choose to take a side trip—which is suggested. One of the first side trips is the Red Spring parking area off Calico Basin Road.

Bike Shops

Broken Spoke Bikes: 11700 W. Charleston Blvd., #190, Las Vegas; (702) 823-1680; brokenspokebikeslv.com. Rents road bikes and sponsors group rides.
Las Vegas Cyclery: 10575 Discovery Dr., Las Vegas; (702) 596-2953; lasvegascyclery.com. Rents road bikes and sponsors group rides.
McGhie's Bike Outpost: 16 Cottonwood, #B, Blue Diamond; (702) 875-4820; mcghies.com
Pro Cyclery: 7034 W. Charleston Blvd., Las Vegas; (702) 228-9460; procyclery.com. Rents road bikes.
REI: 710 S. Rampart Blvd., Las Vegas; (702) 951-4488; rei.com
Southern Highlands Cyclery: 10550 Southern Highlands Pkwy., Ste. 130, Las Vegas; (702) 778-7786; southernhighlandscyclery.com

Following the road for a little over a mile will take you to a picnic area, featuring a boardwalk loop that travels around the spring-fed meadows.

Riding past Calico Basin Road will take you into one of the most scenic areas of the entire trail. Here, to the right of the road, you can see the red and white sandstone formations that give the Red Rock Canyon National Conservation Area its name. If you want to take another side trip, turn into the entrance of Red Rock Canyon and take the road to the Red Rock Visitor Center. A fee is required to pass.

Passing the entrance to Red Rock Canyon will take you farther down SR 159 into an area where Joshua trees grow freely on the right side of the road and Blue Diamond Hill rests on the left. While this hill may not, at first, seem scenic, a second look might just change your mind. As you look closer at Blue Diamond Hill, you can clearly see gray fossil-bearing Kaibab limestone, a remnant of a time, 250 million years ago, when these deposits were left behind from a warm, shallow sea that once covered the area.

While Blue Diamond Hill may appear to be simply a large gray hill, the other side of the road is something completely different. The Joshua trees growing in the valley eventually lead to mountains composed of rock so colorful, they've led to one of the mountains being named Rainbow Mountain. This area provides many great photo opportunities, which are best captured in the early morning hours when the light accentuates the vibrant colors of the surrounding mountains.

Following SR 159 will eventually take you to one of the oldest places in Las Vegas—Spring Mountain Ranch State Park. This once full-functioning ranch is another great detour to take, mainly because once there, it's easy to forget you're in a desert. Here you can find ample picnic areas, some of the oldest buildings in the valley, a large man-made pond—perfect for bird-watching—and some wonderful history of a ranch once owned by both Howard Hughes and Chester "Chet" Harris Lauck, half of the famous Lum and Abner comedy duo. While there is a small fee to enter, it is well worth the price and the time.

Farther down SR 159 is Bonnie Springs, an Old West village that features a hotel, restaurant, and petting zoo. While there is a fee to enter the village, the restaurant is open to the public without the fee. Shortly past the entrance to Bonnie Springs is the little town of Blue Diamond. There are public restrooms next to the park and a small convenience store where you can get drinks. After you cross Arroyo Street, the road curves to the left. Be careful on this stretch of road, as it is a favorite of wild burros, especially in the morning hours, when they like to hang out in the park at Blue Diamond. These burros will typically leave you alone; however, they won't move for you and they have the legal right-of-way, so it is best to get out of their way.

A rider passes the warning sign for burros on the road.

Spring Mountain Ranch State Park

At the foot of the mountains that make up the Red Rock Escarpment once lay one of the most famous trails in American history—the Spanish Trail. The trail got its start in 1829 when merchant Antonio Armijo led a group of sixty men and one hundred mules on a trek from Santa Fe, New Mexico, to Los Angeles, California, following trails blazed by such men as Jedediah Smith. Around 1860, as the trail become more and more popular, a one-room cabin and a blacksmith shop were built on land adjacent to the trail. It is believed these buildings were built as a respite and sort of repair station for weary travelers.

The buildings, which still exist in their original locations, are now part of Spring Mountain Ranch State Park. The park got its start in 1876 when James B. Wilson and George Anderson homesteaded 350 acres and named it Sandstone Ranch. Over the years the ranch was owned by the likes of Chester "Chet" Harris Lauck, half of the famous Lum and Abner comedy duo; billionaire Howard Hughes; and German-born actress Vera Krupp, whose husband's family was once part of Hitler's war machine. The State of Nevada eventually took possession of the ranch and turned it into a state park, bringing the total acreage to 528 in the process. It is now open to the public for hiking, picnics, bird-watching, and outdoor theater.

Follow the road as it winds its way toward SR 160, about 3 miles. When you reach SR 160, turn right and stay to the right of the road. Be careful with this road, as the speed limit jumps to 65 mph. Follow SR 160 to Avery Street, about 1 mile, and turn right. Follow Avery Street back to SR 159 and then turn left. Ride SR 159 back to the Canyon Pointe shopping center to complete the ride.

MILES AND DIRECTIONS

0.0 From the Canyon Pointe shopping center, turn right onto W. Charleston Boulevard.

0.1 Cross the 215 (Bruce Woodbury Beltway). In 0.5 mile, cross Vista Center Drive.

1.0 Cross Desert Foothills Drive, then Sky Vista Drive in 0.5 mile.

4.0 Pass the road to Calico Basin and Red Springs on the right.

5.4 Pass the road to the Red Rock Canyon Visitor Center and entrance to the scenic loop on the right. At 7.2 miles, pass the road to the Red Rock Overlook on the right.

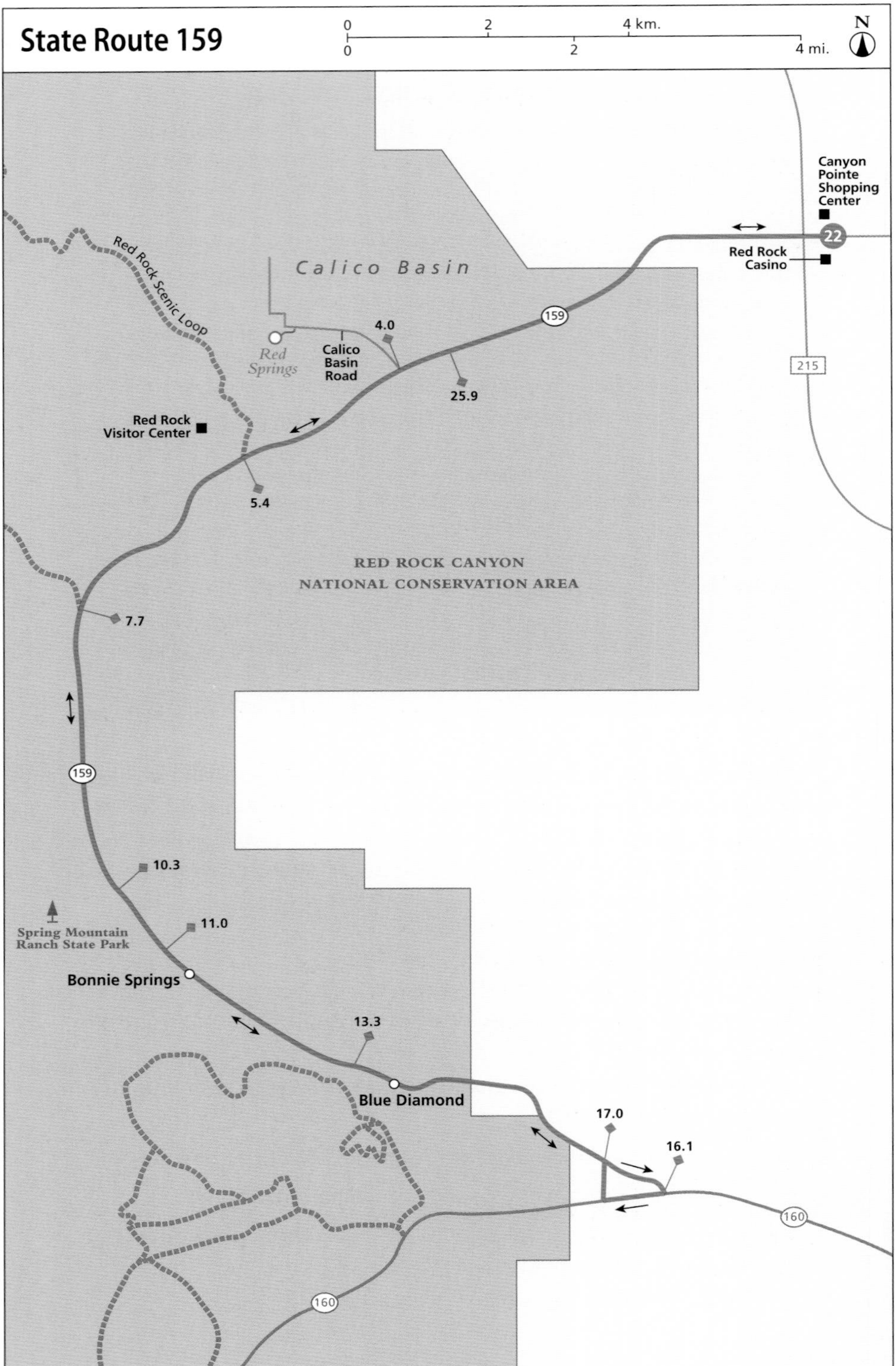
State Route 159
0
2
4 km.
0
2
4 mi.
N
Canyon
Pointe
Shopping
Center
22
Red Rock
Casino
Calico Basin
Red Rock Scenic Loop
159
4.0
Red
Springs
Calico
Basin
Road
25.9
215
Red Rock
Visitor Center
5.4
RED ROCK CANYON
NATIONAL CONSERVATION AREA
7.7
159
10.3
Spring Mountain
Ranch State Park
11.0
Bonnie Springs
13.3
Blue Diamond
17.0
16.1
160
160

7.7 Pass the exit to the scenic loop and dirt parking lot on the right.

9.2 Pass the entrance to Oak Creek on the right. In 0.5 mile, pass the entrance to First Creek on the right.

10.3 Pass the entrance to Spring Mountain Ranch State Park on the right.

11.0 Pass the entrance to Bonnie Springs Ranch on the right. At 12.3 miles, pass the entrance to Wheeler Camp Spring on the right.

13.3 Pass Castalia Street, entrance to Blue Diamond, on the right. In 0.2 mile, pass Arroyo Road on the right.

15.4 Pass Avery Street on the right.

16.1 Turn right onto SR 160/Blue Diamond Road. Stay in the bike lane to the right. In 0.5 mile, turn right onto Avery Street.

17.0 Turn left back onto SR 159 and head back to the Canyon Pointe shopping center.

18.1 Pass the first entrance to Blue Diamond Hill Gypsum Mine on the right, followed by the second entrance at mile 20.0.

25.9 Pass the entrance to the Cowboy Trail Rides on the right.

32.4 Turn left into Canyon Pointe shopping center to complete the ride.

RIDE INFORMATION

Local Events and Attractions

Bonnie Springs Ranch: Visit an honest-to-goodness old-fashioned Wild West town, complete with hangings, shootouts, and an official Main Street; bonniesprings.com.

Horseback Riding: If you'd like to see the scenery of Red Rock Canyon from atop four hooves, you can do so at the Cowboy Trail Rides, just outside the national conservation area; cowboytrailrides.com.

Spring Mountain Ranch State Park: Located close to Red Rock Canyon, this protected park was once a functioning ranch owned at various times by a movie star and a famous billionaire. It is also home to some of the oldest buildings in the valley and is one of the best places to bird-watch; parks.nv.gov.

Super Summer Theatre: Live theater is offered nightly under the summer stars at Spring Mountain Ranch State Park; supersummertheatre.org.

Restaurants

Bonnie Springs Ranch Restaurant: 1 Gunfighter Ln., Bonnie Springs; (702) 875-4400; bonniesprings.com. American-style food located next to Bonnie Springs Ranch.

Islands Fine Burgers and Drinks: 10810 W. Charleston Blvd., Las Vegas; (702) 360-3845; islandsrestaurants.com. Island-style food in Canyon Pointe shopping center.
Lucille's Smokehouse Bar-B-Que: 11011 W. Charleston Blvd., Las Vegas; (702) 220-7427; redrock.sclv.com. A local favorite found inside the Red Rock Casino.

Restrooms

Mile 0.0: Terrible Herbst gas station
Mile 5.4: Red Rock Canyon Visitor Center (fee)
Mile 10.3: Spring Mountain Ranch State Park (fee)
Mile 11.0: Bonnie Springs Ranch Restaurant
Mile 13.3: Next to the park in Blue Diamond

Landmine Loop

Landmine Loop is a challenging trail that climbs up into the hills around Blue Diamond before finishing with a nice, long downhill section. While the trail has some difficult sections, the ride is one of the most popular in Cottonwood.

Start: Asphalt parking lot outside McGhie's Outpost

Length: 7.7 miles

Approximate riding time: 1 to 1.5 hours

Best bike: Mountain bike

Terrain and trail surface: Mostly dirt, some large rocks, and loose gravel

Traffic and hazards: These trails are only open to human power and are mostly used by mountain bikers. However, hikers and runners also use the trail, and it is best to be courteous and give way to them when encountered.

Things to see: Desert plants and animals, Red Rock Mountains, Joshua trees, wild burros

Getting there: **By car:** Take I-15 to the Blue Diamond exit. Head west along Blue Diamond Road (SR 160). Turn right onto SR 159 and follow the road to the town of Blue Diamond. Turn left onto Castalia Street and head to the asphalt parking lot outside McGhie's Outpost. **GPS:** N36 02.835' / W115 24.443'

THE RIDE

This trail starts in the small town of Blue Diamond, beginning on one side of the town and ending on the other. In the meantime the trail makes its way through Cottonwood Valley just outside Red Rock Canyon National

Conservation Area, below the La Madre Mountains and the area known as the Red Rock Escarpment. This area provides spectacular views of the Cottonwood Valley and all it has to offer. Much of the ride is in the hills just behind Blue Diamond, and the height of the trail just adds to the views.

The trail starts in the parking lot outside McGhie's Outpost, a local bike shop, where there is ample parking. Blue Diamond is a small town and the citizens are respectful of the sea of bike riders who invade their community every weekend—that is, as long as those riders return that respect. One of the ways of showing respect is to park where requested. This means not parking at the park or in the dirt at the trailhead, but in the asphalt parking lot outside McGhie's.

Bike Shop

McGhie's Bike Outpost: Rents mountain bikes and gives guided tours of the trails in Cottonwood; 16 Cottonwood, #B, Blue Diamond; (702) 875-4820; mcghies.com

From the parking lot, pull out onto Castalia Street and turn left, heading to Cottonwood Drive. Turn left again and follow Cottonwood Drive up the hill. While traveling up the street, don't be in a hurry to get to the trail. Take time to notice the houses in the area. Many of them are wonderfully decorated and quite quaint. A right turn on Cerrito Street will lead you to the trailhead at the top of the hill. Cerrito Street is a bit of a climb, and you'll know you've found the trailhead when asphalt turns to dirt. There will also be several large rocks at the trailhead, which are meant to deter motorized vehicles from going on the trail.

When you reach the trailhead, you'll find a bit of a drop with a fairly steep but short climb on the other side. Once up that side, continue straight when the trail splits. The trail you are on has a long, storied history. It was once traveled by settlers heading west, looking to make a better life for themselves. So many people traveled the trail that it earned a name—the Old Spanish Trail. As the trail progresses, it makes its way up a very long, very steep hill. There are many rocky spots and some areas are covered with loose gravel. This can be a tricky hill, but it offers a great sense of accomplishment when you reach the top. At the top, just to the left, is a collection of rocks that riders like to arrange into various shapes. One time it may form the outline of a rider on a mountain bike, and another time it may be formed into a large smiley face or a gigantic peace sign.

From here you'll continue on the Old Spanish Trail as it makes its way around one of the hills outside Blue Diamond. This section is a welcome downhill after the rigorous climb you just completed. Be sure to look up into the hills as you travel, as it is a favorite spot for wild burros. When the trail splits a second time, follow it to the right. Shortly after that split, the trail will fork.

You can take either trail because they meet up again a short distance ahead. The trail to the right climbs high into the hills, while the trail to the left follows the foot of those same hills. This guide follows the trail to the left.

Not long after you take that split to the left, there is a short but tricky drop. It is mainly rock, and inexperienced riders may want to walk this section. From here you follow the trail as it makes its way around the bottom of the hills. If you look to the left, you'll see a dirt parking area. Many riders choose to park there instead of Blue Diamond; however, the area is small, only holding five or six vehicles at a time. As you continue, you'll encounter a wash full of gravel. Cross the wash and make an immediate right turn, climbing up the small ridge. From here you'll follow the trail, being sure not to take any offshoot trails on either side of the main trail.

The trail climbs gradually through the desert, offering stunning views of the Red Rock Escarpment—which is the name of the multicolored mountains just to the west of the trail. You'll also ride right by some of the largest Joshua trees in the area. These trees are home to many birds, such as woodpeckers,

A rider makes his way through the many Joshua trees on the Landmine Loop.

The Old Spanish Trail

In 1829 merchant Antonio Armijo led a group of sixty men and one hundred mules on a trek from Santa Fe, New Mexico, to Los Angeles, California. Looking to establish a trade route, Armijo chose trails blazed by trappers, traders, and mountain men such as Jedediah Smith. He also created his own trails, connecting those existing into one main trail that could be used over and over again. Armijo eventually arrived at the San Gabriel mission with his group, for the most part, intact—minus a few mules that were used for meat.

The trail quickly gained the reputation of being the longest, most arduous pack mule route in the history of America. The distinction, however, did not stop it from being heavily used by pack mule trains carrying supplies from New Mexico to California. As different groups made the trek, they created variations on the trail established by Armijo—with some following the Red Rock Mountains and others following what would eventually become SR 160. In 1843 John C. Fremont and Kit Carson were hired to survey the area. Fremont and Carson chose to stick closer to the Red Rock Mountains, taking advantage of the many mountain springs, as they made their way through Cottonwood Valley. The trail they mapped would eventually be named the Old Spanish Trail and eventually the Mormon Trail.

who perch on the branches in search of grubs. At one point the trail makes its way back to the foot of the hills. Here you'll find a large gray rock that can be difficult to ride over. If you can't ride over it, walk your bike. Resist the temptation to ride around the rock on what looks like a trail. This is not an established trail and should not be used. Shortly after the rock obstacle, you'll find another fork in the trail. Take the trail to the right and follow it as it climbs up into the hills. While the terrain isn't difficult, the climb is fairly steep in some places.

After you climb to the top of the ridge next to the hill, you'll cross what looks like a rock bridge and start a little downhill section. When the trail splits yet again at the trail marker, follow the offshoot to the right. Here the dirt turns a rich reddish-brown as you make your way to the crest of a road. When the trail intersects the road at the top of the crest, you'll find a trail map on a kiosk and a large Joshua tree that is commonly used as a landmark. From here take the trail to the right as it veers off the dirt road.

On the other side of the crest, the trail goes downhill, following a dry riverbed. This portion of the trail has some sections filled with soft sand and others filled with smooth but large boulders. The trail is made even trickier by the many cactuses that lay in wait on either side of the trail for the rider to make a wrong move. While it is certainly possible to navigate this portion of the trail, inexperienced riders will want to take their time and may even want to walk some sections.

Once you get past the dry riverbed, the trail continues its downhill trek back to Blue Diamond. However, there is still one hill left to climb. As you begin the climb, looking to the left you'll find an old car—possibly from the '30s or '40s—on its side, down in the valley. The car has been shot up time and again and has often been confused with the car driven by notorious bank robbers Bonnie and Clyde. The confusion is further enhanced by the fact that there is a mountain bike trail in the area known as "Bonnie and Clyde." Rest assured that the bank-robbing duo never made it this far west.

After you complete the final climb, it is an easy downhill ride to the end of the trail. At one point the trail splits again. You can take either trail, as they meet up again a short distance ahead. The upper trail is more difficult, while the lower trail is a bit easier. This guide follows the lower trail. After the trails meet back up, you are home free—that is, except for the final drop. This drop is a little intimidating, but if you have the courage to take the drop without using your brakes, you'll have enough momentum to easily make it up the other side. If you're worried about the drop, there is a more gradual trail leading down into the drop that you can walk with your bike.

Once you've navigated the final obstacle, follow the trail as it curves to the right and makes its way into Blue Diamond. You'll come out on Cottonwood Drive and easily find the parking lot on your left.

MILES AND DIRECTIONS

0.0 Park in the asphalt lot outside McGhie's Outpost. Ride out onto Castalia Street and turn left. Turn left again onto Cottonwood Drive and follow that street. At 0.2 mile, turn right onto Cerrito Street and climb the hill.

0.3 Take the trailhead to the right in the gravel area. The area is marked by large boulders and a trail marker. In 0.1 mile, the trail splits. Take either route into the drop and then make the small climb up the other side. Stay straight. Do not take the offshoot trail to the right.

0.5 Begin the long, steep climb up the hill. At the top of the hill at mile 0.7, stay straight. When the trail splits, take either trail for a short downhill section. The trails will meet back up ahead. Stay straight when another trail on the right merges with the main trail at mile 0.8.

1.2 Follow the trail to the right at the trail marker. When the trail forks, take the trail to the left. The trail takes a short drop over some rocks at mile 1.3. This obstacle is tricky, and inexperienced riders may want to walk it.

Landmine Loop

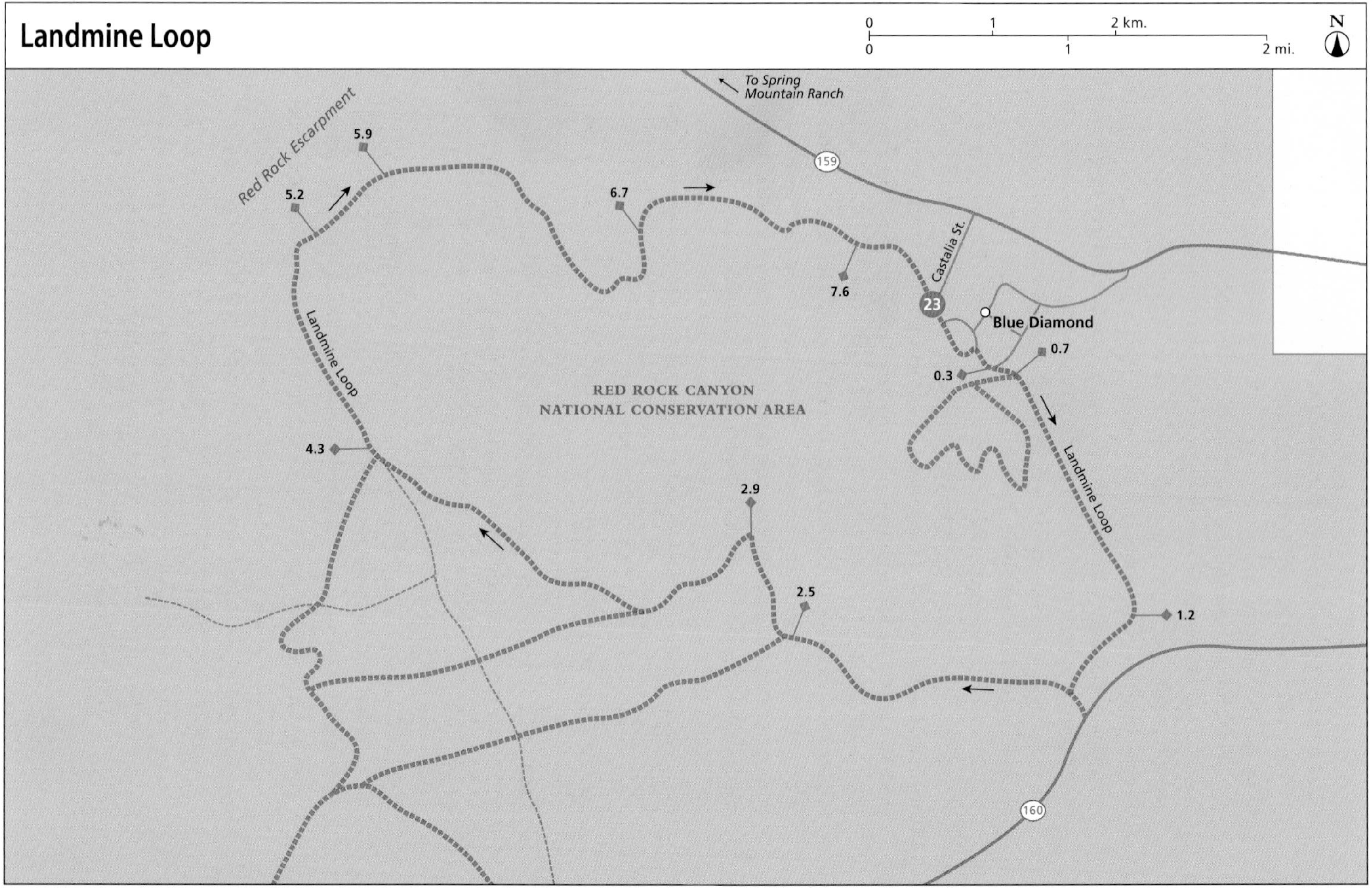

1.4 Stay straight as the upper trail merges with the lower trail. In 0.1 mile, enter the wash and make a sharp turn to the right on the other side. The wash is full of deep gravel. After making the sharp right, make the quick climb up the ridge.

1.6 The trail splits twice. Stay to the right each time. When the trail merges to the right, stay straight.

2.0 Follow the trail along the dry riverbed. Ride over the large gray rock at mile 2.4. Speed is needed to navigate this obstacle. Inexperienced riders may want to walk it.

2.5 When the trail forks, take the trail to the right and cross the riverbed. Follow the trail as it goes to the left and begins a steep climb. The trail makes a short descent at mile 2.7 and then climbs on the other side.

2.9 Follow the trail as it crosses the rock "bridge," then climbs the hill on the other side and curves to the right at mile 3.0.

3.3 Take the quick little drop; be careful of the large, loose rocks. The dirt begins to turn a rich reddish-brown. When two trails cross each other at 3.4 miles, take the trail to the right and climb.

3.5 Follow the trail down and to the left. Shortly after there is another drop and the trail curves to the left.

3.9 Follow the trail to the left and then the right. Stay straight at mile 4.2 as the trail merges with another trail on the right.

4.3 Merge onto the dirt road and turn right. Climb up the hill past the trail map.

4.4 Pick the trail back up at the crest of the road, to the right; do not follow the dirt road. In 0.2 mile, turn right and connect with the dirt road for a short distance. When the dirt road starts to go down, take the trail to the right.

4.8 Follow the trail into the quick drop with large rocks. At the end of the drop, the trail turns sharply to the right and goes into a climb. The trail travels through some very soft dirt and can be hard to navigate.

4.9 Follow the trail through a dry riverbed. There are sections with soft dirt and sections with large, smooth rocks. This portion of the trail is tricky. Stay straight as the trail merges on the right at 5.1 miles.

5.2 End of tricky rock section; stay straight and then follow the trail as it curves to the right. Do not follow the wash straight.

5.8 Stay straight. Do not take the offshoot trail to the left. The offshoot trail leads to an old shot-up car, lying on its side in the valley.

5.9 Stay straight as the offshoot trail on the left meets back up with the main trail. Start a steep climb. Follow the trail to the right at the top of the hill at mile 6.1 and begin a downhill section.

6.2 Take the tricky drop, followed by a steep but short climb on the other side. In 0.3 mile, take the long gradual drop, then follow the trail to the left.

6.7 Take the trail to the left when the trail splits at the marker. This is the lower trail. Stay straight as the upper and lower trails meet back up at mile 7.0.

7.5 Take the last deep drop. Resist the temptation to use your brakes, so momentum will take you up the other side. You can also use the more gradual trail to walk this obstacle. After the climb on the other side, follow the trail to the right.

7.6 When the trail meets up with a dirt road, follow the road to the right as it turns into Cottonwood Drive.

7.7 Turn left onto Castalia Street and then take an immediate right into the parking lot.

RIDE INFORMATION

Local Events and Attractions

Spring Mountain Ranch State Park: Located close to Red Rock Canyon, this protected park was once a functioning ranch owned at various times by a movie star and a famous billionaire. It is also home to some of the oldest buildings in the valley and is one of the best places to bird-watch; parks.nv.gov.

Super Summer Theatre: Live theater is offered nightly under the summer stars at Spring Mountain Ranch State Park; supersummertheatre.org.

Restaurant

Bonnie Springs Ranch Restaurant: 1 Gunfighter Ln., Bonnie Springs; (702) 875-4400; bonniesprings.com. American-style food located next to Bonnie Springs Ranch.

Restrooms

Mile 0.0: Next to the park in Blue Diamond

Landmine/Middle Fork Loop

This trail is an alternate route to the Landmine Loop, adding a little over a mile to the total ride. The ride offers an easy and enjoyable route through the middle of Cottonwood Valley, adding a fun downhill section before it meets back up with the Landmine Loop at the large Joshua tree.

Start: Asphalt parking lot outside McGhie's Outpost

Length: 8.8 miles

Approximate riding time: 1 to 2 hours

Best bike: Mountain bike

Terrain and trail surface: Mostly dirt, some large rocks, and loose gravel

Traffic and hazards: These trails are only open to human power and are mostly used by mountain bikers. However, hikers and runners also use the trail, and it is best to be courteous and give way to them when encountered.

Things to see: Desert plants and animals, Red Rock Mountains, Joshua trees, wild burros

Getting there: By car: Take I-15 to the Blue Diamond exit. Head west along Blue Diamond Road (SR 160). Turn right onto SR 159 and follow the road to the town of Blue Diamond. Turn left onto Castalia Street and head to the asphalt parking lot outside McGhie's Outpost. **GPS:** N36 02.835' / W115 24.443'

THE RIDE

This trail is an alternate route of the Landmine Loop, adding a little over 1 mile to the ride. Just like the Landmine Loop, the trail starts in the small town of Blue Diamond, beginning on one side of the town and ending on the other.

Also like the Landmine Loop, the trail offers great views of the Cottonwood Valley and the Red Rock Escarpment. The difference between the two routes is that instead of staying on the trail that makes up the Landmine Loop, this route takes a detour when the Landmine Loop trail intersects the Middle Fork Trail. Middle Fork, which is an easy, gradual climb, travels directly through the Cottonwood Valley, offering wonderful views of the Las Vegas desert.

After the climb, Middle Fork meets up with another trail called Little Daytona. This aptly named trail takes the rider on a fun, quick ride, eventually leading into a long downhill dash before meeting back up with the Landmine Loop at the large Joshua tree on the crest of a dirt road. From here the trail follows Landmine Loop back to Blue Diamond.

From the parking lot, pull out onto Castalia Street and turn left, heading to Cottonwood Drive. Turn left again and follow Cottonwood Drive up the hill. A right turn on Cerrito Street will lead you to the trailhead at the top of the hill. Cerrito Street is a bit of a climb, and you'll know you've found the trailhead when asphalt turns to dirt. There will also be several large rocks at the trailhead, which are meant to deter motorized vehicles from going on the trail.

When you reach the trailhead, you'll find a bit of a drop with a fairly steep but short climb on the other side. Once up that side, continue straight when the trail splits. As the trail progresses, it makes its way up a very long, very steep hill. There are many rocky spots, and some areas are covered with loose gravel. At the top, just to the left, is a collection of rocks that riders like to arrange into various shapes. One time it may form the outline of a rider on a mountain bike, and another time it may be formed into a large smiley face or a gigantic peace sign.

From here you'll continue on the trail as it makes its way around one of the hills outside Blue Diamond. This section is a welcome downhill after the rigorous climb you just completed. Be sure to look up into the hills as you travel, as it is a favorite spot for wild burros. When the trail splits a second time, follow it to the right. Shortly after that split, the trail will fork. You can take either trail because they meet up again a short distance ahead. The trail to the right climbs high into the hills, while the trail to the left follows the foot of those same hills. This guide follows the trail to the left.

Bike Shop

McGhie's Bike Outpost: 16 Cottonwood, #B, Blue Diamond; (702) 875-4820; mcghies.com. Mountain bike rentals and tours.

Not long after you take that split to the left, there is a short but tricky drop. It is mainly rock, and inexperienced riders may want to walk this section. From here you follow the trail as it makes its way around the bottom of the hills. If you look to the left, you'll see a dirt parking area. Many riders choose

Riders making their way up a difficult climb along the Landmine/Middle Fork Loop

to park there instead of Blue Diamond; however, the area is small, only holding five or six vehicles at a time. As you continue, you'll encounter a wash full of gravel. Cross the wash and make an immediate right turn, climbing up the small ridge. From here you'll follow the trail, being sure not to take any offshoot trails on either side of the main trail.

The trail climbs gradually through the desert, offering stunning views of the Red Rock Escarpment—which is the name of the multicolored mountains just to the west of the trail. You'll also ride right by some of the largest Joshua trees in the area. These trees are home to many birds, such as woodpeckers, who perch on the branches in search of grubs. At one point the trail makes its way back to the foot of the hills. Here you'll find a large gray rock that can be difficult to ride over. If you can't ride over it, walk your bike. Resist the temptation to ride around the rock on what looks like a trail. This is not an established trail and should not be used. Shortly after the rock obstacle, you'll find another fork in the trail. Take the trail to the right and follow it as it climbs up into the hills. While the terrain isn't difficult, the climb is fairly steep in some places.

After you climb to the top of the ridge next to the hill, you'll cross what looks like a rock bridge and start a little downhill section. When the trail splits yet again at the trail marker, continue straight. (***Note:*** Landmine Loop is the trail to the right.) From here you'll take a gradual climb through reddish-brown dirt as the trail makes its way to Little Daytona. You'll know you've reached Little Daytona when the trail dead-ends. Turn right onto Little Daytona and prepare for a fun, easy ride. When you see the wide dirt road, look for the trail on the other side. It is marked by a trail marker—a long piece of brown plastic. Cross the road and take the trail on a downhill section that allows you to go about as fast as you feel comfortable.

The trail will eventually make its way to another dirt road. Keep your momentum up and use it to make the short but steep climb up the hill to the crest of the second dirt road. When the trail intersects the road at the top of the crest, you'll find a trail map on a kiosk and a large Joshua tree that is commonly used as a landmark. From here take the trail to the right as it veers off the dirt road. This is the Landmine Loop.

On the other side of the crest, the trail goes downhill, following a dry riverbed. This portion of the trail has some sections filled with soft sand and others filled with smooth but large boulders. The trail is made even trickier by the many cactuses that lay in wait on either side of the trail for the rider to make a wrong move. While it is certainly possible to navigate this portion of the trail, inexperienced riders will want to take their time and may even want to walk some sections.

Once you get past the dry riverbed, the trail continues its downhill trek back to Blue Diamond. However, there is still one hill left to climb. As you begin the climb, looking to the left you'll find an old car—possibly from the '30s or '40s—on its side, down in the valley. The car has been shot up time and again and has often been confused with the car driven by notorious bank robbers Bonnie and Clyde. The confusion is further enhanced by the fact that there is a mountain bike trail in the area known as "Bonnie and Clyde." Rest assured that the bank-robbing duo never made it this far west.

After you complete the final climb, it is an easy downhill ride to the end of the trail. At one point the trail splits again. You can take either trail, as they meet up again a short distance ahead. The upper trail is more difficult, while the lower trail is a bit easier. This guide follows the lower trail. After the trails meet back up, you are home free. That is, except for the final drop. This drop is a little intimidating, but if you have the courage to take the drop without using your brakes, you'll have enough momentum to easily make it up the other side. If you're worried about the drop, there is a more gradual trail leading down into the drop that you can walk with your bike.

Once you've navigated the final obstacle, follow the trail as it curves to the right and makes its way into Blue Diamond. You'll come out on Cottonwood Drive and easily find the parking lot on your left.

Wild Burros

Just as you enter Blue Diamond, you'll see a sign welcoming you to the town. The welcome is followed by some valuable information: "Elevation—High," "Population—Low," and "Burros—?" Spend any time at all in Blue Diamond, and you are bound to encounter a wild burro. This is because the town welcomes them as much, if not more, than they welcome mountain bikers. Burros can be seen walking the streets of the town in the evening and early morning hours. They are most often found in the town's park, resting in or snacking on the cool grass.

Although they are plentiful in the hills of Cottonwood Valley, burros aren't native to the United States. They're actually native to Africa and were brought to the American continent by the Spanish in the late 1400s as pack animals. As gold and silver were discovered just outside of Las Vegas in the early 1800s, miners used these animals to pack their supplies into the mines and ore out of the mines. The miners eventually abandoned the area, often leaving their pack mules behind.

Wild, or feral, burros are well-suited to the Nevada desert and have thrived in the Red Rock Canyon. If you see one of these animals on your ride, enjoy their beauty from a distance. Most burros are not camera shy and love to have their photos taken—of course, they haven't expressed that, but they do stand still when you take their picture, unless, of course, you get too close. When dealing with these burros, remember they are wild animals. Unfortunately many people ignore the signs and feed them. This combined with the fact that they are welcomed in Blue Diamond make them comfortable around people, which can mistakenly make them seem docile. They are not. They have a strong kick and an even stronger bite. If one brays at you, take it as a warning to back off. And remember, feeding wild animals can make them dependent on a food source that is not reliable. Stop and look at them, take their picture, but let wild animals stay wild.

MILES AND DIRECTIONS

0.0 Park in the asphalt lot outside McGhie's Outpost. Ride out onto Castalia Street and turn left. Turn left again onto Cottonwood Drive and follow that street. At 0.2 mile, turn right onto Cerrito Street and climb the hill.

0.3 Take the trailhead to the right in the gravel area. The area is marked by large boulders and a trail marker. In 0.1 mile, the trail splits. Take either route into the drop and then make the small climb up the other side. Stay straight. Do not take the offshoot trail to the right.

Landmine/Middle Fork Loop

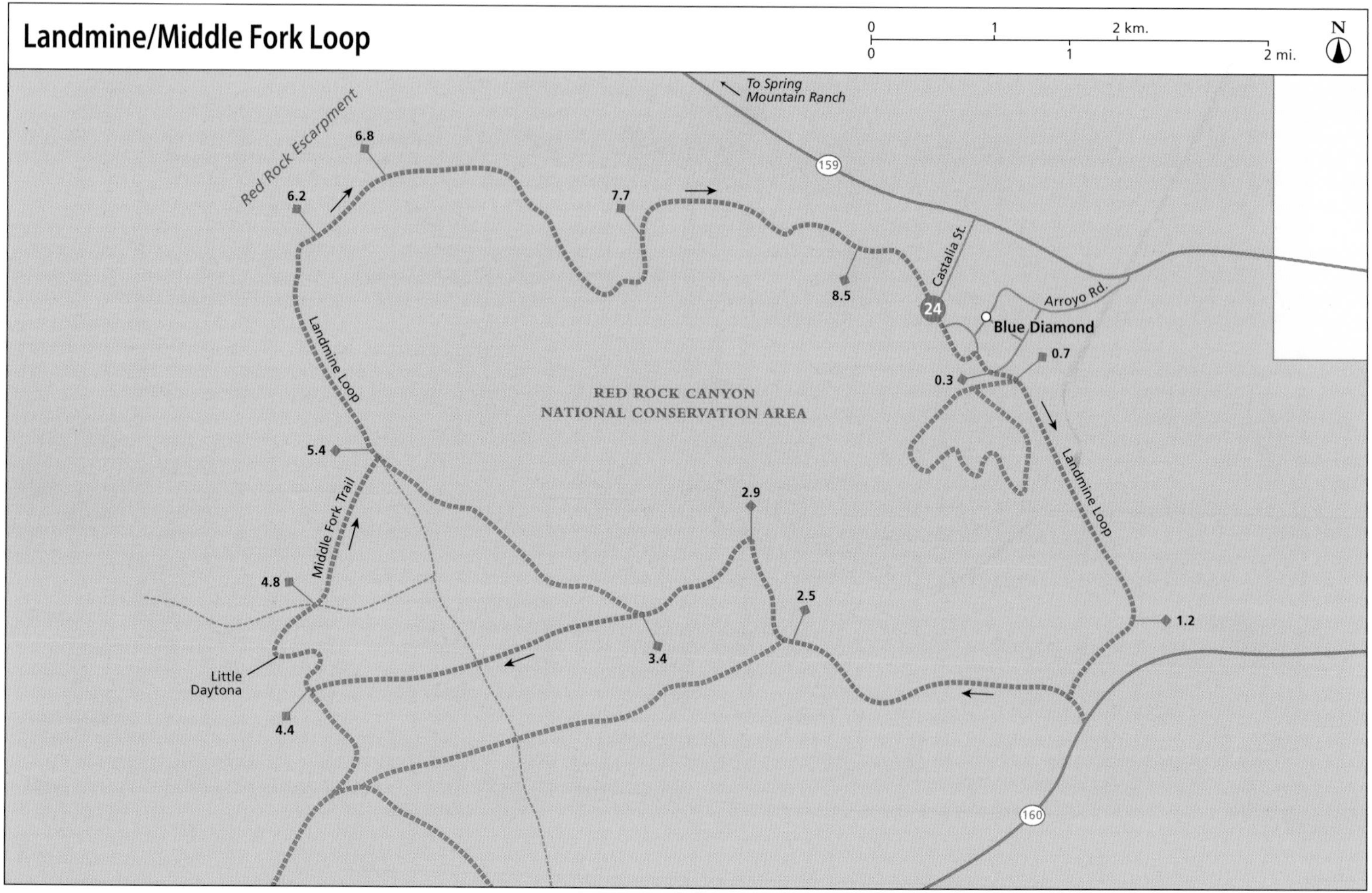

0.5 Begin the long, steep climb up the hill. At the top of the hill at mile 0.7, stay straight. When the trail splits, take either trail for a short downhill section. The trails will meet back up ahead. Stay straight when another trail on the right merges with the main trail at mile 0.8.

1.2 Follow the trail to the right at the trail marker. When the trail forks, take the trail to the left. The trail takes a short drop over some rocks at mile 1.3. This obstacle is tricky, and inexperienced riders may want to walk it.

1.4 Stay straight as the upper trail merges with the lower trail. In 0.1 mile, enter the wash and make a sharp turn to the right on the other side. The wash is full of deep gravel. After making the sharp right, make the quick climb up the ridge.

1.6 The trail splits twice. Stay to the right each time. When the trail merges to the right, stay straight.

2.0 Follow the trail along the dry riverbed. Ride over the large gray rock at mile 2.4. Speed is needed to navigate this obstacle. Inexperienced riders may want to walk it.

2.5 When the trail forks, take the trail to the right and cross the riverbed. Follow the trail as it goes to the left and begins a steep climb. The trail makes a short descent at mile 2.7 and then climbs on the other side.

2.9 Follow the trail as it crosses the rock "bridge," then climbs the hill on the other side and curves to the right at mile 3.0.

3.3 Take the quick little drop; be careful of the large, loose rocks. The dirt begins to turn a rich reddish-brown.

3.4 When two trails cross each other, continue straight. In 0.1 mile, cross the riverbed and make the short climb on the other side.

4.0 Cross the dirt road, and in 0.2 mile, cross another riverbed. There is a bit of a steep climb on the other side. At 4.3 miles, cross the riverbed again.

4.4 When the trail dead-ends, take the trail to the right. This is Little Daytona. In 0.1 mile, cross the riverbed and climb up the other side.

4.7 Follow the trail as it curves to the right, then makes another quick right up the hill.

4.8 Cross the dirt road and look for the trail on the other side. Take that trail into a fun, easy downhill section that eventually makes its way up to the crest of a dirt road.

5.4 Turn left and merge onto the dirt road. Climb up the hill past the trail map. Pick the trail back up at the crest of the road, to the right; do not follow the dirt road. At mile 5.6, turn right and connect with the dirt road for a short distance. When the dirt road starts to go down, take the trail to the right.

5.8 Follow the trail into the quick drop with large rocks. At the end of the drop, the trail turns sharply to the right and goes into a climb. The trail travels through some very soft dirt and can be hard to navigate.

5.9 Follow the trail through a dry riverbed. There are sections with soft dirt and sections with large, smooth rocks. This portion of the trail is tricky. Stay straight as the trail merges on the right at 6.1 miles.

6.2 End of tricky rock section; stay straight and then follow the trail as it curves to the right. Do not follow the wash straight.

6.8 Stay straight. Do not take the offshoot trail to the left. The offshoot trail leads to an old shot-up car, lying on its side in the valley.

6.9 Stay straight as the offshoot trail on the left meets back up with the main trail. Start a steep climb. Follow the trail to the right at the top of the hill at mile 7.1 and begin a downhill section.

7.2 Take the tricky drop, followed by a steep but short climb on the other side. In 0.3 mile, take the long gradual drop, then follow the trail to the left.

7.7 Take the trail to the left when the trail splits at the marker. This is the lower trail. Stay straight as the upper and lower trails meet back up at mile 8.0.

8.5 Take the last deep drop. Resist the temptation to use your brakes, so momentum will take you up the other side. You can also use the more gradual trail to walk this obstacle. After the climb on the other side, follow the trail to the right.

8.6 When the trail meets up with a dirt road, follow the road to the right as it turns into Cottonwood Drive.

8.8 Turn left onto Castalia Street and then take an immediate right into the parking lot.

RIDE INFORMATION

Local Events and Attractions

Bonnie Springs Ranch: Visit an honest-to-goodness old-fashioned Wild West town, complete with hangings, shootouts, and an official Main Street; bonniesprings.com.

Horseback Riding: If you'd like to see the scenery of the Red Rock Canyon from atop four hooves, you can do so at the Cowboy Trail Rides, just outside the national conservation area; cowboytrailrides.com.

Restaurant

Bonnie Springs Ranch Restaurant: 1 Gunfighter Ln., Bonnie Springs; (702) 875-4400; bonniesprings.com. American-style food located next to Bonnie Springs Ranch.

Restrooms

Mile 0.0: Next to park in Blue Diamond

25

Beginner Loop

This trail has a great downhill section that makes for a fun ride. Of course, you have to pay for that downhill with a bit of a climb back to the trailhead, but on the way the trail offers great views of the Red Rocks Escarpment and you may even see a burro or two.

Start: Asphalt parking lot off SR 160

Length: 3.8 miles

Approximate riding time: 45 minutes to 1.5 hours

Best bike: Mountain bike with suspension (either front or full)

Terrain and trail surface: Mostly dirt and loose gravel

Traffic and hazards: This is a singletrack trail that has large ruts in some places. The trail is open mainly to mountain bikes, but hikers and runners can also use it. However, it is not common to see anything other than mountain bikers, and maybe burros.

Things to see: Desert plants and animals, Red Rock Mountains, wild burros

Getting there: By car: Take SR 160 past the Red Rock Conservation Area turnoff (SR 159). Follow the road as it curves to the right and to the left. Look for the asphalt parking lot to the right of the road. The restroom is the only building in the area, so it is easy to spot. **GPS:** N36 00.674' / W115 25.879'

THE RIDE

The Beginner Loop is a fun ride popular with many mountain bikers in the area. The majority of the ride is a great downhill section that you can take as slow or as fast as you feel comfortable. Of course, all that downhill riding does come with a price. Once you complete that portion, you'll have a gradual climb all the way back to the trailhead. Still, the climb is not difficult and the downhill section is worth the price of admission.

The trail begins at a parking lot just off SR 160. The asphalt lot was built specifically for access to the trails in this area, a map of which is carved into a large stone located just to the right of the restrooms. The map is not to scale and is only meant to give an overall idea of the trails. The trailhead for the Beginner Loop is just to the left of the restrooms, which are the only restrooms on the trail. The first part of the trail, before you reach the downhill section, is a climb through loose rocks and gravel. The trail makes its way around the parking lot, eventually turning east at the trail marker and heading towards the Red Rock Escarpment.

About a half mile from the trailhead, the trail splits at another trail marker. Take the trail to the right into a short downhill section. Shortly after the turn there is a small drop, followed by a short climb. A part of the climb goes through a section complete with large, sharp rocks. Close to a mile into the ride, you cross a dirt road and continue straight. Be sure to look up into the hills, as you might just spot

A rider with Ride 2 Recovery starts the Beginner Loop.

a wild burro or two wandering around. You should also watch the trails because these wild animals commonly walk along them and often leave little presents that you'll not want to ride through—if they're fresh.

Bike Shop

McGhie's Bike Outpost: 16 Cottonwood, #B, Blue Diamond; (702) 875-4820; mcghies.com. Mountain bike rentals and tours.

The downhill section begins close to a mile into the ride, just after two separate trails turn into one. Shortly after, the trail splits again. Stay on the main trail to the right and take the drop, allowing momentum to get you up the other side. Shortly after the drop, you'll see a dirt road. Cross the road and continue straight. The ruts in the trail get deep in this section and can be a little tricky to ride. Try to stay in the center so the ruts don't pull you up and off the trail.

A little more than 2 miles into the ride, you'll see the dirt road again. Turn right and either ride down the dirt road or take the trail just to the right. They meet up about 30 or so feet ahead. Turn right at the trail marker and begin the climb back to the trailhead. Time to pay for the fun downhill section you just rode. About 1.5 miles up the trail, follow the trail to the right and head back to the trailhead.

Ride 2 Recovery

Ride 2 Recovery was started in 2008 to help veterans recover from physical and emotional injuries incurred during their service. The organization hosts two events in Las Vegas: an annual mountain bike ride in Cottonwood and an Honor Ride in October during the Interbike convention.

Ride 2 Recovery started with a phone call to John Wordin, a 6-foot, 5-inch man who was once a professional cyclist and director of the acclaimed Mercury Cycling Team, which won 535 races in five years and was named VeloNews Team of the Year seven times in a row. The call came from the Veterans Administration (VA), asking him to lead a group of veterans on a ride as part of the soldiers' physical therapy. Wordin agreed and the first challenge—a road bike ride—occurred in 2008. Fourteen riders showed up for the 490 miles, from Washington, DC, to Charlotte Motor Speedway. "Since then," Wordin says with a slight chuckle, "we've learned to make the rides much shorter."

Like the men and women under his care, Wordin has himself received benefits from being part of the group he founded. "Hanging around these guys and seeing them doing something no one ever thought they could do changes you." Wordin says. "If you see someone with no arms or no legs riding a bike, your life doesn't suck."

MILES AND DIRECTIONS

0.0 Park in the asphalt lot off SR 160. Take the trail just to the left of the restrooms.

0.1 Take the trail to the right at the trail marker. In 0.2 mile, follow the trail through a wash and begin a climb.

0.5 Take the trail to the right when it splits at the trail marker, and start a short downhill section. Take the small drop in 0.1 mile, then follow the trail as it curves to the right and starts to climb.

0.7 Pass through a section with large, sharp rocks, then follow the trail to the right. Do not take the dirt road.

0.8 Cross the dirt road and continue straight. In 0.1 mile, follow the trail to the right after the two trails meet and begin the downhill section.

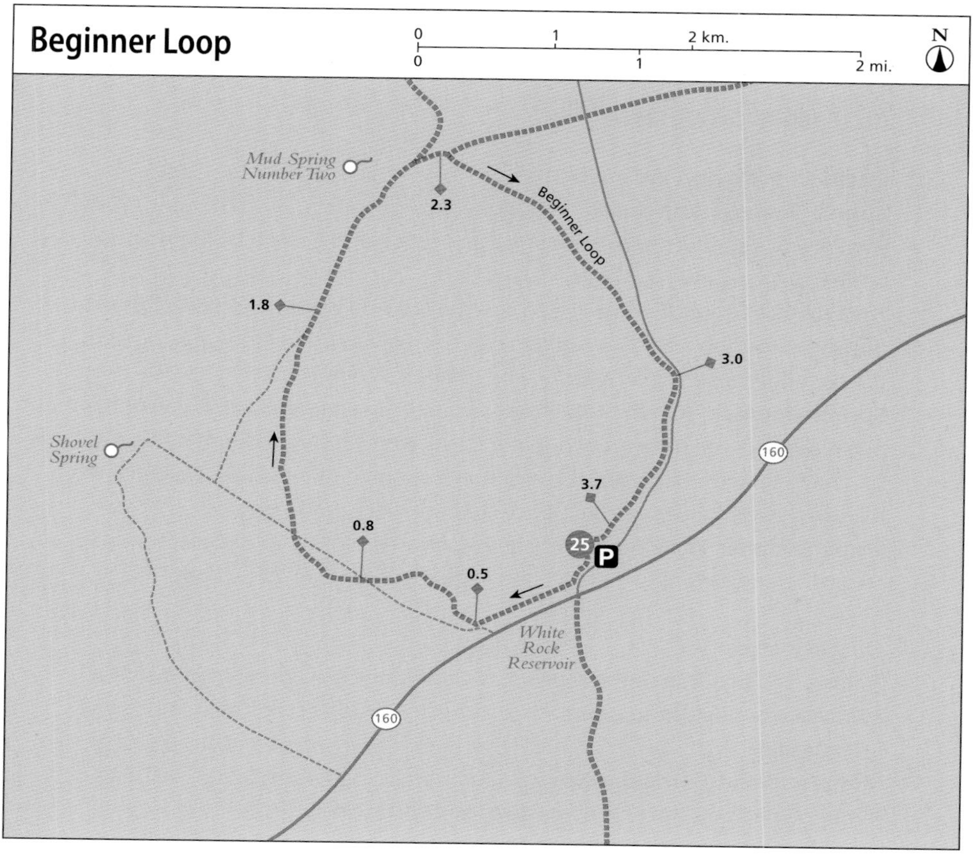

1.0 When the trail splits, stay on the main trail to the right and head down the drop. Follow the trail to the right after the drop.

1.1 Cross the dirt road a second time and continue straight into another drop. Take another short drop at mile 1.2.

1.8 Cross the dirt road and continue straight. Watch for the deep ruts.

2.3 Meet up with the dirt road and turn right. Follow the trail or the dirt road, and take the trail to the right at the trail marker.

2.4 Cross the remnants of a dirt road and stay straight. When the trail splits at mile 2.7, take the trail to the right.

3.0 Start the steeper section of the climb. In 0.2 mile, take the section with long rocks that kind of form stairs up to the dirt road. Stay to the right of the dirt road to meet back up with the trail at the trail marker.

3.7 Take the trail to the right and follow it to the trailhead. You can also take the trail straight to the parking lot.

3.8 Arrive back at the trailhead.

RIDE INFORMATION

Local Events and Attractions

Bonnie Springs Ranch: Visit an honest-to-goodness old-fashioned Wild West town, complete with hangings, shootouts, and an official Main Street; bonniesprings.com.

Horseback Riding: If you'd like to see the scenery of the Red Rock Canyon from atop four hooves, you can do so at the Cowboy Trail Rides, just outside the national conservation area; cowboytrailrides.com.

Spring Mountain Ranch State Park: Located close to Red Rock Canyon, this protected park was once a functioning ranch owned at various times by a movie star and a famous billionaire. It is also home to some of the oldest buildings in the valley and is one of the best places to bird-watch; parks.nv.gov.

Super Summer Theatre: Live theater is offered nightly under the summer stars at Spring Mountain Ranch State Park; supersummertheatre.org.

Restaurants

Bonnie Springs Ranch Restaurant: 1 Gunfighter Ln., Bonnie Springs; (702) 875-4400; bonniesprings.com. American-style food located next to Bonnie Springs Ranch.

Montana Meat Company: 9135 S. Durango Dr., Las Vegas; (702) 407-0362; montanameatco.com. American-style food and steaks.

Mountain Springs Saloon: 19050 US 160, Las Vegas; (702) 875-4266; mountainspringssaloon.com. Actually, the eating establishment BEHIND the Mountain Springs Saloon.

Restrooms

Mile 0.0: At the trailhead

26

The Mini Hurl Loop

This ride is a shorter version of the Hurl Loop, offering different views of Cottonwood Valley. The trail is a favorite of the many wild burros that live in the area, and it is not uncommon to find them walking down the trail on their way to Blue Diamond.

Start: Asphalt parking lot outside McGhie's Outpost

Length: 2.3 miles

Approximate riding time: 30 minutes to 1 hour

Best bike: Mountain bike

Terrain and trail surface: Mostly dirt, some large rocks, and loose gravel

Traffic and hazards: These trails are only open to human power and are mostly used by mountain bikers. However, hikers, runners, and equestrians also use the trail, and it is best to be courteous and give way to them when encountered.

Things to see: Desert plants and animals, wild burros

Getting there: **By car:** Take I-15 to the Blue Diamond exit. Head west along Blue Diamond Road (SR 160). Turn right onto SR 159 and follow the road to the town of Blue Diamond. Turn left onto Castalia Street and head to the asphalt parking lot outside McGhie's Outpost. **GPS:** N36 02.835' / W115 24.443'

THE RIDE

This trail is a shorter version of another trail called the Hurl. As you might guess by its name, the Hurl is a much more difficult trail, requiring more advanced mountain bike skills. The Mini Hurl has some difficult areas, but the trail can be ridden by those with either beginner or advanced skills. The trail also offers views of some interesting rock formations, as it follows a natural wash up into the hills.

This trail is also a favorite of the wild burros who populate the area, and it is not uncommon to see them on the trail. If you do see one, or a group, of these animals, make sure to give them the right-of-way. If they are on the trail, it is best to get off your bike and walk past them. Being off the bike will make you smaller and you'll appear as less of a threat. For the most part, the burros will leave you alone. Unfortunately many people feed them, although it is illegal to do so. This may cause the burros to approach you looking for food, but they will generally avoid you.

Like all wild animals, burros are best viewed from a distance. They have strong teeth and equally strong rear legs. If they bray at you, it's best to put some space between you and them, as most brays are warnings not to approach. The burros, like the residents of Blue Diamond, are used to mountain bikers, so they usually just turn and stare at you. They also like to have their pictures taken, so you may want to bring a camera.

From the parking lot, pull out onto Castalia Street and turn left, heading to Cottonwood Drive. Turn left again and follow Cottonwood Drive up the hill. A right turn on Cerrito Street will lead you to the trailhead at the top of the hill. Cerrito Street is a bit of a climb, and you'll know you've found the trailhead when the asphalt turns to dirt. There will also be several large rocks at the trailhead, which are meant to deter motorized vehicles from going on the trail.

When you reach the trailhead, you'll find a bit of a drop with a fairly steep but short climb on the other side. Once up that side, the trail splits. Take the trail to the right and begin a gradual climb up into the hills behind the town of Blue Diamond. As you climb the hill, there is an offshoot trail to the right and then to the left. Do not take either of these two trails. At the end of the loop, when you come down the hill, you'll be on the trail to the left.

About a half mile into the ride, the trail crosses the wash. Follow the trail into the wash and then into the short but steep climb up the other side. You'll now be on the opposite side of the wash. Follow the trail as it makes its way up a rock ledge. This is a tricky section, and riders with a lower skill level may want to walk it. Once you reach the top of the ledge, you'll find a convergence of trails. Take the trail to the left and follow it as it crosses the ledge and makes a gradual climb. As you cross the ledge, stay straight. Do not take the trail to the right that climbs the steep hill.

Bike Shop

McGhie's Bike Outpost: 16 Cottonwood, #B, Blue Diamond; (702) 875-4820; mcghies.com. Rents mountain bikes and gives guided tours of the trails in Cottonwood.

A tricky rock section of the Mini Hurl Loop

Once you cross the ledge, the trail starts to climb before starting a downhill section. Follow the trail through these sections. The downhill section is a bit rocky, but it is a fun little section and comes right before a steep climb. Follow the trail as it makes the climb. When you come to a spot where several trails meet, take the trail to the left and head downhill. At the end of the downhill section, the trail begins a gradual climb to the original trail. Follow the trail until it dead-ends at the original trail, then turn right and follow the trail down to the large drop. Take the drop, and at the trailhead, take the asphalt road to the left—Cerrito Street. Turn left on Allegro Street and follow it until it turns into Cottonwood Drive. Take Cottonwood Drive back to the parking lot, turning right on Castalia Street and then immediately right into the parking lot.

MILES AND DIRECTIONS

0.0 Park in the asphalt lot outside McGhie's Outpost. Ride out onto Castalia Street and turn left. Turn left again onto Cottonwood Drive and follow that street.

0.2 Turn right onto Cerrito Street and climb the hill. In 0.1 mile, take the trailhead to the right in the gravel area. The area is marked by large boulders and a trail marker.

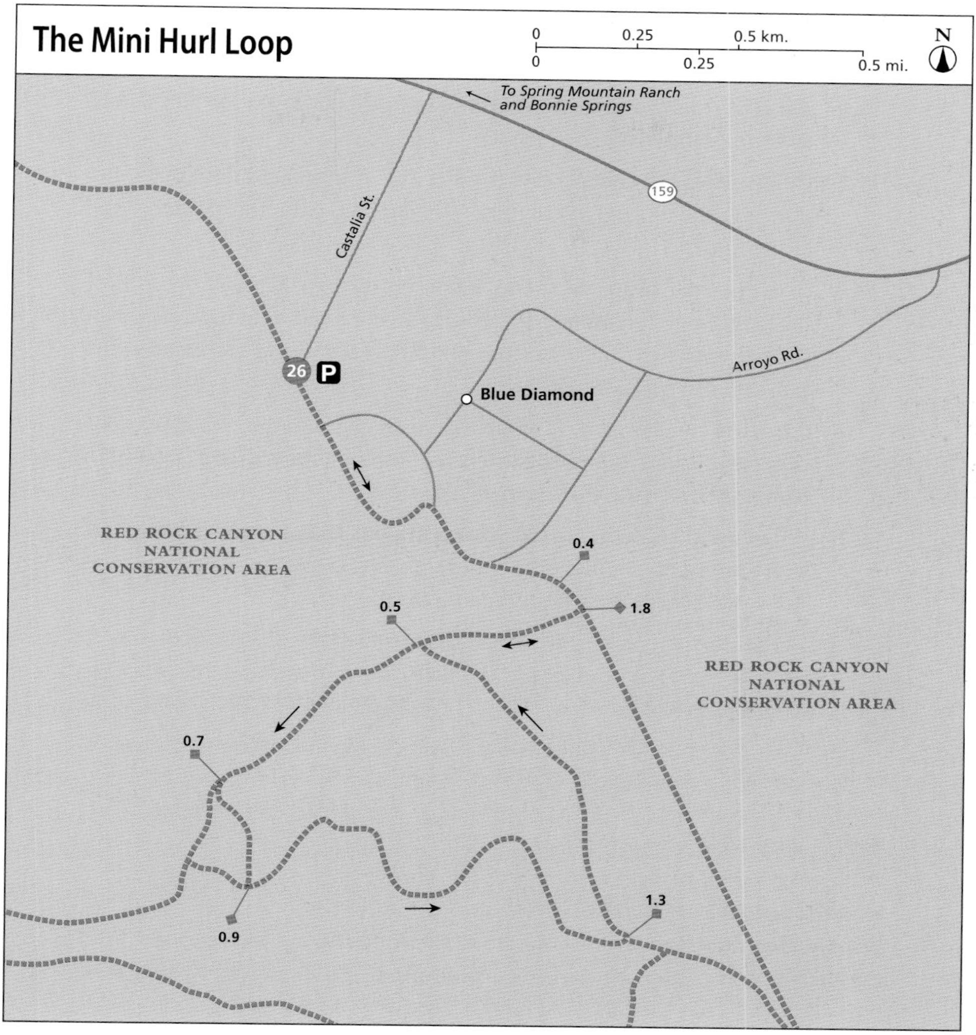

0.4 The trail splits. Take either route into the drop and make the small climb up the other side, then take the trail to the right.

0.5 Stay straight; do not take the offshoot trail to the right or the trail to the left a little farther ahead. In 0.1 mile, follow the trail to the right and take the drop into the wash. Cross the wash and make the short but steep climb up the ridge.

0.7 Go up the tricky rock ledge and follow the trail to the left. When the trail splits at mile 0.8, stay to the left and continue the climb.

0.9 When the trail dead-ends at another trail, turn left and follow the trail down into the valley. This section is a bit tricky, as the trail is filled with large rocks.

1.0 Take the small drop, then follow the trail as it curves to the left. This is the end of the tricky rock section.

1.1 Follow the trail as it curves to the left. This is a fun little downhill section. Begin a steep climb at mile 1.2, then follow the trail as it curves to the right.

1.3 Take the small drop and then the short but steep climb. At the top of the climb, turn left when the trails meet and head downward toward the natural wash. At the bottom of the trail are two large boulders that create a tricky rock obstacle.

1.6 Cross the small wash and begin a gradual climb to the trail you took originally. When the trail dead-ends at the original trail at 1.7 miles, turn right and head down to the large drop.

1.8 When the trails meet, go left, taking the quick drop and then the short but steep climb on the other side. Either trail on the other side will work. Follow the trail as it curves to the left.

1.9 At the trailhead, take the asphalt road to the left—Cerrito Street. In 0.1 mile, turn left on Allegro Street and follow it until it turns into Cottonwood Drive.

2.3 Take a right onto Castalia Street and then another immediate right into the parking lot.

RIDE INFORMATION

Local Events and Attractions

Bonnie Springs Ranch: Visit an honest-to-goodness old-fashioned Wild West town, complete with hangings, shootouts, and an official Main Street; bonniesprings.com.

Spring Mountain Ranch State Park: Located close to Red Rock Canyon, this protected park was once a functioning ranch owned at various times by a movie star and a famous billionaire. It is also home to some of the oldest buildings in the valley and is one of the best places to bird-watch; parks.nv.gov.

Restaurants

Bonnie Springs Ranch Restaurant: 1 Gunfighter Ln., Bonnie Springs; (702) 875-4400; bonniesprings.com. American-style food located next to Bonnie Springs Ranch.

Mountain Springs Saloon: 19050 US 160, Las Vegas; (702) 875-4266; mountainspringssaloon.com. Actually, the eating establishment BEHIND the Mountain Springs Saloon.

Restrooms

Mile 0.0: Next to park in Blue Diamond

27

Badger Pass/3 Mile Smile Loop

This trail has a downhill section that is so well-liked, it was given its own name. Of course, to be able to take that downhill section, you first have to make the gradual climb. Still, this climb offers great views of the Cottonwood Valley and the Red Rocks Escarpment, making it well worth the trip.

Start: Asphalt parking lot off SR 160

Length: 6.4 miles

Approximate riding time: 1 to 2.5 hours

Best bike: Mountain bike with suspension (either front or full)

Terrain and trail surface: Mostly dirt and loose gravel

Traffic and hazards: This is a singletrack trail that has large ruts in some places. The trail is open mainly to mountain bikes, but hikers and runners can also use it. However, it is not common to see anything other than mountain bikers, and maybe burros.

Things to see: Desert plants and animals, Red Rock Mountains, wild burros

Getting there: By car: Take SR 160 past the Red Rock Conservation Area turnoff (SR 159). Follow the road as it curves to the right and to the left. Look for the asphalt parking lot to the right of the road. The restroom is the only building in the area, so it is easy to spot. **GPS:** N36 00.674' / W115 25.879'

THE RIDE

This ride follows two trails, Badger Pass and 3 Mile Smile, to create an enjoyable, easily accessible loop. The trail starts from a paved parking lot on the north side of SR 160 and heads under SR 160 to the other side of the road. This version of the ride doesn't follow the entire Badger Pass Trail, mainly because taking the route as outlined in this guide offers easy access from the parking lot.

The ride starts on the southwest side of the parking lot. Here you'll find a small dirt trail that makes its way toward the asphalt road that leads to the parking lot. Cross the asphalt road and head into the wash towards the tunnels. Go through the tunnels, passing under SR 160. The tunnels are divided into three tubes, and the center tunnel is the one most commonly used; however, you can use any of the three. On the other side of the tunnel, follow the trail as it turns to the left and makes a quick but steep climb. Stay straight at the trail marker, cross the dirt road, and head up into the hills. There is a tricky rock section here.

After the rock section, follow the trail as it makes a gradual climb. While the climb levels out for a bit in certain spots, it is mostly a continuous gradual climb up into the hills. As you are climbing, be sure to pay attention to your surroundings. The Cottonwood Valley is full of all manner of interesting animals—of all shapes and sizes. You can easily find rabbits and lizards, but there are also many different types of birds and, if you're lucky, you might see a wild horse or burro. There are also snakes in this area that blend well into their surroundings. All of this can easily be missed if you pay too much attention to the trail and not enough to the desert around you.

Bike Shop

McGhie's Bike Outpost: 16 Cottonwood, #B, Blue Diamond; (702) 875-4820; mcghies.com. Mountain bike rentals and tours.

About 1.5 miles into the ride, the trail splits. Take the trail to the left. Stay straight a short distance ahead when the two trails meet up. The trail will split again at the marker not far up the trail. Stay left and continue the climb up into the hills. As the trail continues, it hugs the bottom of the hills to the right. When you reach this point, you are about a half mile from the end of the climb. Follow the trail as it snakes around the hills and makes a final, steep climb before heading into the downhill section.

Once you reach the downhill section, you're in for a fun, fast ride. This ride is so popular with mountain bike riders that it has its own name: the 3 Mile Smile. As the name suggests, the downhill section lasts about 3 miles and is designed to make the rider smile. The downhill section starts at the top of the hill where there is a convergence of trails. Stay straight, not taking the trail to the left or the right.

Shortly after you start the downhill section, you'll enter a series of switchbacks that can be tricky due to tight turns at the end of each switchback. Stay straight at the bottom of the switchbacks. Do not take the trail to the left. Follow the trail across a rocky wash as it makes its way up to a dirt parking lot. Pick up the trail directly ahead on the other side of the dirt lot and follow it

The Badger Pass/3 Mile Smile Loop offers great views of the Cottonwood Valley.

across the wash. Here you'll have a bit of a gradual climb, but the trail will head downhill soon enough.

Stay straight when the two trails merge into one, and when the trail splits a short distance ahead, stay to the right. Two trails will merge again just ahead, so stay straight. When the trail nears some large rocks and a telephone pole, turn right and climb the rocks. Cross the dirt road and follow the trail to the left as it drops into the wash and heads toward the tunnels. Go through the middle tunnel, cross the asphalt road, and arrive back at the trailhead.

MILES AND DIRECTIONS

0.0 Park in the asphalt lot off SR 160. Take the trail at the southwest side of the parking lot and cross the asphalt road into the wash.

0.1 Enter the middle tunnel and cross under SR 160. Climb the cement embankment and follow the trail to the right. Follow the trail as it turns to the left in 0.1 mile and makes a quick but steep climb. Stay straight at the trail marker, cross the dirt road, and head up into the hills.

0.3 Navigate a tricky rock section and follow the trail as it begins a long, gradual climb. In 0.2 mile, cross a small gully and continue the climb.

Badger Pass/3 Mile Smile Loop

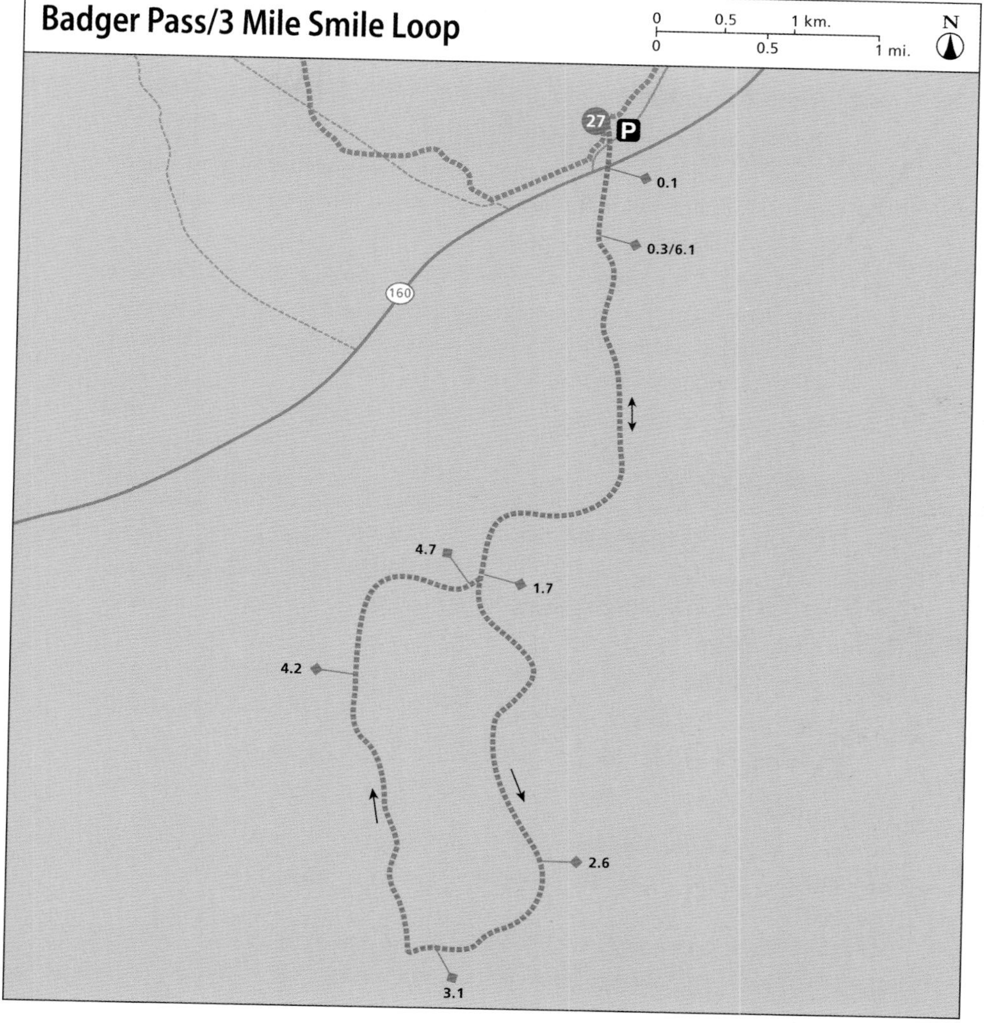

1.5 Take the trail to the left when the trail splits. Stay straight when the two trails meet in 0.1 mile.

1.7 Go left and start a climb when the trail splits at the trail marker. Take the small drop at mile 1.9 and short climb through some large rocks.

2.6 Follow the trail as it hugs the bottom of the hills on the right and then makes a steep climb up the hill. At the convergence of trails at mile 3.0, stay straight and begin the 3 Mile Smile downhill section.

3.1 Enter a series of switchbacks. At the bottom of the switchbacks in 0.3 mile, stay straight. Do not take the trail to the left.

4.0 Follow the trail straight across a rocky wash.

4.2 Follow the trail up to a dirt parking lot and pick up the trail on the opposite side of the lot at the trail marker. Cross the wash at mile 4.3.

4.7 Stay straight when the two trails merge, then stay to the right when the trails split in 0.1 mile. Stay straight when the two trails merge again at mile 4.9.

6.1 Turn right at the large rocks and telephone pole, and climb the rocks. Stay straight and cross the dirt road at mile 6.2, then follow the trail to the left as it drops into the wash. Go through the middle tunnel at mile 6.3 and cross the asphalt road.

6.4 Arrive back to the trailhead.

RIDE INFORMATION

Local Events and Attractions

Bonnie Springs Ranch: Visit an honest-to-goodness old-fashioned Wild West town, complete with hangings, shootouts, and an official Main Street; bonniesprings.com.

Horseback Riding: If you'd like to see the scenery of the Red Rock Canyon from atop four hooves, you can do so at the Cowboy Trail Rides, just outside the national conservation area; cowboytrailrides.com.

Restaurants

Bonnie Springs Ranch Restaurant: 1 Gunfighter Ln., Bonnie Springs; (702) 875-4400; bonniesprings.com. American-style food located next to Bonnie Springs Ranch.

Montana Meat Company: 9135 S. Durango Dr., Las Vegas; (702) 407-0362; montanameatco.com. American-style food and steaks.

Mountain Springs Saloon: 19050 US 160, Las Vegas; (702) 875-4266; mountainspringssaloon.com. Actually, the eating establishment BEHIND the Mountain Springs Saloon.

Restrooms

Mile 0.0: At the trailhead

28

Inner Loop

The Inner Loop is a great trail that gives you a taste of everything Cottonwood has to offer. Before the ride is over, you'll find you've been on just about every trail in the Cottonwood Valley.

Start: Asphalt parking lot outside McGhie's Outpost

Length: 9.7 miles

Approximate riding time: 2 to 2.5 hours

Best bike: Mountain bike

Terrain and trail surface: Mostly dirt, some large rocks, and loose gravel

Traffic and hazards: These trails are only open to human power and are mostly used by mountain bikers. However, hikers and runners also use the trail, and it is best to be courteous and give way to them when encountered. The cactus on parts of this ride are very close to the trail, so it is a good idea to have at least one spare tube and/or to use tubes with some type of flat repellant.

Things to see: Desert plants and animals, Red Rock Mountains, Joshua trees, wild burros

Getting there: By car: Take I-15 to the Blue Diamond exit. Head west along Blue Diamond Road (SR 160). Turn right onto SR 159 and follow the road to the town of Blue Diamond. Turn left onto Castalia Street and head to the asphalt parking lot outside McGhie's Outpost. **GPS:** N36 02.835' / W115 24.443'

THE RIDE

This trail is called the Inner Loop because it makes its way around Cottonwood Valley, for the most part staying in the valley and away from the hills, except, of course, when the trail meets up with the Landmine Loop. However, instead of making the many steep climbs associated with the Landmine Loop, you get to ride down those same trails.

From the parking lot, pull out onto Castalia Street and turn left, heading to Cottonwood Drive. Turn left again and follow Cottonwood Drive up the hill. A right turn on Cerrito Street will lead you to the trailhead at the top of the hill. Cerrito Street is a bit of a climb, and you'll know you've found the trailhead when the asphalt turns to dirt. There will also be several large rocks at the trailhead, which are meant to deter motorized vehicles from going on the trail.

When you reach the trailhead, you'll find a bit of a drop with a fairly steep but short climb on the other side. Once up that side, continue straight when the trail splits. As the trail progresses, it makes its way up a very long, very steep hill. There are many rocky spots, and some areas are covered with loose gravel. At the top, just to the left, is a collection of rocks that riders like to arrange into various shapes. One time it may form the outline of a rider on a mountain bike, and another time it may be formed into a large smiley face or a gigantic peace sign.

From here you'll continue on the trail as it makes its way around one of the hills outside Blue Diamond. This section is a welcome downhill after the rigorous climb you just completed. Be sure to look up into the hills as you travel, as it is a favorite spot for wild burros. When the trail splits a second time, follow it to the right. Shortly after that split, the trail will fork. You can take either trail because they meet up again a short distance ahead. The trail to the right climbs high into the hills, while the trail to the left follows the foot of those same hills. This guide follows the trail to the left.

Not long after you take that split to the left, there is a short but tricky drop. It is mainly rock, and inexperienced riders may want to walk this section. From here you follow the trail as it makes its way around the bottom of the hills. If you look to the left, you'll see a dirt parking area. Many riders choose to park there instead of Blue Diamond; however, the area is small, only holding five or six vehicles at a time. As you continue, you'll encounter a wash full of gravel. Cross the wash and make an immediate right turn, climbing up the small ridge. From here you'll follow the trail, being sure not to take any offshoot trails on either side of the main trail.

Bike Shop

McGhie's Bike Outpost: 16 Cottonwood, #B, Blue Diamond; (702) 875-4820; mcghies.com. Mountain bike rentals and tours.

Three riders make their way along the Inner Loop, heading back to the trailhead.

The trail climbs gradually through the desert, offering stunning views of the Red Rock Escarpment—which is the name of the multicolored mountains just to the west of the trail. You'll also ride right by some of the largest Joshua trees in the area. These trees are home to many birds, such as woodpeckers, who perch on the branches in search of grubs. At one point the trail makes its way back to the foot of the hills. Here you'll find a large gray rock that can be difficult to ride over. If you can't ride over it, walk your bike. Resist the temptation to ride around the rock on what looks like a trail. This is not an established trail and should not be used.

Shortly after the rock obstacle, you'll find another fork in the trail. Take the trail to the left and follow it as it climbs up into the hills. It only stays in the hills briefly before it heads back down into the valley, where it then makes a gradual climb as it heads toward Little Daytona. As the trail makes its way across the valley, take the time to notice the colorful Red Rock Mountains and the many desert plants and animals in the area. There are several offshoot trails, so make sure you stay on the main trail whenever you encounter one of them.

You'll cross a couple of dirt roads—usually the same dirt road—several times. The last time you cross a dirt road, you'll pick up the trail on the other side. Several trails converge in this area, so be sure you take the right trail. You'll know you are on the right trail because there will be a steep drop followed by an equally steep climb on the other side. This is the start of Little Daytona, a trail named for its fun twists, turns, and dips. This portion of the trail is a fun, easy ride, allowing you to go as fast as you feel comfortable.

Towards the end of this trail you'll encounter another dirt road. When you see the dirt road, look for the trail on the other side. It is marked by a trail marker—a long piece of brown plastic. Cross the road and take the trail on a downhill section that again allows you to go as fast as you feel comfortable. The trail will eventually make its way to another dirt road. Keep your momentum up and use it to make the short but steep climb up the hill to this dirt road. When the trail intersects the road at the top of the crest, you'll find a trail map on a kiosk and a large Joshua tree that is commonly used as a landmark.

Before you get to the crest of the dirt road, however, you'll see a trail on the other side. Take this trail, which is part of the Landmine Loop, and start a little downhill section through the valley. You'll be heading back towards where you started. After you climb to the top of a hill, you'll cross what looks like a rock bridge and start another downhill section. Towards the end of the downhill section, you'll cross a riverbed and come out on the other side through some bushes. Here you'll find a familiar fork in the road—the one you encountered near the beginning of the ride. Turn left and make your way back to the large gray rock obstacle. From here follow the trail back the way you initially came, eventually going down the long steep hill you navigated at the beginning of the ride.

At the trailhead, take the asphalt road to the left—Cerrito Street. In 0.1 mile, turn left on Allegro Street and follow it until it turns into Cottonwood Drive. Make a right onto Castalia Street and then another immediate right into the parking lot.

MILES AND DIRECTIONS

0.0 Park in the asphalt lot outside McGhie's Outpost. Ride out onto Castalia Street and turn left. Turn left again onto Cottonwood Drive and follow that street. At 0.2 mile, turn right onto Cerrito Street and climb the hill.

0.3 Take the trailhead to the right in the gravel area. The area is marked by large boulders and a trail marker.

0.4 The trail splits. Take either route into the drop and then make the small climb up the other side. Stay straight; do not take the offshoot trail to the right. At 0.5 mile, begin the long, steep climb up the hill.

Inner Loop

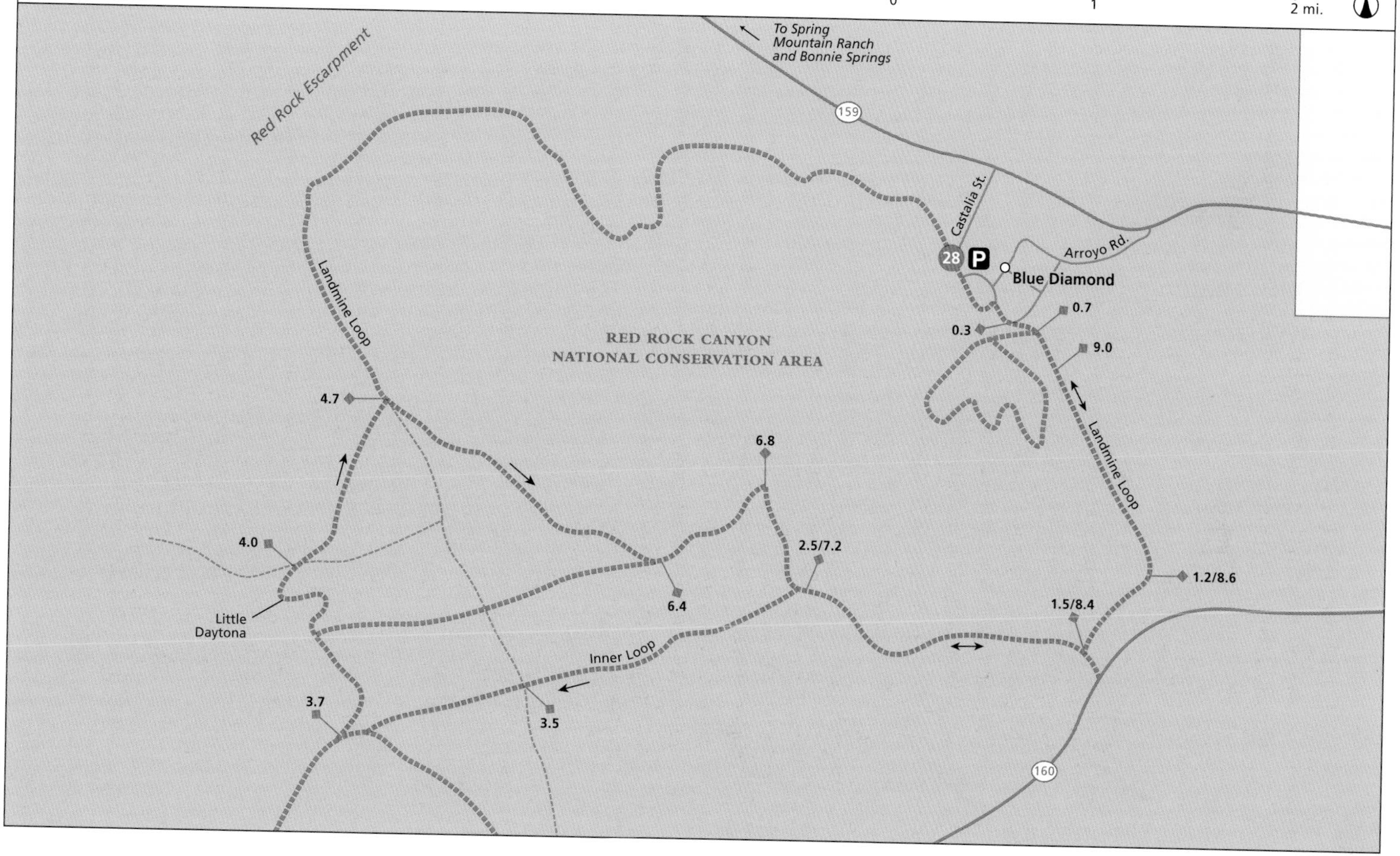
0 1 2 km.
0 1 2 mi.
N
To Spring Mountain Ranch and Bonnie Springs
159
Red Rock Escarpment
Castalia St.
28
P
Arroyo Rd.
Blue Diamond
0.7
0.3
9.0
RED ROCK CANYON
NATIONAL CONSERVATION AREA
Landmine Loop
4.7
6.8
Landmine Loop
4.0
2.5/7.2
1.2/8.6
6.4
1.5/8.4
Little Daytona
Inner Loop
3.7
3.5
160

0.7 At the top of the hill, stay straight. When the trail splits, take either trail for a short downhill section. The trails will meet back up ahead. Stay straight when another trail on the right merges with the main trail at mile 0.8.

1.2 Follow the trail to the right at the trail marker. When the trail forks, take the trail to the left.

1.3 The trail takes a short drop over some rocks. This obstacle is tricky and inexperienced riders may want to walk it. Stay straight as the upper trail merges with the lower trail at mile 1.4.

1.5 Enter the wash and make a sharp turn to the right on the other side. The wash is full of deep gravel. After making the sharp right, make the quick climb up the ridge.

1.6 The trail splits twice. Stay to the right each time. When the trail merges to the right, stay straight.

2.0 Follow the trail along the dry riverbed. Ride over the large gray rock at mile 2.4. Speed is needed to navigate this obstacle. Inexperienced riders may want to walk it.

2.5 When the trail forks, take the trail to the left and cross the riverbed. Follow the trail as it goes to the left and begins a climb. Be careful of the soft dirt on the climb. The trail will crest on a hill and then head back into the valley over a rock section.

2.7 The trail splits twice, first on the left and then on the right. Stay straight each time.

2.8 Stay straight as the trail splits again, following it to the right of the bushes and trail marker. Continue straight when the trail splits at mile 3.1 and climb the small hill.

3.5 Cross the dirt road and pick up the trail on the other side. You'll cross the same road in about a half mile.

3.7 Cross the dirt road a third time. Watch for cactus needles on this part of the trail.

4.0 Cross the wide dirt road and pick up the trail on the other side. The trail is not initially visible, but you will easily see it when you approach the drop. Do not take any of the other trails that seem to merge at this point. Follow the trail as it takes a steep drop and an equally steep climb on the other side.

4.2 Stay straight; do not take the trail to the left. Begin a fun, fast section with lots of turns and little drops. Stay straight when the trail splits at 4.4 miles; do not take the trail to the right. Take the small drop followed by a quick climb.

4.6 Follow the trail to the right, then climb the hill. Do not go straight when the trail seems to split. Stay to the right.

4.7 Cross the dirt road and pick up the trail on the other side at the trail marker. This begins a little downhill section.

5.3 Follow the trail as it turns to the left and meets up with a dirt road. Take the trail directly across the dirt road. This is the Landmine Loop. Stay straight at mile 5.4; do not take the trail to the left.

6.4 At the point where two trails cross, take the trail to the left and begin a short climb.

6.8 Cross the rock "bridge" and begin a downhill section.

7.2 Cross the riverbed and follow the trail through the bushes on the right. When the trail splits, go to the left. Go over the large gray rock at mile 7.3. Riders with less experience may want to walk this obstacle.

8.0 When the trail splits, stay to the right. In 0.2 mile, follow the trail to the left. Do not take either of the offshoot trails to the right. Follow the trail into a gravel section. Turn right, cross the gravel, and pick up the trail on the other side. Stay straight at mile 8.3; do not take the trail to the left.

8.4 Take the steep climb with large rocks. Riders with less experience may want to walk this obstacle. When the upper and lower trail meet at mile 8.5, stay straight.

8.6 Follow the trail as it goes to the left. The trail eventually joins the Old Spanish Trail at mile 8.8. At mile 8.9, stay to the right when the trail seems to split.

9.0 When the two trails meet, stay straight, then follow the trail to the right down the steep hill.

9.3 Stay straight; do not take the trail to the left. Take the quick drop and then the short but steep climb on the other side. Either trail on the other side will work. Follow the trail as it curves to the left.

9.4 At the trailhead, take the asphalt road to the left—Cerrito Street. In 0.1 mile, turn left on Allegro Street and follow it until it turns into Cottonwood Drive.

9.7 Make a right onto Castalia Street and then another immediate right into the parking lot.

RIDE INFORMATION

Local Events and Attractions

Bonnie Springs Ranch: Visit an honest-to-goodness old-fashioned Wild West town, complete with hangings, shootouts, and an official Main Street; bonniesprings.com.

Spring Mountain Ranch State Park: Located close to Red Rock Canyon, this protected park was once a functioning ranch owned at various times by a movie star and a famous billionaire. It is also home to some of the oldest buildings in the valley and is one of the best places to bird-watch; parks.nv.gov.

Restaurants

Bonnie Springs Ranch Restaurant: 1 Gunfighter Ln., Bonnie Springs; (702) 875-4400; bonniesprings.com. American-style food located next to Bonnie Springs Ranch.

Montana Meat Company: 9135 S. Durango Dr., Las Vegas; (702) 407-0362; montanameatco.com. American-style food and steaks.

Mountain Springs Saloon: 19050 US 160, Las Vegas; (702) 875-4266; mountainspringssaloon.com. Actually, the eating establishment BEHIND the Mountain Springs Saloon.

Restrooms

Mile 0.0: Next to park in Blue Diamond

North

The Mojave Desert is so much more colorful than many people realize.

The north area of the valley encompasses everything north of Sahara Avenue and includes what is actually the town of Las Vegas. What most people don't know about Las Vegas is that the town itself officially ends at Sahara Avenue. In fact, Las Vegas hasn't progressed much beyond the original boundaries established by brothers William A. and J. Ross Clark when they first sold lots in their newly established town site in 1905. Must of what people refer to as Las Vegas is actually unincorporated Clark County. This includes all those casinos on the famous Strip.

Many of the trails in this part of the valley follow washes or natural arroyos, making use of land that would otherwise not be used. Some of the trails also follow highways or snake their way around parks, detention basins, and even golf courses. On at least one of the trails in the north part of town, you're almost guaranteed to see wild horses, no matter what time of day you ride the trail. Several trails in this area are still under development, and there are plans to connect many of them, allowing cyclists to travel quite a distance around the valley without having to worry about cars.

29

Cold Creek

This trail offers some of the most scenic views of the Las Vegas desert and mountains, and, depending on the time of day you ride, the colors are spectacular. It is a favorite trail because it is one of the few places in the Las Vegas valley where you are just about guaranteed to see wild horses.

Start: Dirt parking lot at the end of the road to Lee Canyon

Length: 37.5 miles

Approximate riding time: 2.5 to 5 hours

Best bike: Road bike

Terrain and trail surface: Narrow asphalt road

Traffic and hazards: This is a narrow, paved road that leads to a housing community, hiking trails, and camping, all in the Spring Mountains National Recreation Area. There is a significant amount of vehicle traffic, and wild horses often walk alongside or on the road.

Things to see: Desert plants and animals, mountains, small ponds and streams, Joshua trees, wild horses

Getting there: **By car:** Take US 95 north to Lee Canyon Road. Park in the dirt lot at the entrance to the road on the right. **GPS:** N36 28.564' / W115 28.180'

THE RIDE

This trail follows Cold Creek Road to a housing community, hiking trails, and camping sites in the Spring Mountains National Recreation Area. The area, which is part of the Humboldt-Toiyabe National Forest, is one of the most scenic in the valley, offering amazing desert views about as far as the eye can see. Here the untouched desert is surrounded by mountains that cast some of the most interesting shadows in the morning and evening hours. The area is heavily populated with Joshua trees, along with several other varieties of desert plants—many of which flower at certain times of the year. This desert if full of colorful greens, yellows, and reds that all turn a rich golden brown as the sun begins to set.

Bike Shop

Southwest Bikes: 7290 W. Azure Dr., Ste. 110, Las Vegas; (702) 227-7433; southwestbikes.com

The ride is a favorite with locals for two reasons. First, although the area is only thirty minutes from Las Vegas, it is significantly cooler. The surrounding mountains are routinely covered with snow in the winter, and even in the summer, there can be a 30-degree difference between this cool desert climate and the hot Las Vegas temperatures. In fact, the farther you climb the road, the cooler the temperature becomes. This is because

Wild horses are plentiful along Cold Creek Road.

Wild Horses

One of the best parts of the Cold Creek ride are the wild horses that populate the area. These majestic animals roam freely and are beautiful to see, especially when running, heads held high, ears upright, manes flowing in the wind. In fact, there is no more iconic symbol of the American West than a horse roaming wild and free. About half the nation's population of wild horses is in Nevada, living on land managed by the Bureau of Land Management. They were originally brought to the valley by miners, ranchers, and missionaries, among others, during the settlement of the West. Left abandoned, the horses eventually became wild, living in groups—called bands—with one dominant stallion.

Wild horses come in many different colors, with some of the most common being sorrels, which are reddish; bays, which are red or brown with black points; and browns, which have black or brown bodies with light areas around the muzzle, eyes, flank, and inside upper legs. There are also palominos, appaloosas, and red roans, as well as the common blacks, whites, and grays.

As with all wild animals, horses are best viewed from a distance, and it is a federal offense to harass a wild horse. It is also illegal to feed a wild horse, and doing so can incur a significant fine. Unfortunately many people do not abide by this law and feed the horses when approached. You might think you are helping these beautiful animals by feeding them, but you're actually causing them harm for many reasons.

First and foremost, humans are not a reliable source of food. Horses can get used to humans supplying them food, but those humans are usually tourists who only feed the horses the one time they visit the area. Horses that rely on getting food from humans instead of finding food naturally in the area can find it difficult to survive when that source of food is depleted, such as when tourism is low. Additionally, some people tend to feed horses what they think is good for them instead of what actually is. Others just feed the horses whatever they have, including chips and candy. When visiting the area, it's great to see the horses, but please resist the temptation to feed them.

If you choose to camp in the area, Nevada state law prohibits you from camping within 300 feet of a spring or water hole. This is important because doing so can prevent a horse from approaching the life-sustaining water. For this reason, you should only camp in designated areas. For more information visit blm.gov/nv.

there is an almost 2,900-foot gain in elevation from the start of the road to the end.

The second reason is the wild horses. The 316,000 acres that make up the recreation area is home to hundreds of wild horses, and it is not at all uncommon to see them walking alongside or right in the middle of the road. For this reason, it is important to pay attention when riding this road. Not only will the horses not move out of your way, they also tend to leave small *presents* in the road that are not good to ride through.

The ride itself does require a certain amount of road-biking skill. The trip from the start of Cold Creek Road off US 95 is a continuous steep climb from start to finish. There is also no place to park at the beginning of the road. This means you have to park 5.5 miles south in a dirt lot at the entrance to Lee Canyon. You can't park at the entrance to Cold Creek Road because the Southern Desert Correctional Center is located there, eliminating any possible parking. You can, however, drive up Cold Creek Road and park at one of the entrances to the hiking trails. You can then ride down the road to US 95 and back up. However, the way it is mapped out in this guide is the preferred trail.

Start the ride by parking in the small dirt lot just to the right at the entrance to Lee Canyon, on Lee Canyon Road. Turn left and head to US 95, also called Veterans Memorial Highway. Turn left again and ride 5.5 miles to Cold Creek Road. From here you ride 13 miles up the narrow, paved road to the point where the hiking trails start. Once you are on the road, you don't get off it. This means you don't take any of the offshoot dirt roads that border Cold Creek Road.

There is a community of homes at the base of the mountain, and the ride typically stops where the homes begin. The nice thing about this ride is that going back is all downhill. This means you can turn around any time and head back to the trailhead if you don't want to complete the entire ride.

MILES AND DIRECTIONS

0.0 Park in the dirt lot at the entrance to Lee Canyon on Lee Canyon Road. Turn left on Lee Canyon Road and head toward the highway.

0.1 Cross US 95 and turn left. Ride north along the highway.

5.5 Turn left onto Cold Creek Road.

6.2 Pass the road to the Southern Desert Correctional Center on the left. In 0.3 mile, pass the Nevada Department of Corrections Training Academy on the right.

6.6 Pass the road to the Three Lakes Valley Conservation Camp on the left.

7.6 Pass the road to the High Desert State Prison on the right.

29

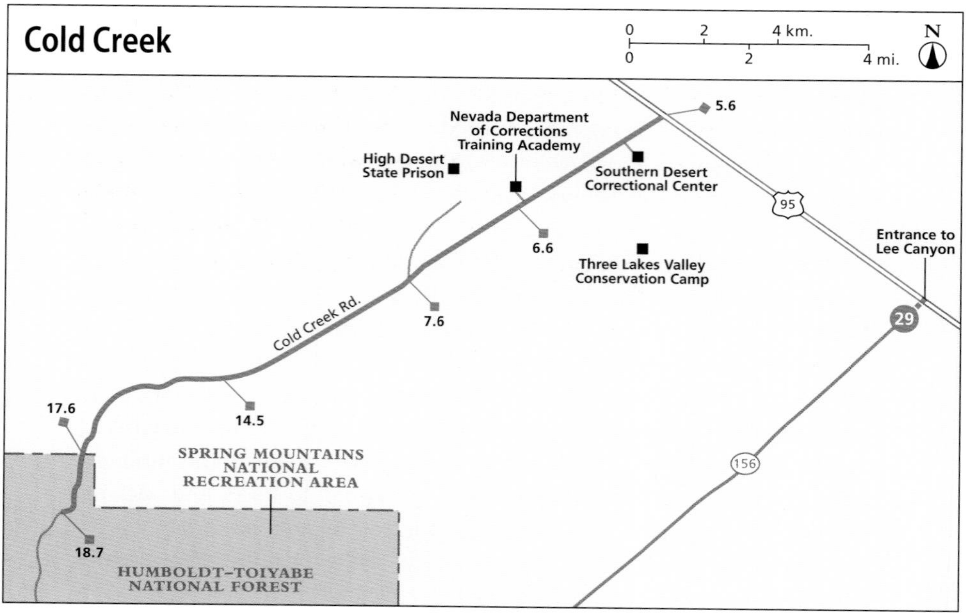

14.1 Pass an entrance to hiking trails on the right.

14.5 Pass an entrance to hiking trails on the left.

15.2 Pass an entrance to hiking trails on the left. In 0.1 mile the road dips, then pass the hiking trails on the left.

17.6 Enter Spring Mountains National Recreation Area and the Humboldt-Toiyabe National Forest.

18.7 Pass the hiking trails, then turn around and head back down Cold Creek Road.

31.9 Turn right on US 95 and ride south.

37.4 Turn right onto Lee Canyon Road.

37.5 Turn right and arrive back at the dirt lot.

RIDE INFORMATION

Local Events and Attractions

Spring Mountains National Recreation Area features several hiking trails. Some can be completed in a day, while others require an overnight commitment. There are also many picnic and camping sites in the 6.3 million acres that make up the Humboldt-Toiyabe National Forest—the largest national forest in the Lower 48. In addition, fishing opportunities abound in Trumbull and Angel Lakes, as well as the many streams in the area.

Restrooms

There are no restrooms on this ride.

30

Lone Mountain Trail

This trail is a nice ride that incorporates many different surfaces and several bridges as it makes its way through urban neighborhoods and parks. The metal bridges, which allow the rider to pass over busy streets, are decorated with artwork representing many of the desert animals and plants found in Nevada.

Start: Charlie Kellogg and Joe Zaher Sports Complex

Length: 9.5 miles

Approximate riding time: 1 to 2 hours

Best bike: Road or hybrid bike

Terrain and trail surface: Cement, asphalt, and partial street trail

Traffic and hazards: This is a multiuse trail that is used by people walking, running, and riding bikes. There are a couple of times when you'll have to ride on city streets or cross streets at crosswalks or lights.

Things to see: Parks and urban areas

Getting there: By car: Take US 95 to Summerlin Parkway. Exit at the Durango exit and turn onto N. Durango Drive. Turn right on W. Washington Avenue and enter the Charlie Kellogg and Joe Zaher Sports Complex. Park on the east end of the complex, around field 9. **GPS:** N36 10.826' / W115 15.919'

THE RIDE

This trail makes its way through urban areas and past several parks. The trailhead is a sports complex, and the turnaround is at a park. Between those two points, the trail snakes through housing communities and goes across two large metal bridges built specifically for the trail that allow you to cross over busy streets. These two bridges are decorated with metal artwork representing plants and animals—such as cactuses, coyotes, tortoises, and snakes—that are common to the desert environment. At certain times of the day, the metal artwork casts interesting shadows on the bridges, reflecting the plant or animal the artwork represents.

This isn't necessarily a scenic ride, but it is an enjoyable ride on a trail that is well-maintained and well-lit. The Lone Mountain theme is also represented at various places along the trail. The name of the trail is posted on the sides of both large bridges, and a mountain graphic appears on both signs and light posts. There are also maps posted on markers along the trail showing the trail itself and indicating where you are in relation to the trail at that marker.

The trailhead is a short distance from the Charlie Kellogg and Joe Zaher Sports Complex; however, the complex is the best place to park. The trail is accessed by following the asphalt path to the south side of the soccer fields. Going to the left of field 9 and turning right will take you to the back of the fields. Once you reach the back, or south side, of the fields, turn left and head east. Here you'll access the trail by entering the trailhead for the Bonanza Trail—which is a cement multipurpose trail. About a half mile down the trail, you'll come to the trailhead for the Lone Mountain Trail. While the trail is well-marked, it's easy to miss, mainly because it doesn't look like a trailhead. Look for a large cement marker on the right side of the trail, as well as a round brass marker embedded in the cement multipurpose trail.

At the trailhead turn left and cross what looks like a parking lot to the cement sidewalk just off to the left. Follow it north and cross W. Washington Avenue at the light, then continue on the trail as it passes Pioneer Park. As you go past Pioneer Park, you'll pass a small bridge on the left. This bridge leads to a housing community, so don't take it. You won't be confused because it is obvious that the trail continues straight.

After you pass Pioneer Park, cross Vegas Drive at the crosswalk. Turn left on the sidewalk and then turn right to meet back up with the trail. About a half mile up the trail, you'll find the first of the two large metal bridges. This bridge takes you across W. Lake Mead Boulevard. At the end of the bridge, turn left and then left again onto the asphalt road. Stay in the bike lane on the right and follow it along the Bettye Wilson Complex.

As the road turns to the right, you'll find a small bridge on the

Bike Shops

Peloton Sports: 911 N. Buffalo Dr., #101, Las Vegas; (702) 363-1991; pelotonsports.com
REI: 710 S. Rampart Blvd., Las Vegas; (702) 951-4488; rei.com
Sport Chalet: 8825 W. Charleston Blvd., Las Vegas; (702) 255-7570; sportchalet.com

Rider crossing the bridge over Lake Mead Boulevard on the Lone Mountain Trail

left. Take the bridge and then follow the asphalt trail to the right, going through the park. There is a sign marking the trail at the end of the bridge.

Follow the trail to W. Smoke Ranch Road and cross the road at the crosswalk. This crosswalk is a little strange. Instead of going straight across the street, the crosswalk turns you to the right before letting you cross a short distance down the street. Once you get across the street, turn left and pick up the trail again by turning right. Follow the trail north, crossing Peak Drive at the crosswalk. On the other side of the street, follow the wide asphalt road as it makes its way through Aloha Shores Park. Turn right on Ronemus Drive and follow the sidewalk to the second of the two large metal bridges. Take the bridge across W. Cheyenne Avenue.

At the end of the bridge, on the other side, take an immediate right and follow the cement trail north to Atwood Avenue. Here the trail is a little confusing. It looks like you should continue straight on Tioga Way; however, the trail doesn't actually go that way. Unfortunately the trail is not well-marked in this area, but it is easy enough to connect back up with the trail. Do this by turning right on Atwood Avenue and following Atwood down to Pioneer Way. Turn left on Pioneer Way and follow it north, passing Buckskin Basin Park. Cross W. Gowan Road at the crosswalk and meet back up with the Lone Mountain Trail, which is well-marked at Gowan.

Follow the trail as it rides along the Gowan North Detention Basin. At the end of the detention basin, cross the bridge and follow the asphalt trail to the right. The trail actually ends by following the cement offshoot to the left; however, the trail to the right is a bit longer and is well-lit—whereas the other trail is not. Just before the trail reaches Tenaya Way, at the bollards, turn around and follow the trail back to the trailhead.

MILES AND DIRECTIONS

0.0 Park at the Charlie Kellogg and Joe Zaher Sports Complex, near field 9. Ride to the back side of field 9 and turn left to find the trailhead for the Bonanza Trail. Ride through the tunnel at mile 0.1 and follow the trail to the right.

0.4 The Lone Mountain Trail starts at the marker. Turn left and head across the parking lot to the cement trail on the left. At 0.6 mile, cross W. Washington Avenue at the light and meet back up with the cement trail on the other side of the street.

0.9 Pass Pioneer Park on the right. Do not take the small bridge to the left.

1.1 Cross Vegas Drive at the crosswalk. Turn left, then meet back up with the trail on the right.

1.6 Take large metal bridge over W. Lake Mead Boulevard. At the end of the bridge, turn left and then left again onto the asphalt road. Stay in the bike lane on the right and follow it along the Bettye Wilson Complex.

1.9 Cross the small bridge on the left marked by a trail sign. Turn right after crossing the bridge and follow the asphalt trail north.

2.2 Cross W. Smoke Ranch Road at the crosswalk. Turn left and meet back up with the trail on the right. At 2.7 miles, cross Peak Drive at the crosswalk and follow the asphalt trail to the left.

3.0 Follow the asphalt road through Aloha Shores Park.

3.3 Turn right on Ronemus Drive. Take the sidewalk to the bridge and use it to cross W. Cheyenne Avenue. At the end of the bridge, take an immediate right to meet back up with the trail. At 3.5 miles, turn right on Atwood Avenue.

3.7 Turn left on Pioneer Way. In 0.1 mile, pass Buckskin Avenue and Buckskin Basin Park.

4.0 Cross W. Gowan Road at the crosswalk, then meet up with the marked trail on the other side.

Lone Mountain Trail

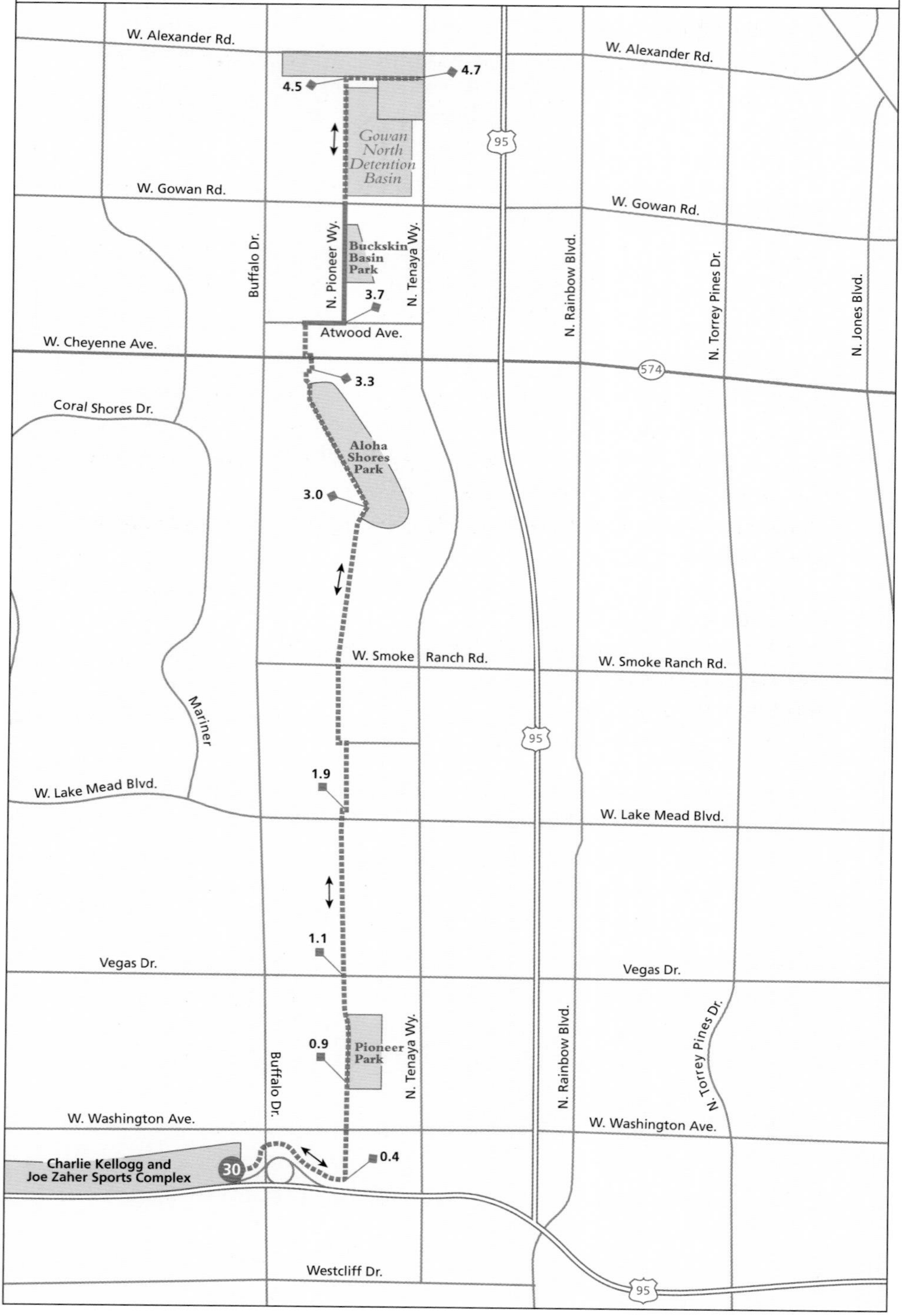
0
0.5
1 km.
0
0.5
1 mi.
N
W. Alexander Rd.
W. Alexander Rd.
4.5
4.7
Gowan North Detention Basin
95
W. Gowan Rd.
W. Gowan Rd.
Buffalo Dr.
N. Pioneer Wy.
Buckskin Basin Park
N. Tenaya Wy.
3.7
N. Rainbow Blvd.
N. Torrey Pines Dr.
N. Jones Blvd.
Atwood Ave.
W. Cheyenne Ave.
574
3.3
Coral Shores Dr.
Aloha Shores Park
3.0
W. Smoke Ranch Rd.
W. Smoke Ranch Rd.
Mariner
95
1.9
W. Lake Mead Blvd.
W. Lake Mead Blvd.
1.1
Vegas Dr.
Vegas Dr.
0.9
Pioneer Park
Buffalo Dr.
N. Tenaya Wy.
N. Rainbow Blvd.
N. Torrey Pines Dr.
W. Washington Ave.
W. Washington Ave.
Charlie Kellogg and Joe Zaher Sports Complex
30
0.4
Westcliff Dr.
95

4.5 Follow the trail over the small bridge and stay on the asphalt trail to the right.

4.7 Turn around and retrace your route to the sports complex.

9.5 Arrive back at the Charlie Kellogg and Joe Zaher Sports Complex.

RIDE INFORMATION

Local Events and Attractions

There are several parks along the trail, many of which have hiking trails, basketball courts, and/or children's play areas. You can also bring a packed lunch or dinner and have a picnic at any of the parks.

Restaurants

The Coffee Bean and Tea Leaf: 7291 W. Lake Mead Blvd., #110, Las Vegas; (702) 944-0030; coffeebean.com

The Cupcakery: 7175 W. Lake Mead Blvd., Las Vegas; (702) 835-0060; thecupcakery.com. Cupcakes—what more is there to say?

Viet Bistro: 7175 W. Lake Mead Blvd., #125, Las Vegas; (702) 463-0009. Traditional Vietnamese cuisine.

Restrooms

Mile 0.0: Charlie Kellogg and Joe Zaher Sports Complex
Mile 0.9: Pioneer Park
Mile 3.0: Aloha Shores Park
Mile 4.7: Wayne Bunker Family Park

31 Angel Park Trail

Angel Park is a golf course, and this trail runs alongside that course. One of the best parts of the ride is the numerous animals that hang out on the course, including rabbits, quail, and geese.

Start: Bruce Trent Park

Length: 5.5 miles

Approximate riding time: 1 to 2 hours

Best bike: Road or hybrid bike

Terrain and trail surface: Mostly asphalt trail with small patches of cement

Traffic and hazards: This is a multiuse trail that is used by people walking, running, and riding bikes. There are a couple of times when you'll have to ride on city streets or cross streets at crosswalks or lights.

Things to see: Park, golf course, desert animals

Getting there: By car: Take Summerlin Parkway to the Rampart exit. Turn onto N. Rampart Boulevard and follow the road to Bruce Trent Park on the corner of N. Rampart Boulevard and Vegas Drive. **GPS:** N36 11.408' / W115 17.432'

THE RIDE

The Angel Park Trail makes its way around the Angel Park Detention Basin towards the Angel Park Golf Course. The ride is mainly on a multiuse asphalt trail, but there are some times when you will have to ride on the sidewalk between sections of asphalt. The trail is well-maintained, and much of it is landscaped. The asphalt sections are lined with lamps, allowing you to ride both during the day and in the evening.

The trail is a favorite with runners, though cyclists use it as well. Be sure to be attentive and courteous when riding and move out of their way. As the trail gets closer to the golf course, many animals become visible, depending on the time of day you ride. The most common animals to see are rabbits. They run all over the golf course and around the detention basin. You can also see Canada geese, quail, and many other birds.

The trailhead, which is well-marked, is at Bruce Trent Park, just east of the parking lot. From here you follow an asphalt trail that winds its way around Angel Park Detention Basin until it reaches Durango Drive. Once you reach Durango Drive, ride south on the sidewalk as it passes over Summerlin Parkway. Before you get on the sidewalk, there is a trail to the right. Be sure not to take this trail, because it is not the Angel Park Trail and will take you in the wrong direction. Follow the sidewalk past the RTC bus depot. There is a parking lot to the north of the depot that is used by people who take advantage of the bus company's Park and Ride program. Large buses come in and out of this area, so it is a good idea to pay attention when riding past the depot.

Shortly after the bus depot, the asphalt trail picks up again on the right. Here you ride past a small park, called Angel Park, and across a nice bridge. Angel Park Golf Course also comes into view to the right. After you cross the bridge, the trail runs alongside the golf course for most of the rest of the ride. Follow the trail to Rampart Boulevard, making sure to stay to the left when the trail seems to split. The trail to the right goes into a tunnel under Rampart Boulevard, but it is the property of the golf course and is not open to the public.

Cross Rampart Boulevard at the light. Once you've crossed the street, turn right and follow the sidewalk down to the asphalt trail on the left. The start of the trail is well-marked and is easy to find. From here the trail climbs upward, alongside the golf course, until it ends at Alta Drive. Be sure to look out onto the golf course as you are riding to see the wildlife that likes to hang out on the fairways.

Bike Shops

Peloton Sports: 911 N. Buffalo Dr., #101, Las Vegas; (702) 363-1991; pelotonsports.com
REI: 710 S. Rampart Blvd., Las Vegas; (702) 951-4488; rei.com
Sport Chalet: 8825 W. Charleston Blvd., Las Vegas; (702) 255-7570; sportchalet.com

Angel Park Trail runs alongside Angel Park golf course.

At the end of the trail, you simply turn around and follow it back down. Be careful when going back down the trail. The climb is steeper than it looks, and it is fairly easy to build up a significant amount of speed when going back down. Remember there will be people running and walking on the trail, and a fast-moving bike can be very off-putting. A bell is helpful here to give notice you are approaching.

Neon to Nature

Neon to Nature is a Clark County program designed to help residents get moving, eat better, and live tobacco-free. The website—gethealthyclarkcounty.org—is an online tool designed to help residents find walking and bicycling trails throughout southern Nevada. Each listing includes information about the trail, a detailed map, and a description of the trail's location. The website also lists the difficulty rating of the trail, from easy to strenuous. Many trails, including the Angel Park Trail, are marked as being a Neon to Nature trail. The marking is placed in the trail itself, no matter if the surface is cement or asphalt, every quarter mile.

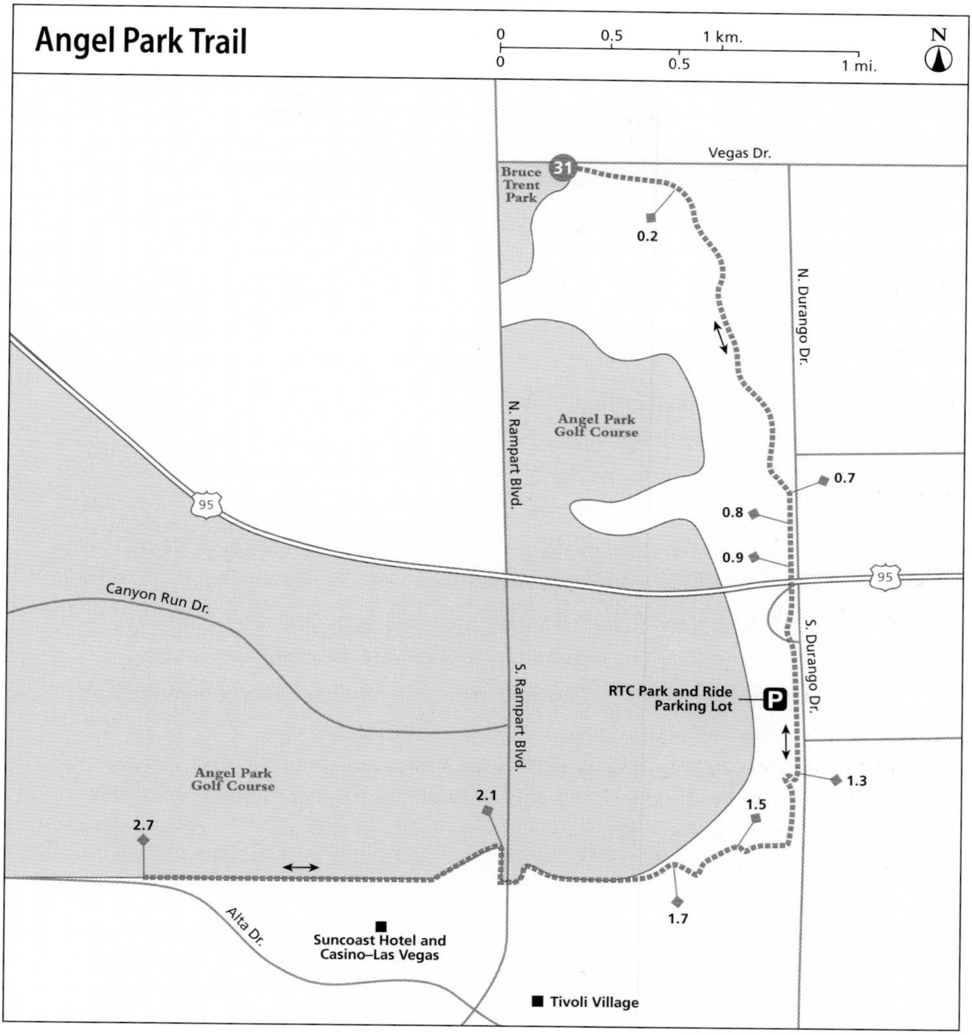

MILES AND DIRECTIONS

0.0 Park in the parking lot at Bruce Trent Park on the corner of Vegas Drive and N. Rampart Boulevard. The trailhead is east of the parking lot. In 0.1 mile, the trail turns from asphalt to cement for a brief time, but then turns back to asphalt.

0.2 Stay straight. Do not take the trail to the left.

0.7 Stay straight. Do not take the trail to the left.

0.8 Follow the trail onto the sidewalk. Turn right and head south. Do not take the trail off to the right.

0.9 Follow the sidewalk as it goes over Summerlin Parkway.

1.0 Cross the entrance to Summerlin Parkway at the crosswalk and follow the sidewalk past the small children's park on the right. In 0.1 mile, cross the entrance to the RTC Park and Ride parking lot.

1.2 Cross Westcliff Drive at the light, then cross the bus entrance to the RTC depot.

1.3 Take the marked asphalt trail to the right. There is a bit of a climb, followed by a curve to the left. Follow the trail to the right past Angel Park at mile 1.4. Do not take the offshoot cement trail to the left.

1.5 Cross the small bridge. Stay straight at mile 1.6. Do not take the cement trail to the left.

1.7 Follow the trail to the right. Do not take the offshoot trail to the left. Cross the long bridge and then start a climb alongside the golf course.

2.0 Cross Rampart Boulevard at the light. Once across the street, turn right and follow the sidewalk north.

2.1 Turn left at the marked asphalt trail. Follow the trail as it climbs between the golf course and the Suncoast Hotel and Casino.

2.7 The trail ends at Alta Drive. Turn around and head back down the trail to the trailhead.

5.5 Arrive back at the trailhead at Bruce Trent Park.

RIDE INFORMATION

Local Events and Attractions

There are several small parks along the trail and an exercise area. Shopping and dining can be found at nearby Tivoli Village and Boca Park.

Restaurants

Embers Grill + Spirits: 740 S. Rampart Blvd., #7, Las Vegas; (702) 778-2160; emberslasvegas.com

Grimaldi's Pizzeria: 7155 S. Rainbow Blvd., Las Vegas; (702) 207-6757; grimaldispizzeria.com

Pizza Lounge: 420 S. Rampart Blvd., Las Vegas; (702) 778-0400; pizzalounges.com

Restrooms

Mile 0.0: Bruce Trent Park

32

Lower Las Vegas Wash Trail

This is one of the many trails that follow a wash as it winds its way through the valley. The trail makes its way to a park that got its start as a working ranch.

Start: Commercial center parking lot off Decatur Boulevard

Length: 13.1 miles

Approximate riding time: 1.5 to 2 hours

Best bike: Road or hybrid bike

Terrain and trail surface: Asphalt trail

Traffic and hazards: This is a multiuse trail that is used by people walking, running, and riding bikes. There are a couple of times when you'll have to cross city streets at crosswalks or lights.

Things to see: Urban scenery

Getting there: By car: Take the Bruce Woodbury Beltway to the Decatur Boulevard exit. Turn south onto Decatur Boulevard and head to the commercial shopping center on the left. Turn left and park anywhere in the commercial center. **GPS:** N36 16.132' / W115 11.839'

THE RIDE

This ride follows a partially man-made, partially natural wash as it makes its way down towards a 170-acre park, considered the crown jewel of the North Las Vegas park system. The asphalt trail is downhill one way, with a gradual climb back to the trailhead. The well-landscaped trail passes through an urban area of North Las Vegas and is, for the most part, easy to follow. There are trail markers and covered benches at most street crossings, and in only one area does the trail turn and follow a sidewalk that doubles as a multipurpose trail. At a couple of places the trail passes cement portions that are imprinted with some of the reptiles and insects that can be found in the wash.

While the trail eventually makes its way to a power plant, I suggest that once you reach Craig Ranch Regional Park, you enjoy the park and then head back up the trail. The last part of the trail is not very scenic, and it requires you to ride on a fairly busy Las Vegas street that has no bike lane. This only takes about 2 miles off the trail, but it really isn't a part you'll miss.

Start the trail at the parking lot of the commercial center off Decatur Boulevard. Pull onto Decatur and turn right. Cross Tropical Parkway at the light and then cross Decatur Boulevard at the light. Follow Tropical Parkway to the trailhead, just past Valley Drive. The trailhead is on the left and is well-marked. Turn left and take the asphalt trail. Once on the trail you won't get off except to cross streets. Cross Willis Street at the crosswalk, then follow the trail and cross El Campo Grande Avenue at the crosswalk. Pick up the trail on the other side of the street to the left.

Cross Allen Lane and follow the trail to Ann Road. When the trail ends at Ann Road, turn left and cross Ann Road toward Ferrell Street. Cross Ferrell and pick up the trail on the left. At the end of the trail, turn right and head to Hammer Lane. Cross Simmons Street at the lighted crosswalk and pick up the trail on the other side and to the left. Follow the trail and cross Clayton Street at the lighted crosswalk. When the trail ends, turn right and follow what looks like a sidewalk but is really a continuation of the multipurpose trail, following Camino Al Norte. You'll know it is the correct way because you'll be able to see the lamp posts continuing to the right.

Cross La Madre Way, then cross Lone Mountain Road at the lighted crosswalk. Follow the crosswalk to the right and pick up the trail on the right. This is the entrance to Craig Ranch Regional Park. Follow the trail as it makes its way around the park. It is at this point that I would recommend turning and heading back. However, if you choose to finish the trail, follow it to N. Fifth Street and then down to Craig Road. Cross N. Fifth Street and then follow Craig Road—on the road—and pick up the trail down the road and to the right. Then follow the trail to the trailhead at E. Alexander Road.

The trail is a little confusing at this point, because a sign on the trail seems to indicate that it continues just across the street. This other trail makes its way down through North Las Vegas into Las Vegas. Unfortunately,

Bike Shop

Southwest Bikes: 7290 W. Azure Dr., Ste. 110, Las Vegas; (702) 227-7433; southwestbikes.com

A trail marker and covered bench along the Lower Las Vegas Wash Trail at Camino Al Norte

North Las Vegas calls this other trail Lower Las Vegas Wash, while Las Vegas calls it simply Las Vegas Wash. You can follow this other trail, which will add approximately 22 miles to the trip; however, the trail is not included in this guide because it is difficult to follow and is not well-marked in many areas.

MILES AND DIRECTIONS

0.0 Park in the parking lot of the commercial center off Decatur Boulevard. Follow the sidewalk up Decatur Boulevard. Turn right onto Decatur and head down to Tropical Parkway.

0.1 Cross Tropical Parkway at the light, then cross Decatur Boulevard at the light. Follow Tropical Parkway, crossing River Landing Street at 0.3 mile.

0.5 Cross Palmilla Street. In 0.2 mile, cross Valley Drive and pick up the asphalt trail ahead and to the right.

1.1 Turn left at the stop sign and cross Willis Street at the crosswalk, then cross El Campo Grande Avenue at the crosswalk and pick up the trail to the left. At mile 1.4, cross Allen Lane at the crosswalk.

Lower Las Vegas Wash Trail

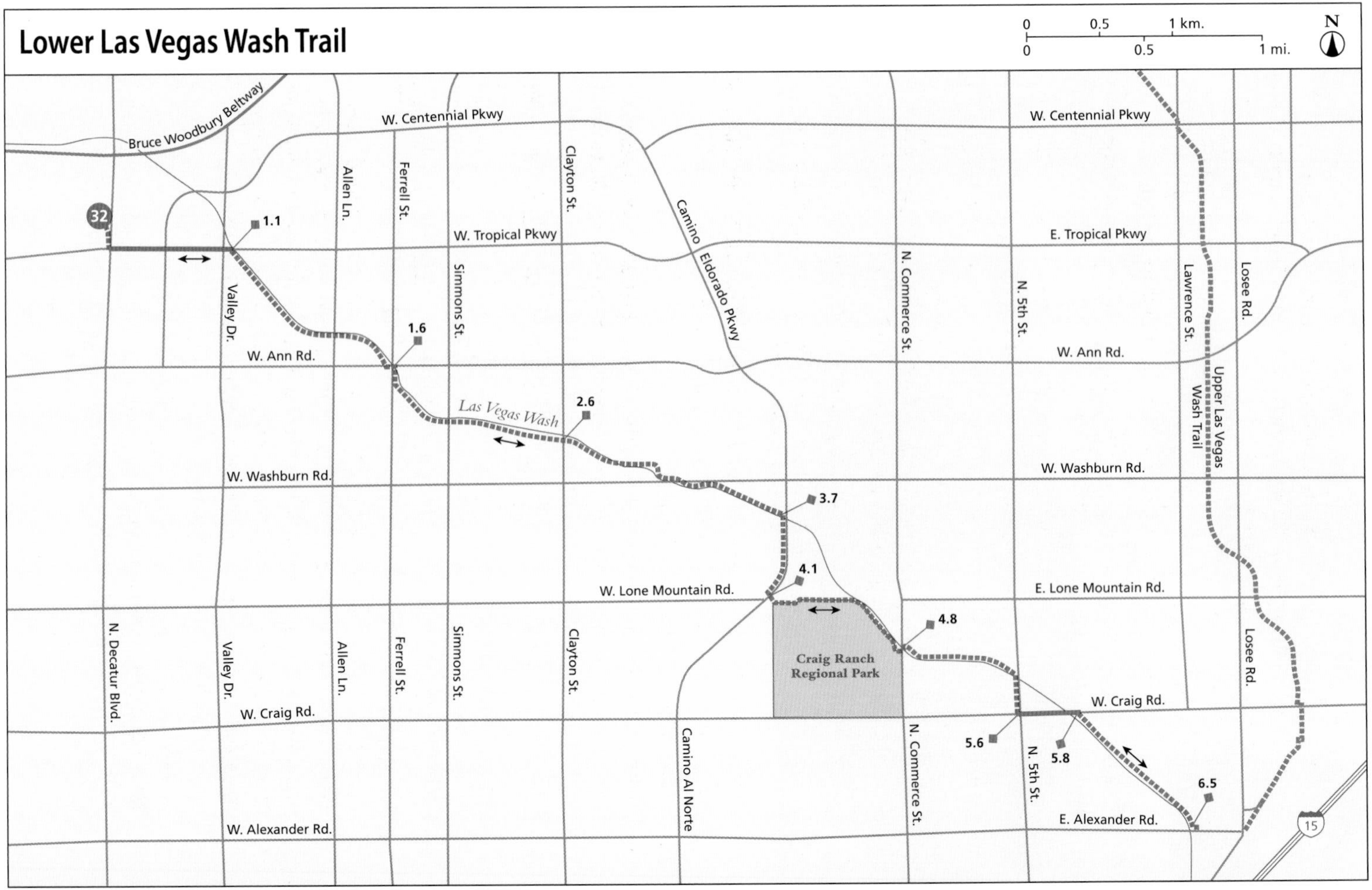

1.6 Turn left when the trail ends and head to Ferrell Street. Cross Ann Road at the lighted crosswalk, then cross Ferrell Street at mile 1.7 and pick up the trail on the left.

2.1 When the trail ends, turn right and head to Hammer Lane. Cross Simmons Street at the lighted crosswalk and pick up the trail to the left. Stay straight at mile 2.4; do not take the bridge to the left.

2.6 Cross Clayton Street at the lighted crosswalk. Stay straight at mile 2.9; do not take the bridge to the left.

3.7 Turn right when the trail ends and head up the sidewalk/multipurpose trail on Camino Al Norte. In 0.1 mile, cross La Madre Way.

4.1 Cross Lone Mountain Road at the lighted crosswalk. Follow the crosswalk to the right and pick up the trail on the right.

4.2 Cross the entrance to Craig Ranch Regional Park and then take the bridge to the right. Follow the trail around the park.

4.8 Take the trail to the left and cross Commerce Street.

5.1 Turn right and cross the bridge, then follow the trail to the left. At 5.4 miles, follow the trail to the right.

5.6 Cross Craig Road at the lighted crosswalk, then cross N. Fifth Street at the light. Follow Craig Road, riding on the street.

5.8 Pick up the trail on the right.

6.5 Take the bridge to the left and then follow the trail to the trailhead on the right at the light. Turn around and retrace your route to the parking lot.

13.1 Dismount and follow the sidewalk up Decatur Boulevard to the parking lot.

RIDE INFORMATION

Local Events and Attractions

Craig Ranch Regional Park: Craig Ranch Regional Park is a 170-acre recreational area that includes a 5-acre dog park, 62 community garden plots, a water feature, a climbing wall for children, a pond, a 7-acre amphitheater, 2 baseball diamonds, 2 basketball courts, a sports plaza, 6 tennis courts, 4 sand volleyball courts, 2 playgrounds, and a skate park.

Restrooms

Mile 0.0: At the commercial plaza

Mile 4.2: Craig Ranch Regional Park

33

Upper Las Vegas Wash Trail

This is a short but nice trail that follows a wash as it winds its way down through the valley. The trail is well-landscaped and is dotted with covered benches and rest areas.

Start: Commercial center parking lot off N. Fifth Street before Deer Springs Way

Length: 8.8 miles

Approximate riding time: 45 minutes to 1 hour

Best bike: Road or hybrid bike

Terrain and trail surface: Asphalt trail

Traffic and hazards: This is a multiuse trail that is used by people walking, running, and riding bikes. There are a couple of times when you'll have to cross city streets at crosswalks or lights.

Things to see: Urban scenery

Getting there: **By car:** Take the Bruce Woodbury Beltway to the N. Fifth Street exit. Turn east on N. Fifth Street to W. Dorrell Lane. Turn right and park anywhere in the commercial center. **GPS:** N36 17.019' / W115 07.705'

THE RIDE

This easy, well-landscaped trail follows the Upper Las Vegas Wash as it makes its way down into the valley, eventually combining with the Las Vegas Wash as it makes its way to Lake Mead. Unlike many of the washes in the valley, this wash is completely man-made, meaning the entire wash is cement. Like the Lower Las Vegas Wash, there is no parking lot at the trailhead. Instead, you'll have to park in the commercial plaza off N. Fifth Street and then make your way down to the trailhead off Deer Springs Way.

From the commercial plaza, turn left on N. Fifth Street and follow it down to Deer Springs Way, then cross that street at the light. Follow Deer Springs Way to the trailhead about a half mile down the road, and pick up the asphalt trail on the right at the trail marker. At the stop sign, pull onto Lawrence Street and turn right. Cross Centennial Parkway at the light, then cross Lawrence Street and turn to the right to pick up the trail on the left. Pass the small park on the right and stay straight when the trails cross.

Bike Shop

Southwest Bikes: 7290 W. Azure Dr., Ste. 110, Las Vegas; (702) 227-7433; southwestbikes.com

Cross Tropical Parkway, Ann Road, and Washburn Road at the crosswalks, then take the bridge to cross Losee Road. Cross Lone Mountain Road and pick up the trail on the other side. At the stop sign, turn left and head toward Berg

One of the covered benches along the Upper Las Vegas Wash Trail

Street. Cross Craig Road with the light. Here the trail turns to cement. Take the bridge across the channel, then cross the road and follow the trail to the left as it follows Frehner Road. The trail ends at Losee Road where the North Las Vegas Fire Department Administration Building is located. Turn and head back up the trail.

As an alternative, you can cross Losee Road and follow the sidewalk/multipurpose trail along Alexander Road. Here you meet up with the trailheads for both the Las Vegas Wash Trail and the Lower Las Vegas Wash Trail. Both trails start at the corner of Arcata Way and Alexander Road. The Lower Las Vegas Wash trailhead is located at the bridge just off Arcata Way, whereas the Las Vegas Wash trailhead is located to the south of Alexander Road. These two trails are a little confusing because the trail off Alexander Road is called Las Vegas Wash by Las Vegas, but is called the Lower Las Vegas Wash by North Las Vegas. In fact, the sign at the trail marker labels the trail as the Lower Las Vegas Wash Trail. Most of the trail follows the Las Vegas Wash and is in Las Vegas—meaning their label is more commonly used. Taking this trail adds about 22 miles to your ride. The trail is not included in this guide because it is difficult to follow and is not well-marked in many areas.

MILES AND DIRECTIONS

0.0 Park in the parking lot of the commercial plaza off N. Fifth Street. Turn left out of the parking lot and head down to Deer Springs Way.

0.2 Cross Deer Springs Way at the light with the crosswalk and turn left. In 0.1 mile, cross Donna Street.

0.4 The trailhead to the Upper Las Vegas Wash on the right.

1.0 Pull onto Lawrence Street at the stop sign and turn right. Cross Centennial Parkway at the light, then cross Lawrence Street and turn right. Pick up the trail on the left.

1.1 Pass the small park on the right. Stay straight when the trails intersect at mile 1.6, then cross Tropical Parkway at the crosswalk.

2.1 Cross Ann Road at the crosswalk. In 0.5 mile, cross Washburn Road at the crosswalk.

2.9 Take the bridge over Losee Road. In 0.3 mile, cross Lone Mountain Road and pick up the trail on the other side of the street.

3.8 Turn left at the stop sign and head toward Berg Street, then cross Craig Road with the light. Here the trail turns to cement.

3.9 Take the bridge across the channel. In 0.4 mile, cross the access road and follow Frehner Road.

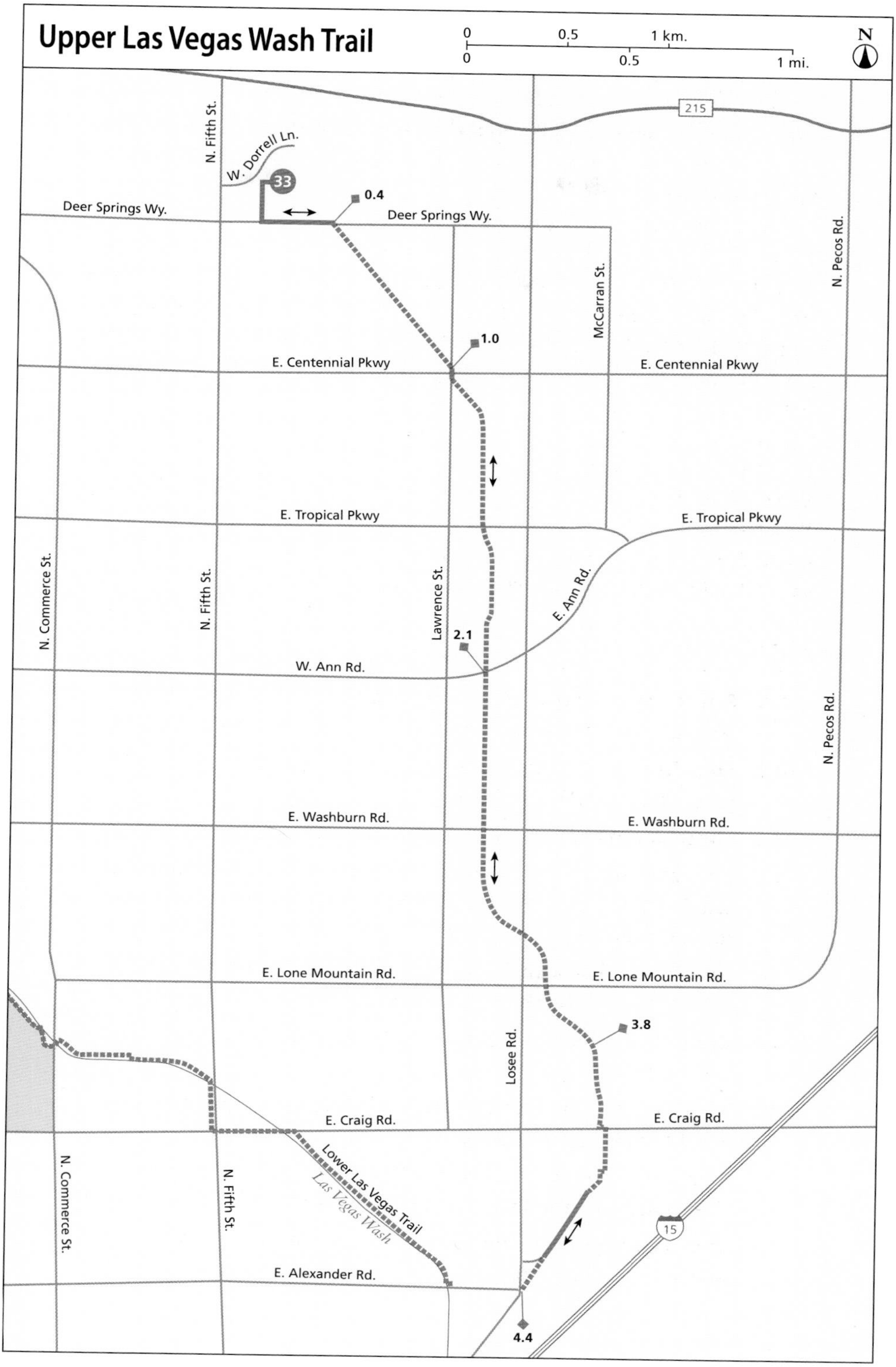
Upper Las Vegas Wash Trail
0
0.5
1 km.
0
0.5
1 mi.
N
215
N. Fifth St.
W. Dorrell Ln.
33
0.4
Deer Springs Wy.
Deer Springs Wy.
McCarran St.
N. Pecos Rd.
1.0
E. Centennial Pkwy
E. Centennial Pkwy
E. Tropical Pkwy
E. Tropical Pkwy
N. Commerce St.
N. Fifth St.
Lawrence St.
E. Ann Rd.
2.1
W. Ann Rd.
N. Pecos Rd.
E. Washburn Rd.
E. Washburn Rd.
E. Lone Mountain Rd.
E. Lone Mountain Rd.
3.8
Losee Rd.
E. Craig Rd.
E. Craig Rd.
N. Commerce St.
N. Fifth St.
Lower Las Vegas Trail
Las Vegas Wash
15
E. Alexander Rd.
4.4

4.4 The trail ends at Losee Road. Turn around and head back to the parking lot.

8.8 Turn into the commercial plaza and arrive at the parking lot.

RIDE INFORMATION

Local Events and Attractions

Broadacres Marketplace and Event Center: Located at 2930 N. Las Vegas Blvd., North Las Vegas, Broadacres is a 44-acre swap meet that features food, music, and retail spaces. It is open every Friday from 4 to 11 p.m. and Saturday and Sunday from 6 a.m. to 5 p.m. There is live music on Saturday and Sunday; broadacresmec.com.

Restrooms

Mile 0.0: At the commercial plaza

Western Beltway Trail

The Western Beltway Trail follows the Bruce Woodbury Beltway, with the beltway on one side and a mountain range on the other. The mountains have edges that look as if they were pushed up by some volcanic eruption, creating ramp-like shapes that might attract the likes of Evel Knievel. This fun trail is one of the most popular in all the valley, being heavily used on most weekends.

Start: Small park at the west end of Alexander Road

Length: 23.8 miles

Approximate riding time: 1 to 2 hours

Best bike: Road or hybrid bike

Terrain and trail surface: Asphalt trail

Traffic and hazards: This is a multiuse trail that is used by people walking, running, and riding bikes. There are a couple of times when you'll have to cross city streets at crosswalks or lights and other times when you get to ride under these streets.

Things to see: Desert scenery, the Las Vegas valley, Red Rock Mountains

Getting there: By car: Take the Bruce Woodbury Beltway to the Cheyenne Avenue exit. Turn west on Cheyenne and follow it to Cliff Shadows Parkway. Take Cliff Shadows Parkway to Alexander Road. Turn left on Alexander and follow it to the end. Park in the small park to the left. **GPS:** N36 13.917' / W115 20.023'

THE RIDE

Many of the rides in this book have great scenery, interesting views, or beautiful landscapes. The Western Beltway Trail doesn't really fall into any of those categories. Sure, the trail passes by the mountains that surround Las Vegas, and yes, you can get great views of the Las Vegas valley from the trail, but neither of these are the reason this trail is so well-used. Part of what makes the Western Beltway Trail so popular is that it is one of the few trails that run down the entire west side of the valley—from just above Cheyenne Avenue all the way down to Tropicana Avenue. It also has a limited number of road crossings, allowing riders to pass under busy streets at least three times and over them twice. But the main reason this trail is so popular is because it's just a fun ride.

Of course, like all fun things, there is a price to pay. The price of this ride comes during the first few miles with one of the longest climbs of all the trails in the valley. The climb is so long, there are no less than six resting spots along the left side of the trail. Don't worry, though: The trail is ADA compliant, meaning there are flat spots on all the climbs that allow you to catch your breath before you continue up the trail. Once you complete the climb, however, you are rewarded with a fun, easy downhill section that makes this one of the most fun trails in the valley. Of course, you'll have to ride up that trail on the

One of the two bridges along the Western Beltway Trail

way back, but it is more gradual than it feels going downhill. You can also simply take the trail only one way and avoid the climb back—but you'll have to figure out how to get back to your car.

The trail starts at a little park off Alexander Road. Turn right out of the park and take the bike lane to Cliff Shadows Parkway. Cross Cliff Shadows at the light and continue in the bike lane. Cross Rainwater Drive and then Alexander Road. Turn right on the sidewalk and follow it down to the trailhead on the left. Enter the asphalt trail just before the pedestrian bridge and follow it into the hairpin turn to the right. Follow the trail under the bridge and then to the right. From this point, except to cross some streets, you don't really get off the asphalt trail.

A little less than a mile into the trail, you'll start the long climb. About 1.5 miles into the ride, you'll meet Cliff Shadows Parkway again. Cross Cliff Shadows at the light with the crosswalk signal. Pick up the trail on the other side and continue the climb. As the climb progresses, you'll see several benches on the left side of the trail. Some are pointed towards the mountains, while others are pointed towards the Las Vegas valley. You may want to take the time to enjoy the scenery by resting on at least one of these benches during your climb.

When the climb seems to finally end, follow the trail across Lake Mead Boulevard. This portion of Lake Mead is not complete, so there are no lights or crosswalks; however, there are also no vehicles to worry about because they aren't allowed. Once you cross Lake Mead Boulevard, continue the climb another mile or so, then cross Summerlin Parkway, which, like Lake Mead, is not yet finished. After you cross Summerlin Parkway, you'll start the downhill section. About a mile down the trail you'll find a bridge. Cross the bridge, being sure not to take the offshoot trail to the right.

About 5.5 miles into the ride, the trail splits. Taking the trail to the right leads to Alta Drive; however, the trail to the left allows you to pass under Alta Drive and continue the ride without having to stop or worry about traffic. Follow the trail to Charleston Boulevard and cross it at the light with the lighted

Bike Shops

Las Vegas Cyclery: 10575 Discovery Dr., Las Vegas; (702) 596-2953; lasvegascyclery.com. Rents road bikes and sponsors group rides.
Southern Highlands Cyclery: 10550 Southern Highlands Pkwy., Ste. 130, Las Vegas; (702) 778-7786; southernhighlandscyclery.com
Vegas Bike Store: 3955 S. Durango, Ste. B-1, Las Vegas; (702) 586-5500; vegasbikestore.com. Sponsors bike rides.

crosswalk. When the trail ends at Summerlin Center, turn left and follow the sidewalk down, then cross Hughes Park Drive West at the crosswalk signal. Pick up the trail on the other side and follow it to Sahara Avenue. Cross Sahara at the light with the crosswalk.

When you get to Desert Inn Road, the trail splits just like it did at Alta. Take the trail to the left and go under Desert Inn. At Town Center Drive, take the trail to the right and use the bridge to cross Town Center. At Hualapai Way, take the trail to the left and cross under the street. This is the last place you get to go under the streets. From here on you'll have to cross all the streets at the light. The first of these streets is Flamingo Road. Cross Flamingo at the light and pick up the trail on the other side. When you get to the stop sign at Fort Apache Road, turn right and follow the sidewalk to the light at Peace Way. Cross Peace Way at the light with the crosswalk signal, then cross Fort Apache with the light. Pick up the asphalt trail on the other side of Fort Apache and follow it to Tropicana Avenue, which is the end of the trail, then turn and head back up.

MILES AND DIRECTIONS

0.0 Park in the parking lot at the small park off Alexander Road. Turn right out of the park and take the bike lane to Cliff Shadows Parkway. In 0.1 mile, pass Shawnee Ridge Street and Attleboro Park.

0.2 Cross Cliff Shadows Parkway at the light with the crosswalk, then continue straight in the bike lane. Continue straight in the bike lane at mile 0.3 (do not take the cement trail to the left), then cross Rain Water Drive.

0.4 Cross Alexander Road, turn right, and follow the sidewalk down to the trailhead.

0.5 Enter the asphalt trail on the left, right before the pedestrian bridge that crosses the Bruce Woodbury Beltway. Follow the trail as it takes a hairpin turn to the right.

0.6 Follow the trail under the bridge and then turn to the right. At mile 0.9, start the long climb.

1.3 Stay straight on the asphalt trail. Do not take the cement trail to the right.

1.5 Cross Cliff Shadows Parkway at the light with the crosswalk. Pick up the trail on the other side and continue the climb. The first of several benches is on the left side of the trail at mile 1.8.

2.6 End of the first section of the climb.

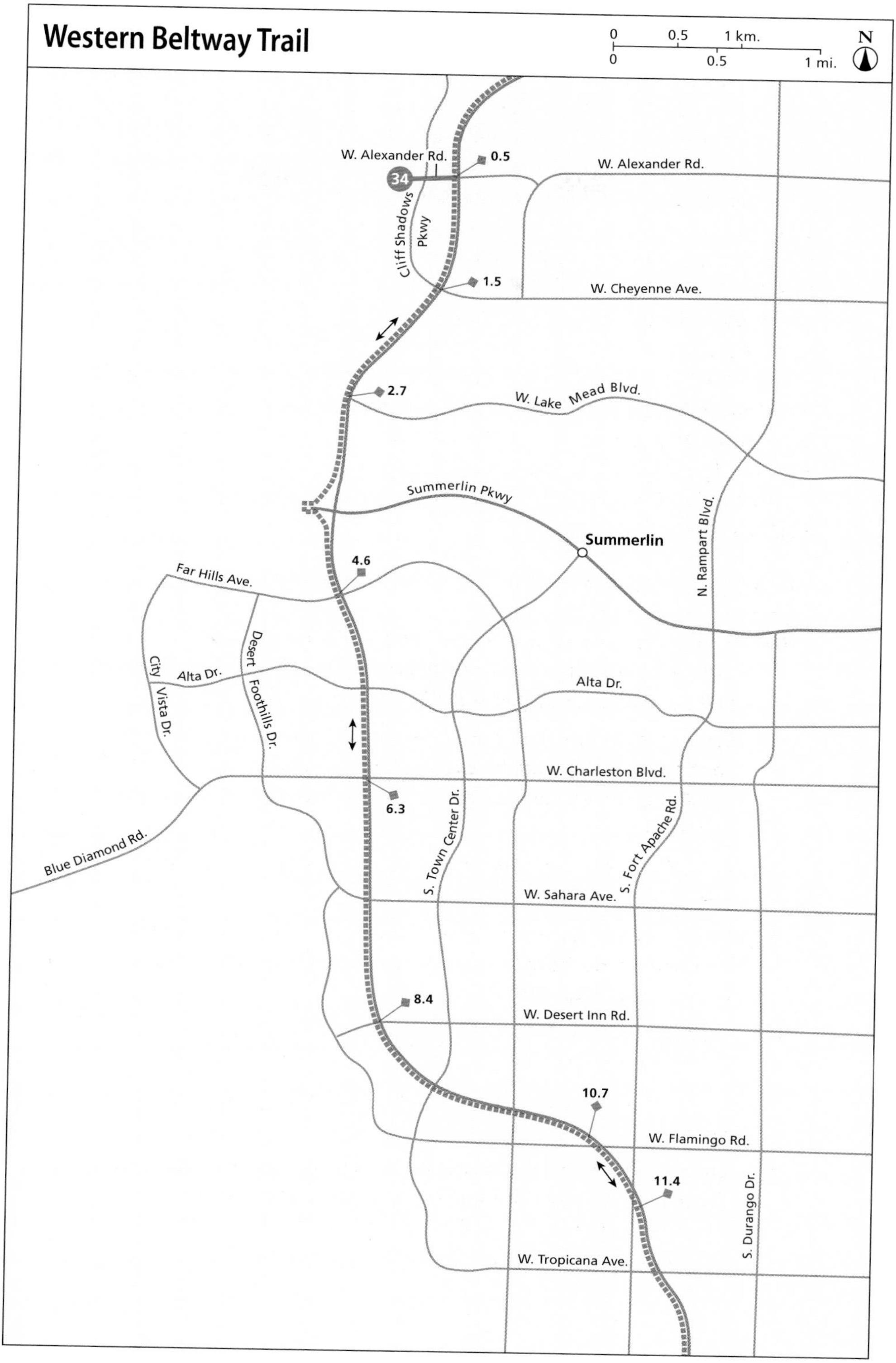

Western Beltway Trail
0 0.5 1 km.
0 0.5 1 mi.
N
W. Alexander Rd.
0.5
W. Alexander Rd.
34
Cliff Shadows Pkwy
1.5
W. Cheyenne Ave.
2.7
W. Lake Mead Blvd.
Summerlin Pkwy
Summerlin
N. Rampart Blvd.
4.6
Far Hills Ave.
Desert Foothills Dr.
City Vista Dr.
Alta Dr.
Alta Dr.
W. Charleston Blvd.
6.3
Blue Diamond Rd.
S. Town Center Dr.
S. Fort Apache Rd.
W. Sahara Ave.
8.4
W. Desert Inn Rd.
10.7
W. Flamingo Rd.
11.4
S. Durango Dr.
W. Tropicana Ave.

2.7 Follow the trail across Lake Mead Boulevard. The Red Rock Mountains start to come into view on the right.

3.8 Cross Summerlin Parkway and start the downhill portion of the ride.

4.6 Stay straight and take the bridge over Far Hills Avenue. Stay straight at mile 4.8; do not take the turn to the right.

5.4 Take the trail to the left and cross under Alta Drive.

6.3 Cross Charleston Boulevard at the light with the crosswalk signal.

6.6 Turn left when the trail ends at Summerlin Center Drive and follow the sidewalk down to Hughes Park Drive West. In 0.1 mile, cross Hughes Park Drive West at the crosswalk signal.

7.3 Cross Sahara Avenue at the light with the crosswalk signal. Do not take offshoot trail to the right at 7.6 miles.

8.4 Take the trail to the left and cross under Desert Inn Road.

9.2 Take the trail to the right and cross the bridge over Town Center Drive.

10.0 Take the trail to the left and go under Hualapai Way.

10.7 Stay straight at the stop sign. Go left at the light and cross Flamingo Road at the light with the crosswalk signal. Turn right at the stop sign at mile 11.3 and take the sidewalk to the light.

11.4 Cross Peace Way at the light with the crosswalk signal, then cross Fort Apache Road at the light with the crosswalk signal. Pick up the asphalt trail on the other side of Fort Apache Road to the right.

11.9 Arrive at the trailhead on Tropicana Avenue. Turn around and head back the way you came.

23.8 Arrive back at the small park off Alexander Road.

RIDE INFORMATION

Local Events and Attractions

Farmers Market: Held in Gardens Park, 10401 Garden Park Dr., this festival-type market features home-grown produce, local entertainment, and festive foods. Growers, gardeners, artists, crafters, and culinary artists are all featured. The event is held every Thursday night from 4 to 8 p.m.; summerlink.com.

Strawberry Festival: This strawberry-themed annual event, held in the Gardens Park every May, features various contests, such as a strawberry toss, a shortcake-eating contest, and a relay race; summerlink.com.

Restaurants

Islands Fine Burgers and Drinks: 10810 W. Charleston Blvd., Las Vegas; (702) 360-3845; islandsrestaurants.com. Island-style food located in Canyon Pointe shopping center.

Roadrunner Saloon: 9820 W. Flamingo Blvd., Las Vegas; (702) 243-5329; roadrunnersaloon.com/Flamingo.htm

Siena Italian Authentic Trattoria and Deli: 9500 W. Sahara Ave., Las Vegas; (702) 360-3358; sienaitalian.com

Restrooms

Mile 0.0: At the small park

Mile 1.5: At the gas station right off the trail

35

Pueblo Park Trail

This hidden trail is one of the most beautifully landscaped in all of Las Vegas. It is heavily used and populated by all manner of wildlife. This is one of the best places in the city to ride with the family.

Start: Bruce Trent Park

Length: 3.7 miles

Approximate riding time: 30 minutes to 1 hour

Best bike: Hybrid bike

Terrain and trail surface: Cement

Traffic and hazards: This is a multiuse trail that is heavily used by people walking their dogs and by families with children. At most times of the day there are a lot of people on the trail.

Things to see: Desert plants and animals, parks

Getting there: By car: Take Summerlin Parkway to the Rampart exit. Turn onto N. Rampart Boulevard and follow the road to the Bruce Trent Park on the corner of N. Rampart Boulevard and Vegas Drive. **GPS:** N36 11.408' / W115 17.432'

THE RIDE

Although this trail is one of the shortest in the guide, it is one of the best for families and for viewing wildlife. Las Vegas is a city that understands how to take an otherwise desolate area and turn it into something that can be used and appreciated by members of the community. The Pueblo Park Trail snakes its way through a functioning desert arroyo between communities. An arroyo is a natural wash, or a normally dry gulch, that can fill with water after sufficient rain. Instead of just leaving this area vacant between several existing communities, the city created a multiuse area complete with a biking/walking path, benches, picnic areas, a basketball court, and a couple of small parks. The area is also landscaped with desert trees and plants, making it an appealing home for many species of wildlife.

While this trail is beautifully landscaped and full of birds, rabbits, and lizards, it can be dangerous as well. Because it is constructed in an area meant to be a natural path for runoff water, the trail can quickly become flooded after a Las Vegas downpour. Rains in Las Vegas do not happen often, but when they do, large volumes of water are typically dumped in a short period of time. Ground that has been baked in the sun for months is not equipped to absorb large amounts of rainwater. This means when the rain falls, flash floods are common. When it rains in a desert arroyo, water doesn't just collect, it streams down the arroyo like a river, sweeping plants, rocks, sand, and debris in its path. This can pose a significant danger to anyone riding along the trail. For this reason, the Pueblo Park Trail should never be used during a rainstorm, even a small one. After it rains, some areas of the trail can become littered with small rocks, sand deposits, plants, and other types of debris. Parts of the trail can also become covered with water. Care should be taken whenever riding the trail after a rainstorm.

However, because it seldom rains in Las Vegas, the trail is available for use most of the year. The Pueblo Park Trail is really hidden. In fact, if you didn't know it was there, you'd pass right by it without seeing it. This does not stop the residents of the communities it borders from using the trail, and it is common to see many people on the trail at all times. For this reason, it is best to have a bell mounted on your handlebars. A bell is very useful in notifying people that you are approaching them. Voice signals, like telling people which side you are approaching from, are also helpful when riding this trail.

The trailhead is off N. Rampart Boulevard, just north of Vegas Drive. There is a large sign warning of the downhill slope that starts the trail. The slope is steep and turns quickly to the right before entering a tunnel that goes under N. Rampart Boulevard. On the other side of the tunnel, the trail splits. Stay straight and do not take the offshoot trail to the right. There are several of these offshoot trails, which serve as access points for the communities the trail borders. You will not be taking any of them.

From here the trail meanders downward through the desert

Bike Shops

Peloton Sports: 911 N. Buffalo Dr., #101, Las Vegas; (702) 363-1991; pelotonsports.com
REI: 710 S. Rampart Blvd., Las Vegas; (702) 951-4488; rei.com
Sport Chalet: 8825 W. Charleston Blvd., Las Vegas; (702) 255-7570; sportchalet.com

arroyo. Shortly down the trail there is a small outdoor exercise area to the right. Much of the trail is bordered by mesquite trees and it is easy to forget you are riding in the desert, let alone an area meant to be a natural water runoff. There are a couple of small parks along the trail. One of these has a basketball court and a children's play area, and the other has a large grassy area and picnic tables. Benches along the way allow for resting or just sitting and taking in the wildlife.

Starting from the N. Rampart Boulevard trailhead makes the ride a gradual slope downhill, meaning you'll have a slow, gradual climb back to the trailhead. However, you can also start the trail at the parking lot adjacent to the lower park. This can be accessed from W. Lake Mead Boulevard. If you start at this parking lot, you have a gradual climb upward, but an easy downward slope back to the lot. When you get to the lower park, take the trail as it turns to the right and makes its way around the grassy area back to the main trail. You can then turn right and follow the trail back to the N. Rampart Boulevard trailhead.

A young rider enjoys the Pueblo Park Trail.

Pueblo Park Trail

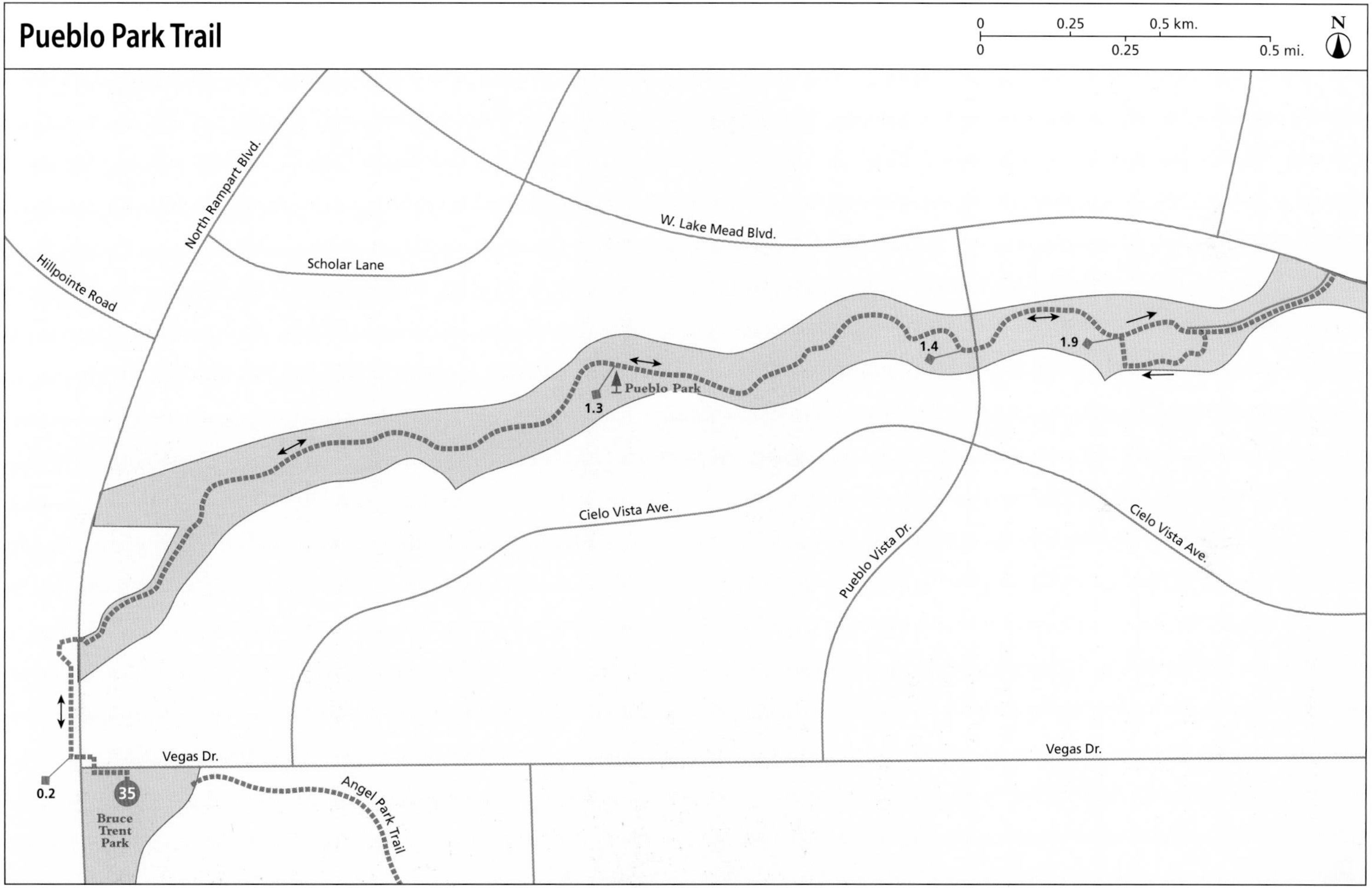

MILES AND DIRECTIONS

0.0 Park in the parking lot at Bruce Trent Park on the corner of Vegas Drive and N. Rampart Boulevard. Pull out of the parking lot and turn left on the sidewalk, then head to the intersection of Vegas Drive and N. Rampart. Cross Vegas Drive at the crosswalk, then cross N. Rampart Boulevard at the crosswalk. Turn right and follow the sidewalk north.

0.2 Take the trailhead to the left at the Caution Steep Grade sign. Follow the trail downward and to the right and go through the tunnel under N. Rampart Boulevard.

0.3 Follow the trail to the left; do not take the offshoot trail to the right. In 0.1 mile, pass a small exercise area to the right of the trail.

0.7 Continue straight; do not take the offshoot trail to the right. Also continue straight at miles 0.8, 0.9, and 1.2.

1.3 Pass Pueblo Park on the right.

1.4 Continue straight. Do not take the offshoot trail to the right or the next offshoot trail to the left. Follow the trail as it passes under the tunnel for Pueblo Vista Drive.

1.5 Continue straight. Do not take the offshoot trail to the left or the two offshoot trails that follow at miles 1.6 and 1.7.

1.8 Follow the trail as it turns to the right and loops back to the main trail through the grassy area.

1.9 Turn to the left and follow the trail back to the trailhead.

3.7 Arrive back at the Bruce Trent Park parking lot.

RIDE INFORMATION

Local Events and Attractions

There are several small parks along the trail and an exercise area. You can play basketball or visit the children's play area if you have brought kids on the ride. You can also bring a packed lunch or dinner and have a picnic.

Restrooms

Mile 0.0: Bruce Trent Park
Mile 1.8: Lower park on the trail

Honorable Mentions

A BOULDER HIGHWAY TRAIL

Start: Parking lot near Water Street
Length: 7.4 miles
Approximate riding time: 45 minutes to 1 hour
Best bike: Road or hybrid bike
Terrain and trail surface: Asphalt
Traffic and hazards: This is a multipurpose trail open only to walking, running, and biking. There are some intersections with traffic lights and some without.
Things to see: Wildlife, urban environments
Getting there: By car: Take US 95 to the Lake Mead exit. Head east on Lake Mead Parkway and turn left on Water Street. Pick up the trail at the end of Water Street. **GPS:** N36 02.876' / W114 59.326'

The Ride

When the construction of Hoover Dam was announced, the struggling town of Las Vegas celebrated. They got out the fire trucks and held an impromptu parade down Fremont Street. The celebration would soon be tempered when Secretary of the Interior Ray Lyman Wilbur announced he was building a company town to keep his workers away from the wild influences of alcohol, gambling, and prostitution that Las Vegas offered. Undaunted, Las Vegas built a road, connecting the town to Wilbur's Boulder City. The road became known as the Boulder Highway and still exists today.

As the name suggests, the Boulder Highway Trail follows this road originally created in the 1930s. It starts at the corner of Water Street and Boulder Highway and makes its way up to Equestrian Drive, where it crosses to the other side of the street. Once you cross the street, you can either go back down Boulder Highway on the other side or ride east to Magic Way before turning and heading back down. The trail passes one of the best museums in Las Vegas, the Clark County Museum. Be sure to take the time to visit this bit of Nevada history.

B LAKE MEAD PARKWAY TRAIL

Start: Fiesta Henderson parking lot
Length: 12 miles
Approximate riding time: 1 to 2 hours
Best bike: Road or hybrid bike
Terrain and trail surface: Asphalt
Traffic and hazards: This is a multipurpose trail open only to walking, running, and biking. There are some intersections with traffic lights and some without.
Things to see: Wildlife, urban environments
Getting there: By car: Take the Bruce Woodbury Beltway until it turns into Lake Mead Parkway. Turn right into the Fiesta Henderson parking lot. **GPS:** N36 02.051' / W115 00.691'

The Ride

Lake Mead Parkway is so named because it eventually leads to Lake Mead. While this trail does not go as far as the lake, it does connect with the River Mountains Loop, so you could take that trail and actually reach Lake Mead from this trail.

The Lake Mead Trail starts across the street from the Fiesta Henderson Hotel & Casino and can be reached by crossing Fiesta Henderson Boulevard. The trail actually starts closer to US 93, but there is no reason to go to the head of the trail. Once you cross the street, turn right and follow the asphalt trail. The trail passes through a well-landscaped section before heading into an urban area as it makes its way toward a community called Lake Las Vegas. When it meets up with the River Mountains Loop, turn and head back.

C COTTONWOOD CANYON TRAIL

Start: Off Pavilion Center Drive
Length: 2.8 miles
Approximate riding time: 25 to 35 minutes
Best bike: Road or hybrid bike
Terrain and trail surface: Cement

Traffic and hazards: This is a multiuse trail that is heavily used by people walking their dogs and by families with children.
Things to see: Desert plants and animals, parks
Getting there: By car: Take the Bruce Woodbury Beltway to the Charleston Boulevard exit. Turn east onto Charleston Boulevard then left at Canyon Pointe and park in the commercial parking lot. The trail can be found to the north of Costco off Pavilion Center Drive. **GPS:** N36 09.921' / W115 19.978'

The Ride

The Cottonwood Canyon Trail is another one of those trails that take advantage of a space that would otherwise be unused. It is located between several housing communities in a natural wash. This is a perfect trail for families because you don't have to cross any streets to get to the trail and once on it, you can avoid vehicles by accessing the tunnels that go under the streets. The trail is a fun one because it is really just a path that winds around the natural wash, with circular, curving, and, of course, straight portions.

D TROPICANA/FLAMINGO WASH TRAIL

Start: Off Hacienda Avenue
Length: 8.8 miles
Approximate riding time: 35 minutes to 1 hour
Best bike: Road or hybrid bike
Terrain and trail surface: Asphalt
Traffic and hazards: This is a multipurpose trail open only to walking, running, and biking. There are some intersections to cross.
Things to see: Urban scenery
Getting there: By car: Take the Bruce Woodbury Beltway to the Tropicana Avenue exit. Turn east onto Tropicana Avenue and left at Durango Drive. Park in the commercial lot across from Hacienda Avenue, then take Hacienda Avenue and pick up the trailhead on the right. **GPS:** N36 05.549' / W115 16.657'

The Ride

This trail isn't the most scenic, but it is an easy trail to follow and offers some nice views of the valley. The trail starts just off Hacienda Avenue and makes its way down to Russell Road, following a flood control canal and passing a golf course, high school, and large medical center. About halfway through the ride, the trail makes a giant U-shape along Dewey Drive. In this portion you'll have to leave the asphalt trail and ride on the street. Turn right on Timber Creek Street, left on Russell Road, left on Rainbow Boulevard, and right on Dewey Drive to form the U. The trail picks up again on Dewey Drive.

Rides at a Glance

ROAD AND TRAIL RIDES

Under 10 Miles

35. Pueblo Park Trail: 3.7 miles
3. Paseo Verde Trail: 5.0 miles
31. Angel Park Trail: 5.5 miles
8. Wetlands Park Trail: 6.2 miles
2. Pittman Wash Trail: 8.8 miles
33. Upper Las Vegas Wash Trail: 8.8 miles
4. Amargosa Trail: 9.5 miles
30. Lone Mountain Trail: 9.5 miles

10 to 30 Miles

1. St. Rose Parkway: 10.4 miles
20. Hoover Dam: 10.5 miles
7. Union Pacific Railroad Trail: 13.1 miles
32. Lower Las Vegas Wash Trail: 13.1 miles
21. Red Rock Scenic Loop: 14.6 miles
9. Outer Wetlands Trail: 20.2 miles
34. Western Beltway Trail: 23.8 mile

31 to 40 Miles

22. State Route 159: 32.4 miles
10. River Mountains Loop: 34.4 miles
29. Cold Creek: 37.5 miles

More Than 40 Miles

18. Valley of Fire: White Domes: 47.6 miles
11. Lakeshore/Northshore to Callville Bay: 53.2 miles
19. Valley of Fire: Overton: 63.8 miles

MOUNTAIN BIKE RIDES

Under 5 Miles

26. The Mini Hurl Loop: 2.3 miles
17. Inner Caldera Loop: 2.5 miles
13. Middle and Lower Lake View Loop: 2.7 miles
14. POW/Par None/IMBA Loop: 3.7 miles
15. Girl Scout/West Leg/Mother Loop: 3.7 miles
25. Beginner Loop: 3.8 miles
16. Caldera Loop: 4.3 miles
5. Anthem East Trail: 4.4 miles

Over 5 Miles

27. Badger Pass/3 Mile Smile Loop: 6.4 miles
12. Historic Railroad Trail: 7.5 miles
23. Landmine Loop: 7.7 miles
24. Landmine/Middle Fork Loop: 8.8 miles
28. Inner Loop: 9.7 miles
6. McCullough Hills Trail: 14.8 miles

Resources

CLUBS AND ADVOCACY GROUPS

Bike Henderson: Website for the city of Henderson, listing all of the bike routes with maps; cityofhenderson.com/public_works/bicycle/bike_hend erson_index.php.

BikingLasVergas.com: Cycling forum where you can find information and maps of trails in and around Las Vegas. There is also a calendar of events, including bike rides organized by local clubs and bike shops; bikinglasvegas .com.

Green Valley Cyclists: Riding club based in Henderson but includes Las Vegas; greenvalleycyclists.org.

Green Valley Ridez: Not an official riding club, but a good source for riding with a group; gvridez.com.

Las Vegas Valley Bicycle Club: Riding club based in Las Vegas; lasvegasbikeclub.org.

Mountain Bike Las Vegas: Promotes safe cycling practices, physical achievement, and the social benefits of group cycling; mountainbikelasvegas.com.

Southern Nevada Mountain Bike Association: Advocacy, trail building and maintenance, and group rides in and around Las Vegas; snmba.net.

The Wizard of Vegas: This site has a little bit of everything for everyone, including reviews of trails ridden by the creator of the site; wizardofvegas.com.

BIG BIKE RIDES AND EVENTS

Callville Bay Classic: This is a 90-mile, two-day, stage road bike race from Las Vegas to Callville Bay.

CrossVegas: The largest cyclo-cross race in the United States, this annual event is held at night and attracts bicyclists from both America and abroad; crossvegas.com.

Downhill Mountain Bike Skills Camp: This event is designed to improve the skills of all downhill riders; betterride.mycustomevent.com.

Goldilocks Las Vegas: A women-only event that incorporates 20-, 40-, 60-, 80-, and 100-mile rides through the western part of Las Vegas; goldilocksride.com.

Ironman 70.3 Silverman Triathlon: An annual race in October where competitors swim, bike, and run. The event starts at Lake Mead and finishes in Henderson; ironman.com.

Las Vegas Tour de Cure: Annual 20-, 35-, 65-, and 100-mile rides to benefit the American Diabetes Association, with team and individual events; tour.diabetes.org.

Mountain Bike Skills Camp: This event is designed to improve the skills of all riders; betterride.mycustomevent.com.

MS 150 Las Vegas: An annual 30-, 65-, and 100-mile ride to benefit the National MS Society; bikenvl.nationalmssociety.org.

North Las Vegas Century: A 100-mile ride in North Las Vegas; lvvbc.org.

Pedal to the Medal: An annual 25-, 50-, and 100-mile ride benefiting Special Olympics; sonv.org.

Ride 2 Recovery Honor Ride: This 39- and 75-mile team and individual event, sponsored by Mandalay Bay, allows the public to ride alongside healing heroes from all branches of the armed forces; ride2recovery.com.

3 Feet for Pete: Annual event to raise awareness of cycling safety. The *3 Feet* refers to the Nevada state law that requires vehicles to give road bikes a 3-foot leeway on the road. There is both a 16- and 28-mile course that goes from Las Vegas Boulevard to Jean and back; threefeetforpete.org.

Tour De Fire: An annual 100-plus-mile ride into the Valley of Fire State Park to benefit the Nevada Childhood Cancer Foundation.

Tour de Summerlin: Touted as the "most rider-friendly" bicycling event, this yearly ride is either 100, 75, or 40 miles, depending on how far you wish to ride, and is done for charity. The ride is around the west area of Las Vegas known as Summerlin; tourdesummerlin.com.

Viva Bike Vegas: This event, which benefits close to twenty charities, includes a 101-mile, 62-mile, and 25-mile race, as well as a Fun Rides of 10 miles, 5 miles, and 0.25 mile.

XTERRA West Championship: This event includes a full-length XTERRA championship race (1.5K swim/28.2K mountain bike/10K run) and a shorter distance XTERRA Sprint race, along with 5K, 10K, and 21K runs; xterraplanet.com.

References

BOOKS AND ARTICLES

Bureau of Land Management. "Go Wild Horse and Burro Watching" pamphlet.

Carroll, Laura. "Lost City Museum a Hidden Nevada Cultural Gem." *Las Vegas Review–Journal*, October 28, 2013.

DeHaven, James. "'Beautiful' New Park to Reveal Treasures." *Las Vegas Review–Journal*, October 20, 2013.

Hoffman, Rick. "How Turtle Fence Can Protect the Threatened Desert Tortoise." *The Fence Post*, July 18, 2013.

Lake, Richard. "Law Says Bicyclists Don't Need Helmets . . . I Don't Get It." *Las Vegas Review–Journal*, August 4, 2013.

Land, Barbara and Myrick. *A Short History of Las Vegas*. Reno, NV: University of Nevada Press, 2004.

Moulin, Tom. *Red Rock Canyon Visitor Guide*. Las Vegas, NV: Snell Press, 2013.

Nordli, Brian. "In North Las Vegas, a Crown Jewel Finds Itself in Need of a White Knight." *Las Vegas Sun*, March 12, 2013.

Papa, Paul W. *It Happened in Las Vegas: Remarkable Events That Shaped History*. Guilford, CT: Globe Pequot Press, 2009.

Shine, Conor. "Henderson Ready to Break Ground on $9.6 Million Walking Trail." *Las Vegas Sun*, August 18, 2011.

Stutz, Howard. "Railroad Pass Celebrates 80th Anniversary This Week." *Las Vegas Review–Journal*, August 2, 2011.

Sweet, Phoebe. "Leave the Wild Burro Be." *Las Vegas Sun*, May 21, 2008.

WEBSITES

bikinglasvegas.com: Bike trails, group rides, and events around Las Vegas.

birdandhike.com: Promotes the hiking trails and wildlife in the area around Las Vegas.

blm.gov/nv: Bureau of Land Management

fs.usda.gov: US Forest Service

getoutdoorsnevada.org: Promotes outdoor activities throughout the state.

hooverdambypass.org: Hoover Dam Bypass Project

lvvbc.org: Las Vegas Bicycle Club

mtbproject.com: mountain bike trails in America

nps.gov/lake/planyourvisit/hike.htm: National Park Service

parks.nv.gov/parks/valley-of-fire-state-park: Valley of Fire State Park

ride2recovery.com: Ride 2 Recovery

rivermountainstrail.org: River Mountains Loop

secure.defenders.org: Defenders of Wildlife

wizardofvegas.com: bike trails around Las Vegas

About the Author

Paul W. Papa is an avid bicyclist who can often be found in the hills and on the trails throughout the Las Vegas valley. He started his riding career in the early 1990s when he worked at the Sands Hotel and Casino as a security bike officer—logging close to 10,000 hours on a bike. Paul is a full-time writer who has written several books about Las Vegas, including *It Happened in Las Vegas*, *Haunted Las Vegas*, and *Discovering Vintage Las Vegas*. Visit his website and blog at paulwpapa.com.